# Libertarianism: Pro and Con

By
George R. Ingham

# Table of Contents

# Introduction

If men were angels, no government would be necessary. If angels were to govern men, neither external nor internal controls on government would be necessary.
—James Madison

If there were omniscient men ... there would be little use for liberty.
—F.A. von Hayak

...the sole end for which mankind are warranted, individually or collectively, in interfering with the liberty of action of any of their number, is self-protection.
—John Stuart Mill

A free man is he that ... is not hindered to do what he has a will to.
—Hobbes

We are living in perilous times for civil liberties. The United States of America is facing its most serious threat to democracy from right-wing authoritarianism since the height of the Ku Klux Klan's power in the mid-1920s. We are in the midst of a new Gilded Age, which threatens the survival of our democratic institutions. Europe is under siege from a resurgence of fascist nationalism. And yet, Dr. Martin Luther King Jr.'s arc of the moral universe has been slowly bending toward justice in recent decades, with more and more groups gaining rights that had been denied to them since the beginning of civilization. However, though stoking old prejudices for economic and political gain, for example against certain immigrants, is a very old practice, it has, unfortunately, only gotten more sophisticated, with new technologies and methods. Although we may be even more aware today of these subtle and not so subtle vulnerabilities of democratic government, we still fall into the same traps because eternal vigilance is so hard to maintain.

Then, how have we arrived at this crisis of liberal democracy, and what can we do about it? After all, both sides in this debate claim to be promoting the maximum amount of individual liberty and both share our culture's glorification of wealth. A big part of the difficulty is that we fiercely disagree about almost every political value; disagreements that are carried on by shouting and with acrimony, rather than anything that resembles civil discourse or rationality. Each camp and sub-camp ends up forming into their own tribe, defining their very own truths and facts. This balkanization and the accompanying incivility has been facilitated and encouraged by the development of social media. The human tendency to form into political tribes is reinforced by our equally human tendency to favor evidence that confirms our bias, and to ignore any evidence we don't like. Specifically, we tend to look for and report historical events that confirm our theory and to ignore any events that counter it. Individuals who are historically challenged tend to utilize examples from their personal experience. This disposition was described by Francis Bacon and others, long before psychologists labeled it *confirmation bias* and confirmed it, to their own satisfaction, with experiments.

It is important at this time to note that America began with two competing sets of core values: on the one hand the desire for minimal government, one that governs least, combined with the promotion of an independent individual citizen with freedom to choose her own goals and lifestyle; on the other side is an equally exalted commitment to active government to protect the vulnerable and to promote the common good. This liberal family feud can be seen at the founding in the debates between the Federalists and the anti-Federalists, with the latter most closely representing the libertarian position today. For most of American history, laissez-faire, minimal state liberalism has been the guiding philosophy of political life. American history has also been marked, over and over again, by periods when the first set of traditional convictions has led to social problems that threatened the stability and, even, survival of our freedoms, followed by periods of resurgence of active government intervention; followed, in turn, by yet another resurgence of economic individualism, or what President Harding called a "return to normalcy." The reaction to Hamiltonian active government contributed to the development of political parties, and, eventually to the era's reaction under President Andrew Jackson. The Gilded Age, in the last decades of the nineteenth century, was followed by the Progressive reforms of the first decades of the twentieth. The New Deal, of course, followed the Great Depression. The ending of American expansion westward and the increase in America's population beyond the capacity of industry to meet demands, by the beginning of the twentieth century, led to new challenges, and expansion of government power, and challenges to the myth of rugged individualism. The belief that public power should check the excesses of corporate power has itself been checked by a deep distrust of government power. Libertarian or neoliberal values have usually been supreme, followed by economic crises, leading to briefer periods of active state liberalism, when those classes most adversely affected react with anger, as they are today. Inequality has, once again, become a political, and not just a social challenge.

Another critical danger to any democracy comes from idealists who are unwilling to compromise, who want a revolution, or who refuse to vote for a candidate who does not meet their exacting standards of political rectitude; thus leaving the field open for authoritarian leaders to emerge. The book before you is an effort to bridge the divide of misunderstanding between these widely divergent and competing political viewpoints.

Books by libertarians and about libertarianism would fill a library. What's more, like any group of economic and political thinkers, they are far from monolithic. But, almost all of these works are highly partisan, written by true believers, for and against. They only serve to create ideological uniformity, and to further our already extreme and acrimonious, political polarization. There is evidence that the growth of media news and social websites has only increased such ideological alignment and rigidity. This book demonstrates that there is more that unites us than people realize. At a time when established political parties in western nations appear to be fracturing and realigning along ideological fault lines, it is even more important to understand these shared principles. Some question whether or not parties that were established to deal with the Great Depression and the Cold War are fully equipped to solve problems created by very different demographic and economic realities.

This book is also written in the hopes of furthering what the poet, John Keats called, "negative capability." This virtuous disposition, which Keats felt Shakespeare "possessed so enormously," is the capacity "of being in uncertainties, mysteries, doubts, without any irritable reaching after fact and reason."[1] Few people welcome having their most forcefully held convictions challenged by the best counterarguments. Individuals who possess this rare capacity also tend to display the virtues of humility and empathy. Educators who wish to promote this ability aim "to start little insurrections in the realm of their [student's] convictions."[2] The American philosopher of education and democracy John Dewey gave his own prescription, recommending the "incorporation of the scientific method into individual disposition[s]."[3]

One great example of someone with negative capability from American history is Abraham Lincoln. In a speech as a freshman Representative before the U.S. House of Representatives on June 28, 1848, Lincoln notes that, as a rule, there are only degrees of good and evil in ideas and policies. "Almost everything, especially of governmental policy," he states, "is an inseparable compound of the two; so that our best judgment of the preponderance between them is continually demanded."[4] This receptive attitude was expressed by the most respected libertarian thinker, Robert Nozick, who wrote that "intellectual honesty demands that, occasionally at least, we go out of our way to confront strong arguments opposed to our views … only the refusal to listen guarantees one against being ensnared by the truth."[5]

The philosopher Kwame Anthony Appiah is fond of summarizing his philosophy as "that everything is more complicated than you thought."[6] An important part of the professional ethic of a philosopher is that you need to be able to fully understand and counter the very best arguments of the opposing viewpoint. This engenders a realization and appreciation of the complexity of ideas. This book is written with that ethic in mind. Since it is rarely the case that the most extreme or orthodox theorists, on either side of the political spectrum, provide the most sophisticated arguments, some will object to my choice of representatives for libertarianism and its critics. The extreme positions on both sides, namely, socialist and libertarian anarchists would require a radical transformation of human nature into something much more positive. Mankind is a given, with all our imperfections, including the harsh aspects of self-interest. H.L. Mencken said it best: "the urge to save humanity is almost always a false-face for the urge to rule. Power is what all messiah's really seek; not the chance to serve."[7] Abigail Adams, in a famous letter to her husband, admonished him to "remember the ladies," as "all men," and she meant *men* "would be tyrants if they could." Therefore, this is a book that accepts these negative realities; and, moreover, one that is meant to challenge, not to reinforce political bias. A character in the Tom Stoppard play, *Professional Foul,* refers to a prominent example of such a challenge: "There would be no moral dilemmas if moral principles worked in straight lines and never crossed each other."

The need that the human mind has to think in categories has long been established. In his 1954 classic, *The Nature of Prejudice,* Gordon Allport showed how this dependency can lead to great harm, especially when applied in social and political relationships. A very important component of prejudice is prejudgment. Prejudice as prejudgment has been styled as "conditions of understanding."[8] Also, exaggerated claims for any political position have usually led to human misery. Each party sees itself as the Children of Light and the opposing party as the Children of Darkness. As one popular and well-respected economic historian put it, "whenever one speaks about the distribution of wealth, politics is never far behind, and it is difficult for anyone to escape contemporary class prejudices and interests."[9]

Simple-minded hostility toward capitalism, as only fostering greed, fraud, and deception; and, similar characterization of government as always coercive, inefficient, and arbitrary, are the opposite of a nuanced and complex analysis. In his classic study of propaganda during World War 1, Harold Lasswell showed how this conscious selective manipulation of symbols of value is motivated by self-interest.[10] Political positions are hardened by presenting extreme opposite viewpoints: free market anarchy versus central government planned economic socialism.[11] George Orwell quipped that "nearly all creators of Utopia have resembled the man who has a toothache, and therefore thinks happiness consists in not having toothache."[12] The last century repeatedly brought reminders that political ideologies can be very dangerous. They represent systems of thought that purportedly tell us, not only how things supposedly are, but how they should be. This utopian aspect or program for perfection often leads to a justification for compulsion. Each group of advocates readily sees this danger in the opposing 'ism, but finds it hard to see the same tendency in their own political position. Libertarians tend to attack any program they dislike as a form of socialism. Meanwhile, socialists fail to see the real dangers in the enlarged role for a centralized government in their programs for reform. Each group remains proudly confident that they are on the right side of history. In fact, as John Dewey noted, "in spite of itself any movement that thinks and acts in terms of an 'ism becomes so involved in reaction against other 'isms that it is unwittingly controlled by them."[13]

Historically, in fact, American reformers have usually not wished to abolish capitalism, but rather to preserve it by reigning in its worst impulses. They have not wished to eliminate the wealthy, but only to share in their bounty. One such great reformer, the philosopher of American democracy John Dewey, devoted much of his work to trying to counter dualistic, "us" versus "them," political categories that threaten our freedom. Dewey also cautioned citizens of a democracy to be attentive to "concealed economic aims" and "secret manipulations."[14] We all have a tendency to be fooled by the many biases that psychologists and others have identified.[15] Dewey cautioned us to approach political issues with a pragmatic spirit, noting that "all intelligent political criticism is comparative. It deals not with all-or-none situations, but with practical alternatives; an absolutistic indiscriminate attitude, whether in praise or blame," he warned, "testifies to the heat of feeling rather than the light of thought."[16] The complexity of the issues involved in understanding and being open to the libertarian viewpoint can be seen by the use of an example that goes beyond narrowly political or economic concerns.[17]

Do citizens have a right to health care? Do they also have a right to good health? The first thing to notice is that both libertarians and their critics often confuse these two, very different, questions. Is saying that a person has a *right* to health care the same as saying they are *entitled* to certain goods? What do these terms even mean in this context; and, does use of one, rather than the other, already bias the healthcare debate. Libertarians have some interesting things to say about these very complex concepts. What about the government *promoting* good health or wider access to healthcare, as opposed to *guaranteeing* it? Few people would deny someone injured the right to emergency care. But would they also say that there is a right to cosmetic surgery? What if the individual was disfigured by a fire? Should a very elderly person have a right to a kidney transplant? Does it matter whether or not viable kidneys are in very short supply? Should the fact that wealthy parents are able to purchase life-saving medical treatment for their child be considered more unjust than their ability to buy a luxury automobile?[18]

Answers to questions in political discussion, like those about medical care above, are often strongly determined by which questions are asked and how they are worded. For example, a critic of libertarianism, Michael Sandel, characterizes Milton Friedman's complex discussion about the effects of licensure of physicians by writing that Friedman believes that, "if I want a bargain appendectomy, I should be free to hire anyone I choose, certified or not, to do the job." Sandel adds that Friedman believes that private organizations could rate physicians like "*Consumer Reports* or the *Good Housekeeping* seal of approval."[19] Friedman, however, raises some interesting questions about whether the effect of state licensure has been to reduce "both the quantity and quality of medical practice."[20] Yet, some of Friedman's ideas are very similar to Paul Starr's classic history of American medicine, which won the Pulitzer Prize in 1984.[21] The point is not to take away from Sandel's sophisticated analysis of libertarianism, which I will come back to below, but to note the subtle effects that the wording of political discussion can have on the appreciation of ideas.

Most would agree that a right to good health means that the state has an obligation to protect its citizens from the effects of toxic waste, the pollution of water and the air, as well as the spread of infectious diseases. However, does the state also have an obligation to protect us from the consumption of drinks with an "excess" of sugar? Should an individual's personal lifestyle choices be the concern of anyone but themselves, and should the government intervene to protect citizens from choices with negative health consequences. Does the fact that citizens in the top economic percentile have better health, as measured, for example, by life-expectancy, determine your answer to any of these questions? Does the state have any obligations when it comes to preventing diseases known to be caused by economic factors, such as malnutrition; or should it rely entirely on the expectation of private charity? Those who oppose the libertarian viewpoint often accuse those who support it with being callous, greedy, or lacking in compassion. Yet, both sides say that they are concerned for the poor, and often the only real difference between them is the empirical question of what is the best way to provide services such as healthcare or the resources needed to maintain good health. But, that empirical question itself is based on differing assumptions about what is being measured. Some libertarians and their critics would argue that the empirical questions about economic outcomes are secondary to the principles of free choice or beneficence. For example, should a cost-benefit analysis be the only or primary method to determine the allocation of scarce healthcare resources? Another empirical question with implications for libertarians and their critics concerns the cost of medical care, especially, the cost of drugs. Do government' policies have the effect of driving up the cost of pharmaceuticals, or do they actually serve to put a lid on these and other healthcare costs? What are the ultimate consequences of government oversight or inaction when it comes to drugs and other medical procedures? Is there anything unique about medicine that makes it a very different kind of marketplace; one requiring governmental regulation?

Political ideologies work by creating false dualisms or dichotomies, as well as unrecognized biases. An example from medicine concerns innovation, especially as it relates to the development of new technologies and drugs. There can be no doubt that market forces have led to a renaissance of scientific development in all areas of medicine. However, there are times when the creative incentives central to the market mechanism do not prove sufficient for the creation of an effective curative agent. A case in point involves the production of drugs for very rare diseases. Leading promoters of contemporary libertarian ideas were often open to the desirability, even necessity, of a role for government in such cases. The libertarian economist, Milton Friedman, admitted that "government may enable us at times to accomplish jointly what we would find difficult or expensive to accomplish severally."[22] Other prominent dichotomies in the debate about government and medicine include: autonomy vs. paternalism; freedom vs. responsibility and obligation; efficiency vs. wastefulness; greed vs. beneficence; negative vs. positive rights and liberties; and, the central dualism of individual vs. government, or, more broadly, society. Libertarians have also been described, with some justification, as "individualist puritans."[23]

As with other political theories, the central concepts of both libertarians and their critics, as well as many of the arguments between them have a lot in common with debates going back at least as far as the early Enlightenment. For example, there are many reminders of arguments on both sides of the debates over ratification of the United States Constitution.[24] Kant was right to warn about the dangers of paternalism in his essay, "An Answer to the Question: What is Enlightenment?"[25] But, it usually comes down to whose ox is being gored as to which particular law or regulation is promoted or opposed. It is also the case that, like all other political philosophies libertarianism and opposing "collectivist/statist" ideas are grounded in opposing viewpoints about human nature and social psychology; in the words of Supreme Court Justice Felix Frankfurter political philosophers seek "illumination for the problems of politics from the slow accretions of insight into human behavior."[26]

Also, like other political terms, 'libertarianism' is quite fungible and malleable, and it can, therefore, be confusing. The result of such a lack of clarity can be that important areas of agreement become obscured, leading to greater partisan conflict and misunderstanding. Both sides can also be confused by accepting certain origin myths. This is particularly true when it comes to the extremes of socialist or libertarian anarchism. However, the term libertarian and its key concept can be stated simply enough: an individual should have the right to live his or her life in any way the person chooses so long as he or she respects the equal right of others to do likewise. Yet, even though the principle that we should all be entitled to equal consideration appears to be built into our nature, like other reactions to injustice, it is not at all clear what equal consideration, or even the concept of *equal*, really means, as well as what should be the policy implications of these ideas about justice. Minimal state economic policies have sometimes been held by individuals, like Ronald Reagan, alongside conservative and sectarian social policies that call for active government intervention. Still, there is at least one thing that the dueling economists Friedrich Hayek and John Maynard Keynes could agree on, which also has the virtue of being true, and that is that the ideas of economists and political philosophers have important consequences for the politics of the future; often, as Hayek noted, long after they have been put forward.[27]

Historically, American governments have been pushed to become more active in order to address inequities and to force the inclusion of more and more previously excluded groups of people into receiving the blessings of democracy.

A central concept is the idea of *ownership*, especially, *self-ownership*. Aspects of this concept are easier to understand today, with our more abstract ideas about labor, intellectual capital, and even human capital. These earlier concepts about freedom and property were, of course, key to the political ideas of John Locke; but, they also can be found in the works of Benjamin Constant, Wilhelm von Humboldt, David Ricardo, and some key Scottish Enlightenment philosophers. They were given modern form by, arguably, the greatest contemporary libertarian philosopher, Robert Nozick, in his classic *Anarchy, State, and Utopia*. A key question is whether or not individuals have rights to property that are independent of any rules, laws, or regulations?

Part of the terminological confusion is that there are right-libertarians and left-libertarians. Although the former group tends to dismiss the latter as "bleeding-heart libertarians," both groups generally accept this concept of self-ownership. To oversimplify, their differences are mostly about the proposed obligations of ownership, as well as an acceptance of some form of egalitarianism by left-libertarians when it comes to natural resources.[28] This major difference about the ownership and use of such things as rivers and lakes means that both groups often differ on procedural issues regarding the environment and global warming.

Since libertarians seem to support the founding American principles of individual liberty, private property, and free markets, one might be excused for asking: "what's not to like?"But, there are contradictions at the heart of every political persuasion, and libertarianism is no exception.

A major focus of opposition comes with the last mentioned key American principle, free-markets, and ideas around the importance of markets and how they operate. This leads to yet another terminological confusion, namely, the use of *neoliberalism*. This equally fuzzy concept has been largely used by academics and Europeans, and mostly with a pejorative connotation. This particular loose terminology can cause the most confusion for my purposes in this book, and I will offer further clarification in chapter 2 below. A case in point is that the massive *Encyclopedia of Libertarianism*, not only does not have an entry on neoliberalism, but even a mention of it in the index.[29] Meanwhile, neoliberalism can, roughly, be distinguished from libertarianism by the use of American and European intervention abroad to promote the interests of large corporations, by all major parties, as opposed to an emphasis placed by the Libertarian Party on traditional free market global policies of unbridled market competition and the liberalizing of international trade. Neoliberal foreign interventions are the direct result of the same values and some of the same policies of libertarianism. I will argue that neoliberal interventionism, though directly opposed to the libertarian policies and rhetoric of negative liberty and protection from fraud, is an unintended negative consequence of mistaken views of human nature, freedom, and power, as well as misunderstandings about the culture and values of capitalism. The libertarian formula that free trade brings a free people, though partially true, is ultimately based on certain assumptions that are unsustainable. The combining of the newly formed Tea Party with the Republican Party, in order to gain American political influence, has been a major cause leading to this confusion.[30] European financial organizations, led by Germany, have imposed austerity measures on smaller countries in a similar muscular interventionist manner. All of these policies run counter to the libertarian ideology of nonintervention. Neoliberalism is largely the same as libertarianism when it comes to values or ideology, but with the addition of these few similar economic doctrines.[31]

This introduction is not the place to go into the complex and tortured history of the use of the terms liberal and liberalism in American history. In the 1956 Preface to his most popular book, *The Road to Serfdom,* Friedrich Hayek called the use of *liberal* for welfare state programs "muddleheadedness."[32] He argued that libertarianism was forward looking, and that it looks forward to progress through "spontaneous change," rather than being held back by government controls. Despite the liabilities associated with any generalization, it is not unreasonable to state that the use of these terms was closely associated with American democracy until the so-called Reagan revolution. One of the remarkable transformations that began with Reagan's presidency was to associate these terms with negative connotations for a majority of the population. Reagan's attempt to combine libertarian fiscal policies with morally and religiously conservative social traditions has led to a crisis of cohesiveness in the American Republican Party that is threatening its very survival. Reagan, like Russell Kirk and other conservatives, expressed views more reminiscent of the Puritan leader, John Winthrop, than of Jefferson, Madison, or, for that matter, almost any libertarian.[33] Democrats had their own crisis of identity, one that has caused them to resort to calling themselves "progressives." Milton Friedman could still call himself a "liberal," and libertarians with more of a historical sense refer to their ideas as "classic liberalism," but, most libertarians, especially members of the Tea Party, are known as conservatives (they would be called *minimal* state, as opposed to active state, liberals in Europe). Yet, the conservative political philosophy, as defined by someone like Russell Kirk, combines some libertarian ideas with a moralistic and religious prescriptivism that is quite anathema to most libertarians.[34]

It has also been the case that, at least in America, so-called *neoconservatives* have sometimes joined forces with libertarians in order to achieve some political power or goal, especially when it comes to foreign interventions. To add to the terminological and political confusion, neoconservatives, even though sometimes aligned with libertarians, have often been interventionists when it comes to opposing non-traditional lifestyles and related values, and have backed foreign interventions to supposedly promote or impose these so-called conservative values on other nations.[35] Meanwhile, the American Libertarian Party has strongly promoted free choice, when it comes to lifestyles, and has mostly opposed foreign adventures. I will argue that, if we need a label, it is more accurate to think of the critics of libertarianism as *communitarians,* rather than liberals or even progressives.

The American political organization known as the Tea Party was founded around the 234th anniversary of the famous Boston Tea Party in 2007.[36] The Tea Party received a significant boost in numbers and importance as a result of the negative reaction to the bank bailouts at the end of the George W. Bush administration and beginning of President Obama's first term. As noted above, it is often confused with the Libertarian Party, which began in 1971, and is quite distinct in significant ways. Both groups accuse liberals of being too anxious to use government power to achieve their social ends at the cost of sacrificing individual freedom. Many individuals in both these parties like to refer to their group as "the Freedom Party." But, both groups have also been able to find common cause with some American liberals in certain areas, such as concerns about an overzealous, governmental, security system, and other similar threats to civil liberties.

There are a number of government programs, such as Social Security and Medicare that are popular even among American conservatives. When a conservative makes a statement such as "keep your government hands off my Medicare," the humor comes from the obvious cognitive dissonance of combining the concepts of an effective program and government run. The libertarian effort to privatize such services builds on this conceptual conflict. The dogma that the private market is always more efficient than government run programs has a hard time explaining the far greater efficiency of Medicare over any private insurer.

At risk of adding to the confusion, the Tea Party could be designated a right libertarian organization. Democrats tend to dismiss libertarian fiscal views, but are happy to join forces with Tea Party members on questions regarding the expansion of social or cultural freedom, such as gay marriage. More germane to purposes of this book, the Tea Party has aligned itself with the Republican Party. This uneasy alliance has been repeatedly challenged by actual Republican fiscal behavior, as opposed to fiscal rhetoric and policies. This whole use of the labels conservative and liberal has been confusing for Europeans, for whom ideas of "laissez-faire" capitalism are referred to as neoliberalism. There is an important difference, however, between libertarianism and neoliberalism, and it is not just a question of emphasis or political acceptance. The emphasis on economic liberalism, in the latter, has consequences that will be important throughout this book. The important thing to note, at the outset, is that all these political ideologies, when looked at closely, can be seen to come in a wide variety of ambiguous flavors. Yet, there are very similar concepts and assumptions that set libertarians apart.

These fundamental questions involve the nature of power and some of the biggest ethical issues of our time. American libertarians like to summarize their position by calling themselves fiscally conservative, but socially liberal. What they mean by this will be examined in chapter 1. They are also not afraid to take on corporate power, when the large corporations engage in practices that reduce individual choice or freedom. It cannot be denied that ideas about the morally privileged status of individual liberty, as separate from political liberty; that individual rights are inalienable and need to be protected from exploitation and coercion; and, that market principles of ownership apply equally to such rights, have all been traditionally associated with liberalism. Passages in John Stuart Mill's great work, *On Liberty,* express sentiments that could be embraced by just about any libertarian. But, Mill's political philosophy, like that of other major thinkers usually referred to as liberals, such as Locke and John Rawls, have complex ideas about liberty and equality that can mislead when quoted out of context, as they often are by libertarians and their critics. For example, Rawls's first principle of justice sounds very much like a libertarian conception.[37] Many libertarians would agree that wide economic inequality threatens the stability of political equality, that it greatly reduces the political potency of the vast majority of citizens, but they would strongly differ with active state liberals about the empirical question as to what specific economic policies have brought about such gross differences in wealth and standard of living. The libertarian equality, however, is more reminiscent of the equality of chances of the Social

Darwinist, William Graham Sumner, who wrote that "rights do not pertain to results, but only to *chances*."[38]

To make matters even more confusing, one of the leading libertarian thinkers, Friedrich A. Hayek, wrote a Postscript to his major work, *The Constitution of Liberty,* with the title "Why I Am Not a Conservative."[39] However, in all this confusion about political terminology it is important to recognize that most conservatives and liberals, like most libertarians, share a deep skepticism about political power and government. Also, it is important to acknowledge that there exists no neutral and independent standpoint, outside the political and moral spheres, from which to offer an absolute judgment about these positions; but this does not mean that one cannot offer rational and moral judgments about them. This book is written from the perspective expressed by Roger Scruton that, "political understanding, as a form of practical judgment, does not readily translate into universal principles."[40] It is an attempt at a critique of ideologies, without fostering its own ideology.

An argument can be made that all these different views can be seen as disagreements within the same political tradition, one that accepts more principles than it realizes. This tradition, for example, recognizes that the attainment and preservation of the freedom of the individual has been and continues to be the most significant achievement and goal of society. Moreover, most people would accept that some inequalities are inevitable in any society. They might also agree that the extreme inequality prevalent in Renaissance Italy led to the creation of masterpieces that would never have been created, even though it also led to great pain and political conflict. The fact is that, as with any political philosophy, there are purists, often dismissed as "extremists" or "dogmatists," and there are those who are open to more nuanced positions but still wish to maintain what they see as certain fundamental ideals. For example, just as there are libertarians who acknowledge that markets can fail and that society needs to have a safety net to support the poor, so there are critics of libertarianism who recognize the many failures of liberal government. Much of the criticism, on both sides, turns out to assume the same principles of justice and equality before the law, such as the conviction that bad regulations include ones that are unjustly enforced only against small businesses. These regulations give power to unelected officials, which can sometimes lead to abuse or even corruption. The rule of law, mere "parchment barriers" to borrow James Madison's phrase, have not proved sufficient to preserve liberty, when the other branches of government have been subverted or corrupted by money or powerful economic interests. Are laws and regulations just meant to keep us from physically assaulting and stealing from each other? Can we have markets without laws and regulations, such as those dealing with contract and fraud? If the answer to these questions is that we cannot, then we can start to have a constructive debate about which laws and regulations work to promote competition, efficiency, and innovation, and which tend to retard these virtues of capitalism.

A major area of criticism involves the growing role of bureaucracy in modern life, with libertarians focusing on the extreme negative manifestations of bureaucratic mismanagement in modern government, as opposed to the more general and positive view of the great German sociologist, Max Weber. Once again, the issues involved here are highly complex, and call for an appreciation of the contributions of both libertarians and their critics. This is another area, I will show, where both sides can learn from each other; and, where solutions can and have been found by a younger and more open generation of entrepreneurs. During the twelve years that I was the head of a large organization, I insisted that we periodically examine whether or not our rules and regulations were still necessary, or were getting in the way of the efficient operation of that organization. I found that employees appreciated this effort, as it tended to make their work easier, but also more constructive and rewarding.

It is also the case that citizens of a representative government can hold quite contradictory positions and desires: for example, on the one hand to be left alone to do their own thing, while at the same time being protected from the predatory practices of other individuals and institutions. One of the great contributions of the Scottish Enlightenment thinkers, Adam Smith, David Hume, and Francis Hutchinson to America in the constitutional period was the understanding that individuals tend to prefer their own interests and goals over those of others, leading to the central role that faction plays in any political arrangement. Hume's analysis of irrationality and, specifically, the envy we tend to display toward the rich and powerful, has important relevance for a richer understanding of market transactions.

An important issue is the exact role of what Hayek called "the rule of law."[41] At one extreme is the libertarian, Murray Rothbard's "Anarcho-capitalism," a form of individualist anarchism. At the risk of oversimplifying, this is the view that individual rights and free markets are all that we require, and that governments are, not only, not necessary, but they are dangerous and inefficient. Much more prevalent is the ideal of a minimal state, the proponents of which are sometimes referred to as "minarchists." This is the view dismissed with the phrase "night watchman state" by the socialist Ferdinand Lassalle, and dismissed by Thomas

Carlyle as a society held together only by the "cash-nexus" leading to "anarchism plus the constable." However, the same Thomas Jefferson who wrote that "that government is best that governs least," and that any taxation for purposes of equality of distribution was to violate a person's right to acquire and enjoy the fruits of his labor, also promoted state run services to help citizens gain individual autonomy and agency, government services that almost all libertarians would object to.[42] The best arguments for such a minimal state were put forward by Robert Nozick, in his classic work referred to above. Nozick admits that he began his study with the goal of refuting libertarianism, especially the extreme version advocated by Rothbard. He ended up, instead, by giving a classic justification of the argument that we can have a state that does not violate individual rights, so long as such a government does not attempt redistribution of assets and resources. Such egalitarian redistribution, Nozick argues, requires ongoing, coercive, interference with personal rights.

The focus of the arguments of Hayek and most libertarians is on the economic and political consequences of governmental actions, where Robert Nozick's concerns were more abstract issues, such as the nature of human rights. All libertarians accept the simple formula: where there is more government there is less freedom; where there is less government, there is more freedom. However, since power abhors a vacuum, we need to ask the equally important question, when does *less* government promote the will to power of private individuals and institutions? Since *soft* power very readily turns into *hard* power, through a process of propaganda and other forms of manipulation, eternal vigilance is a virtue that needs to be taught. The capacity to recognize falsehood and the signs of manipulation is a necessary virtue in all relationships, including political. The psychological and sociological lessons that I covered in my book, *Love of Having: Compulsive Buying, Spending, and Hoarding,* are highly relevant to political power as well as to intimate relationships.[43] As Henry Adams pointed out "knowledge of human nature is the beginning and end of political education."[44] What's more, honesty and trust is as essential to political legitimacy as it is to all personal and social relationships. Libertarians are fond of pointing to the many unintended consequences of laws, such as prohibition of alcoholic beverages. But, it is also important to note historical examples where it was the lack of laws or regulations that led to serious negative consequences. James Madison's reminder, quoted at the beginning of this chapter, that we are not angels is relevant here.

It was John Locke, a very important political philosopher for libertarians, who noted that, "the end of law is not to abolish or restrain but to preserve and enlarge freedom … [and] where there is no law, there is no freedom."[45] Locke also warned, in a different context, that some "men are so foolish that they take care to avoid what mischief can be done by polecats and foxes, but are content, nay think it safety, to be devoured by lions."[46]This view of both liberty and property is that it should be enabling and expand individual capabilities. The extension of guarantees of civil rights to more categories of citizens is a paradigm for the use of legislation; the establishment, for example, of a democratic marketplace, one that includes people of all backgrounds. Laws and regulations prevent consumers from having to renegotiate every aspect of market relationships at every deal. Everything should not always be up for grabs, whenever we buy or sell in the marketplace. For example, most libertarians acknowledge the need to protect individuals from fraud. Some regulation, therefore, serves to enhance individual freedom and autonomy; but, it is equally the case that other regulations restrict individuals or businesses from providing for the common wealth and unduly interfere with their freedom.

The common goal should not be to oppose markets but to open them up in such a way that they serve the greater good. But, should freedom of contract and exchange be totally unrestricted by any governmental agency? The history of regulation and deregulation shows that both these actions, including the inaction, have consequences. I recently learned that I was not the first person to call attention to the intended but hidden consequences of lack of government action. In fact, some economists have not only developed a similar concept, but they have come up with a term, *passive deregulation,* to help explain how the lack of oversight of financial institutions, which led to the Great Recession began with a deliberate effort to first create and then fill a vacuum of power. This form of subtle maneuvering, or soft power, is hard for citizens of a democracy to discern, even without the added feature of highly effective propaganda. In order to access these issues correctly, it is important to avoid caricaturing the founders of laissez-faire capitalism, especially Adam Smith and David Hume, as having opposed the necessity for a system of laws and rules and assuming some magical rationality and harmony.[47] It is important to acknowledge that reality is also more complicated for opponents of libertarianism than they acknowledge. For example, that a much greater proportion of today's super-rich, as opposed to those in the nineteenth century, have earned their wealth from hard work and merit. America's Progressive Era did not bring about a significant decrease in inequality, and the issues of technology and global trade agreements are much more complicated than many of our current progressives seem to realize.

Also, people sometimes need to be reminded that a fire in my neighbor's home may become an issue for me. We all need to be reminded, from time to time, of the wisdom of the golden rule. Liberty is actually a common goal for both libertarians and their critics in our society. We differ as to how to define and how best to achieve this common virtue. The issue is the role that the state should play, if one accepts at least a limited obligation to protect citizens from coercion or injustice? For example, what should be the limited government's role in the economy and the protection of property? An example will make this clearer.[48]

Shortly after the terrorist attacks on September 11, 2001, Omaha, Nebraska resident Donald Lamp, acting like so many patriotic citizens, decided to display the American flag from the balcony of his condominium. The condominium association proceeded to order Mr. Lamp to take down the flag, which violated a rule about any such display on aesthetic grounds. What makes this case relevant to the concerns of this book is, not only that Mr. Lamp happened to be the father-in-law of Supreme Court Justice Clarence Thomas, or even that the controversy surrounding the case led the U.S. Congress to pass a law prohibiting such a rule, but rather the reaction it created between two self-described libertarian students when Professor Joseph William Singer discussed the case before his Harvard Law School class. Singer gives a fair and nuanced presentation of their differing arguments in his excellent book on the role of regulation in the economy and a free society. One student put forth good libertarian reasons why the condominium association had the right to order Lamp to remove the flag. After all, Lamp had voluntarily entered into a contractual relationship with his neighbors, a contract that included the provision prohibiting the flying of any flag from his balcony. The association as a whole had ownership rights that were being violated by the United States contract. The other student felt strongly that Lamp was the victim of interference and coercion in this case. The venerable common law principle that an owner has absolute right over the use of his property, and especially his own home, as well as his freedom of speech, was violated, when he was told he could not display the flag. Singer is careful not to take sides in this dispute between libertarians. His concern is to show that the dispute is not simply one about property rights or a free market. What also needed to be considered was the validity of a more fundamental right of an American citizen to display the flag as an expression of their patriotic support when the country was thought to be in peril.

Another example of the complexity surrounding questions of ownership, so central to libertarian thinking, came my way when a friend asked me to attend a meeting of a branch of our city's local government. The friend works for our local Preservation Society, a private, non-profit agency mainly dedicated to preserving local buildings deemed worthy of such concern. The Historical Commission is a department of the executive branch of our city, charged with the authority to rule on the "appropriateness" of changes to such structures. The private Preservation Society was hoping to delay the demolition of a large, beautiful, but not very old building, standing in the middle of a massive urban renewal project. The building in question was now owned by the developer. The conflict of values, aesthetics versus commerce, though relevant to the subject of this book, turned out not to be the best example. Rather another case before the Commission involved the owner of a home in one of the city's historic neighborhoods. The neighborhood had been designated by a vote of the majority of citizens, as a Local Historic District; one of 2,300 such locations in the United States. For many people in our society, this whole process of preservation of structures deemed to be worthy, whether aesthetically or historically, is a very positive example of democracy in action. For most libertarians, the process raises questions of individual rights and private ownership, similar to the issue of the right to display the flag. These issues were starkly before the Commission on this occasion. An owner in the Historic District had made several improvements to his property. It turned out that he was supposed to have gotten permission from the Commission, prior to making such changes. The Commissioners retroactively approved two of his major improvements, including his new roof, as consistent with the style of the mid-nineteenth century, when almost all of the 205 buildings were built. However, the unfortunate owner, had also installed a new, plastic, fence; and, they ordered him to take that down. The reader can, no doubt, think of many similar examples of restrictions on owners, such as zoning laws. In my neighborhood one can have chickens, but there is a zoning law against having a rooster, for obvious reasons having to do with a right to sleep.

Political philosophers think of property *rights* as a group of such social rules. There is very little disagreement that there is a need for some sort of rules about ownership; for example, certain restrictions usually apply to the use of natural resources, such as water. The issues involving ownership and private property are more complicated, not only because of the complexity of modern, especially urban, living, but, also, because of a growing awareness of the importance of environmental concerns and our collective responsibility for preserving the earth for our posterity. The Fifth Amendment of the United States Constitution contains the Eminent Domain clause prohibiting government from taking private property for public use without "just compensation." The issues around the multiple rights involved in this so-called "takings clause" are too involved to go into here.[49] There are, also, multiple reasons why such a restriction on government is important, including questioning whether or not government can be trusted to make the best decisions about our property. As a matter of historical record, courts have tended to interpret "public use" in a broad way. However, as noted earlier questions about the rights involved in the use of private property are, inevitably, subject to societal sanction.

John Locke recognized this fact when he sought to justify the existence of private ownership in a religious context, in which he accepted that God had granted the earth to all humans. In a famous argument to justify the morality of private property, Locke noted "that every man has a property in his own person. This nobody has a right to but himself. The labor of his body and the work of his hands ... are properly his."[50] A little over a hundred years later, James Madison expanded on Locke's principle in a short article on property, in interesting ways I will explore in the next chapter.[51] Locke has been criticized for his "possessive individualism," and for his views on scarcity, accumulation, labor, tacit consent, and the origin and effects of money. His answer to these potential problems is central for the justification of capitalism and libertarianism, and they will be examined briefly in the next chapter. Jean-Jacques Rousseau's famous attack on the concept of private property has also had a profound political influence. Rousseau's argument came out of his understanding of the psychology of envy and selfishness. This use of social psychology, taking into account inherited and educational differences in attributes and in opportunities, as well as the promotion of insatiable desire, led Rousseau to argue that the first use of "mine" was the source of wars and social conflict.[52] The great anthropologist Mary Douglas listed individualism and egalitarianism as two of her five biases that show how close or distant a culture happens to be.[53] Richard Ellis applies Douglas to provide a useful perspective on American political culture that is very relevant to a full assessment of libertarianism.[54] A central aspect of a person's political culture, as Ellis notes, is a person's views about human nature. The concluding chapter of this book builds on modern insights about human nature from my earlier book, *Love of Having,* and adds some very important recent psychological analysis on the nature of political power.[55]

Politically contentious debates are often fueled by hidden ideological presuppositions that need to be exposed and questioned by historical evidence. For example, a central issue about taxation has often been framed by the following dichotomy: should taxes be reduced in order to stimulate employment, or should taxes be increased in order to pay for socially necessary services? The first part of this sentence presupposes historical evidence that reducing the tax burden of employers and corporations has always or usually led to an increase in hiring of new employees. The second hidden premise begs the question by using the phrase "socially necessary." For both sides, however, historical evidence can, and should, be the determining factor in any rational determination about the effects of taxation. This book rejects historical relativism, while recognizing that any evaluation of economic and political successes and failures necessarily involves certain value judgments. Although there are always varying degrees of evidence for any past event, the past occurred as it did: agents lived, economies thrived or collapsed, nations survived as free or declined into tyrannies. Any rewriting of historical fact to conform to political assumptions should and will be condemned.

Chapter 1 presents the best arguments for the libertarian political viewpoint, and why libertarian ideas have proved so attractive over many years. Central to the libertarian viewpoint is the question, what happens when we take individual rights very seriously. The chapter begins with a brief look at some of the major historical influences on contemporary libertarian views. It is important to understand that modern libertarianism was, in large part, a reaction to the negative consequences that resulted from government economic planning and intervention in Europe between the world wars. A good example is what happened from the implementation of rent control by Social Democrats in Vienna during this period; and, the influence this experience had on Friedrich Hayek and other economists. This historical example is followed by a brief recognition of the positive benefits for economics and innovation that come from unhindered free market competition. The focus will be on the limited state arguments of minarchists, rather than the extreme Anarcho-capitalist view of someone like Murray Rothbard. The emphasis is on the *moral* arguments for the libertarian political program, rather than on specific economic positions, since the latter are often the weakest justification for libertarianism.

Key components of this moral argument concern differences between negative and positive liberty and rights, as well as the important issue of self-ownership, rather than defending the role that the existence and level of taxation plays in the dampening or the promotion of economic productivity. Although widely publicized stories about welfare "queens" driving expensive cars have proven to be propaganda, no one should deny that there are always some people who game any system, that much of the money goes to maintain a growing bureaucracy of workers, and that welfare can and does sometimes promote a dependency, rather than enhancing personal autonomy in recipients. As one commentator on Friedrich Hayek sums up his position: "the safety net must not be allowed to become a hammock."[56] Reform of this system in the 90s, at least initially, was a social good.[57]

One professor I know of, who considers himself a libertarian, jokes that he would love to live in the eighteenth century, if it weren't for the fact that he is afraid of horses. There is no doubt that one of the appeals of the libertarian outlook, for many people, is their antipathy or rejection of the complexity of modernity, especially urban modern life, our all-pervasive therapeutic and litigious culture, and all modern forms of bureaucratic collectivism. The question is how much of this complexity can be directly blamed on active state liberalism, and how much would persist with any modern political system. After all, it has recently been true that those opposed to libertarianism have also been reacting against some aspects of modern economic reality. Anyone who looks at the mind-boggling amounts of money sent to Iraq after 9/11, with little or no oversight, should be able to understand the appeal of the libertarian arguments about government inefficiency and waste.[58] This is only one of countless examples of such staggering incompetence. Libertarians, such as Hayek, have often been at the forefront of warnings about the insidious effects of so-called experts on the freedom of individuals.[59]

This first chapter also looks at the fascinating new studies of social and moral psychology that illuminate the emotional appeal of different political world views. An understanding of these personal differences does not provide an argument for or against any particular political theory; but, it does go a long way toward helping us bridge the divisions that have made political discourse so toxic. Leading libertarians, such as Hayek, Buchanan, and Friedman maintained that their views were based on a value-free, scientific, economic foundation. Whether or not we accept the possibility of such value-neutral analysis, it must be admitted that the economic, psychological, and sociological tools available today call for a more complex set of arguments about political economy than were available when they wrote. The concept of a rational consumer, who always maximizes her returns, while minimizing her risks, is no longer tenable. In his Inaugural Address in 2009, in the midst of the Great Recession, Barack Obama summed up the positive and negative aspects of capitalism: "Nor is the question before us whether the market is a force for good or ill. Its power to generate wealth and expand freedom is unmatched. But this crisis has reminded us that without a watchful eye, the market can spin out of control." Contrary to its critics, few libertarian economists would deny this need for some oversight. How and to what extent we can allow markets to function without any interference from government, however, is still a major remaining question.

It is important to acknowledge that the leading intellectuals on both sides of this debate agree that, in our pluralistic society, the government should remain neutral as to questions of what moral behaviors promote a good life. However, libertarians argue that this liberal ideal of neutrality is often violated by the modern state. Furthermore, libertarians would add that the welfare state tends to foster a dependency in its citizens that leaves them more vulnerable to such promotion of a moral consensus on how we should live and what we should believe.

Chapter 2 presents my main negative arguments directed at the libertarian/neoliberal political ideology, utilizing tools from history, psychology, sociology, economics, and political philosophy. Economic inequality is much more than socially unjust and painful; it is, also, a major threat to the stability, and even the survival, of any government that wishes to establish and defend individual liberty. This is why even those citizens who are well-off or comfortable should be very concerned about our current extreme inequality of wealth. It has been recognized, ever since Greek and Roman times that the greatest threat to the security and preservation of republican forms of government has been material inequality. Privilege tends to perpetuate itself if left alone. We need a mixed economy, in part, for the same reason that we need mixed government, to check concentrated power, and, thereby, preserve liberty. To combat special privileges for some at the expense of others, as Abraham Lincoln, as well as the rise of Jim Crow showed, requires active intervention by the government, in order to counter the realities of power. We all benefit when citizens, and even foreigners, are provided with the capacities and resources to reach their full potential and achieve their personal goals.

Contrary to libertarian dogma, extreme inequality, the concentration of wealth, and monopoly are the direct result of the *lack* of regulation and oversight. Rather than unregulated free competition being the guarantee of equality of opportunity, free competition is itself the result of regulation. This economic rule should not be surprising since it accords with what we know about power and the motivating effects of self-interest. It also fits better with the historical record. James Madison was right to point to the many factions or interest groups in any great nation: a landed interest, a manufacturing, labor, commercial, financial, and other powerful interest groups. In order to preserve liberty the power of one interest group needs to be balanced against the other, just as each department of government needs to check the power of the other.

A small example is the collective formed by the largely Latino day laborers in Oakland, California. These workers were being exploited by the random groups that hired them for daily jobs, with low or no pay, unsafe conditions, and no recourse despite laws that were meant to protect them. They decided to band together, in a manner similar to the early labor movement and, among other things, to register those who called to employ them in a central registry. The conditions under which they worked improved considerably as employers knew they were being registered. Freedom for one group becomes a threat to others; to their economic, cultural, religious, or, ultimately, political privilege and status. Plutocracy is defined as government by and in the interest of the wealthiest. Technically, the term oligarchy means rule by the few. Under conditions of extreme inequality, as we have today, those with political power are relatively few. I will tend to use the terms plutocracy and plutocrats, for this specific form of oligarchy.[60]

Historically, the financial interest of banking and securities has proven the most dangerous to economic equality. Alexander Hamilton agreed that given these many powerful interest groups, "the vigor of government is essential to the security of liberty." Madison argued that the vast lands of North America and the related slowness of communication would help prevent organized interest groups from combining their power to subvert democracy.[61] This safeguard, of course, no longer holds. But, there are good reasons why libertarians tend to live in more rural areas; and, why they also tend to reject certain aspects of modernity. It is ironic to note that rural states usually receive back a significantly higher percentage of Federal government benefits for their tax dollars. For example, in 2013 New Jersey only received back sixty-one cents in benefits for every dollar in taxation, whereas a rural state like Wyoming received a dollar and eleven cents for every dollar sent to Washington.[62]

The philosopher of American democracy, John Dewey, directed some arguments against libertarian views in a little book he wrote in 1935. Dewey notes that the first Article (Section 8) of the United States Constitution explicitly gives Congress the power to "provide for the "public welfare."[63] He could have added that the Constitutional clauses that further spell out what this power implies include taxation, duties, and other commercial regulation. Dewey goes on, however, to warn that the people should not simply rely on the government to institute policies that will promote the welfare of all the people rather than a favored few. He notes that reforms have to come from the grass roots, from an informed and motivated public opinion and action that will force the government to act in the public interest.[64] The Founders knew this, and that is why they stressed the importance of a well-educated and informed electorate, a vigorous free press, free speech, and the other rights enshrined in the Bill of Rights. Dewey rejected both the crude misreading of Darwin by Sumner and the libertarian theorists, but he also argued with other reformers, like his friend Jane Addams, that struggle was required to bring about a just society. She described her pragmatic work as "an attempt to relieve, at the same time, the over-accumulation at one end of society, and the destitution at the other."[65] Dewey's interpretation of evolutionary struggle was much closer to the recent view: teamwork and social cooperation, he argued, was needed for a just democracy and economic progress. In the words of one of his best interpreters, Dewey believed that "equality of opportunity should enhance rather than inhibit individuality."[66]Dewey's was a more effective critique of Social Darwinism, because of his more realistic view of human nature, society and the reality of change and struggle.

The principle of equal justice before the laws, including financial and other regulations, is a cornerstone of liberal justice. This is not a question of redistribution or socialism, but rather active state intervention to achieve economic opportunity, a fair deal, for the widest possible number of citizens without imposing significant harm to any one citizen or group of citizens. It is the belief that such government actions not only can provide political stability, but will serve to promote the most flourishing economy possible. It is the belief, furthermore, that, instead of such direct action interfering with the free operation of the capitalist market, they can serve to promote its smoother operation, while ensuring the widest possible sharing of its blessings. In other words, such active state intervention has been shown at times to be the only way to save capitalism from the worst features of its own functioning. After all, what does it mean to say that an individual has freedom but not the capability or the necessary resources to act on or employ that freedom for his or her own advancement? What does it mean to any society if only a select few individuals actually possess those resources and capabilities? Most libertarians profess to believe in equal opportunity for all citizens. However, they have a narrow view of what constitutes equality of opportunity and an unrealistic view of how to achieve this essential goal.

It has also been known since ancient times that broad views about how governments and societies should be organized are based on specific conceptions about human nature. Libertarianism is no exception. In this latter case, these conceptions are based on certain ideas from the

Enlightenment, bolstered by other "scientific" ideas about human psychology and social relations which were popular in the nineteenth and early twentieth century under the label of Social Darwinism; what has been called "the biological apology for laissez-faire" capitalism.[67] Placing the adjective *realistic* in front of human nature, of course, does not add anything substantive to the concept. However, the extremes of optimism and pessimism have led historically to utopian, and/or totalitarian political regimes. Pessimists, with their belief that the principle goal of governments should be security, usually produce the authoritarian regimes. The very best contemporary contributions to political theory, much of it by feminist political thinkers, has drawn on more recent empirical research into how people think and behave, and the nature of emotions and power in human relationships.

Just as there are fundamental differences between negative and positive liberty and freedom, there is a vital distinction to be made between power-over and power-to. This is not simply a distinction between power and the use of power, but a fundamental component of my critique of some libertarian core beliefs in Chapter 2. This examination builds on my previous books, as well as some additional fundamental analysis of power and human nature in order to critique some fundamental flaws in the libertarian views and political procedures. My view of power, in those earlier works, draws from the valuable contributions of feminist psychologists and philosophers on the nature of power, human autonomy, and empowerment. These views encourage the promotion of pluralistic human values, without the use of coercion or manipulation. The view of human nature presented is *realist,* in the sense used by John Rawls. I argue that a perilous level of inequality is generated as an unintended negative consequence of governmental inaction. In order to understand why this is the case, it is essential to take into consideration this more realistic understanding of certain psychological tendencies of human nature, as well as to examine much more subtle forms of manipulation and coercion than direct government paternalism and power. It is the case that majorities often tyrannize over minorities; but, there is an essential difference between the goal of promoting minority interests and promoting minority rights, especially when the interests being protected are those of the master class. This is a lesson that should have been learned from the struggle between promoters of slave rights and the champions of abolition and civil rights.

Integral to the critical analysis of Chapter 2 is a conception of instrumental values, going back at least as far as Aristotle, as well as Alasdair MacIntyre's argument about goods internal and external to a social practice. An example that most of us can easily relate to is the relationship known as instrumental friendship. Libertarians sometimes supplement their strong methodological individualism with a realistic recognition that the privileged and powerful have strong incentives to perpetuate their advantages and maintain their power. These passages also make unacknowledged communitarian assumptions about a harmony of interests, a weakening of the social fabric, or about the common good. The libertarian value system can be seen most starkly in the "rational choice theory" of James Buchanan and other economists. Whether or not one agrees with Milton Friedman's assertion that the only interest of the chief operating officer of a corporation is the maximizing of profits, the question remains as to the overall impact such a restricted value system has on the social fabric. The analysis here addresses the vexing problem for libertarians of pure luck, as well as morally arbitrary and unfair advantages, such as the so-called genetic lottery of good health and greater intelligence. The limitations of our moral imagination, which Adam Smith helped us to understand, are very relevant here. Lessons from history play an important role in this chapter. For example, what can be learned about this from the heyday of the influence of Social Darwinist ideas? Are such discredited concepts still influential on libertarianism today? What lesson can be learned about power from the true history of "free trade?" Most importantly, what can be learned about the long term, unintended, social and political consequences of inequality?

Difficult questions arise about the justice of the original acquisition of primary goods in Robert Nozick's Entitlement Theory. The historical example, captured by Aldous Huxley in his *Brave New World,* of individuals bargaining away their freedom for goods such as pleasure, highlights the importance of values and character in political theory. This chapter also exposes certain common logical mistakes regarding more practical or procedural concerns about efficiency and regulations that reinforce opposition against government interference in the marketplace, even for those who accept that efficiency should be the only economic value. Specifically, there is a very common confusion about the just or fair application of laws or regulations and whether these rules are necessary or desirable. Also, a number of very prevalent self-fulfilling prophecies regarding the functioning of government bureaucracy have played a key role in building support for libertarian opposition.

One of these interesting manipulations can be seen most clearly in the anti-state, privatization aspect of libertarianism. This chapter shows why such privatizing has been so very problematic. All but the most utopian of libertarians accept the fact that the state has an important role to play in protecting its citizens against violence, fraud, and other criminal behaviors. However, libertarians are often vague or simplistic about what constitutes behaviors such as fraud. Few would disagree that there is a necessity for police and firefighters, though many argue that such services could be more efficiently provided by private companies than by government. Experience and logic contradict such claims. Some libertarians would also agree that government has a role to play in providing and maintaining the infrastructure required for modern life, for both private and commercial activity and safety. Some would even agree that the state has a responsibility to ensure the reliability of contracts, banking, credit, and other financial transactions, to prevent monopolistic practices, as well as to protect the integrity of trademarks and innovative discoveries through patents. All can agree that these various services ought to be provided as fairly, justly, and efficiently as possible. However, even those who accept the need for these minimal governmental protections and services tend to argue that taxation is a form of theft, and not justified in a free society.

This concluding chapter ends by summarizing the main points in favor and in opposition to libertarianism, and builds on these insights in order to develop a pragmatic political program that will advance cooperation to address the many needs we all share in common. Laissez-faire absolutists present the virtues of free markets and the vices of government intervention, while socialists and communitarians have done an equally good job demonstrating the vices of markets and the necessity of collective action to address numerous evils. But, the best libertarian theorists understand that without some regulation large corporations would have too much monopoly power, especially, as with utilities, they control a certain technology or resource. The unintended consequences of invisible hand market transactions may, as Adam Smith believed, lead to positive results, but as he well knew, they do not always promote good outcomes for society. Smith argued that markets need to work within society's customs and traditions. Like his friend David Hume, and like Michael Oakeshott and others, Smith had a political skepticism about ideology, including free market ideology. He understood that all humans have a limited capacity for empathy, one that tends to reduce quickly with distance, combined with a marked tendency to promote our own self-interest.

I show that issues separating the best defenders of both libertarianism and active state liberalism often are not really about philosophical principles, such as justice, but actually revolve around empirical questions of history, politics, and economics. I present an alternative to the bloated, coercive, bureaucratic, behemoth state, with its indifference and corruption, and the narcissistic, self-absorbed, equally corrupt, fragmented, radically individualist, anti-state, corporate-led society. We have developed the worst of both worlds, because we have ignored the best in both political philosophies. Alexis de Tocqueville expressed concern about an extreme form of individualism in America that threatened its democracy in an entirely new way. He voiced his concern about "an innumerable multitude of men, alike and equal, circling around in pursuit of the petty and banal pleasures with which they glut their souls. Each one of them, withdrawn into himself, is almost unaware of the fate of the rest."[68] On the other hand, Tocqueville was equally concerned by the kind of conformity that can come from a judgment based on misguided commitment to a communitarian ideology.[69]

A brief examination of the corrupting effects of "economic imperialism," or the spread of commercial values to all areas of our life, only confirms the worst fears of classical republicans, including America's Founders. In addition, the long term, negative consequences of inequality have too often been ignored in this political debate. Distinctions about the relationship between freedom and equality have been central in debates about libertarianism. However, confusion about the various uses of the concept *equality* has contributed to misunderstandings on both sides. Martha Nussbaum has introduced the useful concept of an institutional concern for equal human dignity that I show helps to bridge the gap between extreme viewpoints about equality.[70] Democratic government has an affirmative role to play in promoting a vibrant middle class, insofar as extreme inequality is a threat to the survival of a free society.

The fact that Lenin embraced, at least rhetorically, American Taylorism or "scientific management" should alert us to the similar subject-object fundamental assumptions of both collectivists and libertarians. Libertarian critics of the very real dangers and inefficiencies of big government inadvertently end up by encouraging the equally dangerous power of giant, international, corporations. Though libertarians should not be blamed for the negative usage that has often been made of their attack on an active state government, it is also impossible to ignore the history of Southern segregationist attacks on civil rights efforts by the Federal government.[71] This concluding chapter demonstrates that this dichotomy, as well as other distorting assumptions, contributes to the legitimation crisis facing all forms of governance in the twenty-first century. This concluding chapter rejects the false dichotomy that holds that protecting citizens against the corrupting power of financial elites and international corporations will only enhance a swollen government bureaucracy at the expense of individual freedom. All groups, not just bureaucracies, governments, unions, but also financial institutions and large corporations, aim to increase their own power and control. A good example is labor unions. On the one hand, the labor movement played a very significant role in the rise of a vibrant American middle class, just as the decline in unionization has been an important factor in decline of the middle class and today's inequality.[72] On the other hand, some unions have promoted policies that have run counter to the public interest. For example, teacher unions have largely resisted efforts to start high schools later in the day, even though the consensus of experts is that adolescent sleep patterns would make this change helpful to students. What is central here is that the unions serve as a faction, in James Madison's sense, and exercise power, in Thomas Hobbes's sense, of promoting or obtaining a particular self-interest. Some of this power is what has come to be called, *soft* power, which is not always as apparent as governmental actions. If we accept the principle that it should be the individual that is the ultimate source of value, that we are free to choose, then it should follow that development of a person's capacity to promote her self-interest, as she sees fit, should be a major goal of any just society. Balancing factions and opposing power centers, so that no one group is dominant should be the function of a just and healthy republic.

Drawing on a deeper understanding of human nature and power, I conclude with a brief discussion of what has been called a "third concept of liberty," one that combines the best aspects of negative and positive concepts, while avoiding the negative consequences associated with government by only one of these traditional foundations of a republic.[73]

A brief note about economic statistics: the joke that, Bill Gates walks into a bar and immediately the income of the others in the bar goes way up, even though they do not feel any wealthier, not only helps students to understand the *mean*, it also should alert them to more general problems with data. Although Thomas Piketty and his team have done the most exhaustive and sophisticated collection and analysis of data on income and wealth, Piketty would be the first to caution that all such mathematics is only as good as the information it is based on. He uses the stark illustration that many trillions of dollars, Euros, and other world currencies have been very successfully hidden in offshore accounts. Piketty calls for the return of economic analysis based on the use of historical, social, and political information. This book adheres to that prescription, while including psychological, moral, and other inputs.[74] Democracy cannot function without information and education. The so-called post truth politics promoted by our contemporary media is arguably the greatest threat to the survival of our freedom.

Chapter One

# PRO

It seems clear, at all events, that there is an intimate connection between freedom of enterprise and freedom of discussion and that political liberty can survive only within an effectively competitive system.

—Henry Simons

Laissez-faire …means let the consumers, i.e. the people decide—by their buying and by their abstention from buying what should be produced and by whom. The alternative to laissez-faire is to entrust these decisions to a paternal government. There is no middle way. Either the consumers are supreme or the government.

—Ludwig von Mises

The society that puts equality before freedom will end up with neither. The society that puts freedom before equality will end up with a great measure of both.

—Milton Friedman

The municipal government known as "Red Vienna" comprised an experiment in socialist democracy following World War I which lasted till a right wing authoritarian Austrian takeover in 1934.[75] It was meant to be a democratic, Marxist alternative to the communist regime that had recently taken over Russia. The ideal expressed in the very extensive social reforms of the Social Democratic Party was to improve the living conditions of the working class through education, improvements in family and women's roles, daily health, including sports and exercise, working conditions, including shorter work hours, and living arrangements, especially housing. There had been a huge influx of new citizens into Vienna during the war. Rent controls and other regulations, such as making it harder for landlords to evict tenants, were introduced to prevent landlords from taking advantage of this severe shortage of apartments through gouging these new refugees and all tenants. The refugee problem and the shortage of housing was even greater by 1919, in part because of an understandable lack of new building in wartime, but also because of a reduced incentive caused by this restriction in rents. The result was the imposition of even stronger tenant protections by the socialist government. These efforts, as well as the extensive public housing development were praised and imitated by socialist parties throughout Europe. The immediate effect was a reduction in the housing shortage. But the longer term effects of all this government intervention were to prove important in the rise of contemporary libertarian economics and social theory.

Friedrich August von Hayek was born in 1899 into an upper class, intellectual, nominally Catholic family in Vienna. The city had been and remained one of the largest, most cosmopolitan, culturally stimulating capitals in the world.[76] Hayek was a distant cousin of the great Austrian philosopher, Ludwig Wittgenstein, about whom he later wrote a biographical essay.[77] Hayek saw action on the Italian front for a little over a year, and he came close to being killed at least twice. It was during this last year that the city suffered most. It was not surprising that these experiences changed his academic interests from biology to the social sciences, especially economics, when he was at the University of Vienna following the war.[78] In addition to the housing crisis, postwar Vienna suffered from hyperinflation, food and fuel shortages, and the world-wide influenza pandemic. Hayek's idea of a "Great Society" has been succinctly summarized as "a model of society and political organization that aims to achieve the greatest possible individual liberty compatible with social order."[79] Hayek later wrote about the collectivist political ferment that rose up in reaction to all these crises, in his most famous work, *The Road to Serfdom.* Hayek's economic thinking had been influenced by the prevailing socialist ideology. However, at the University of Vienna, he soon came under the influence of economists, especially Carl Menger and Friedrich von Wieser, who maintained that it was an open market, supply and demand that determined price, and, therefore, the real value of commodities. Classical economic ideas about supply and demand, at least in the more sophisticated formulation of David Ricardo, had, as John Maynard Keynes noted, "conquered England as completely as the Holy Inquisition conquered Spain."[80] However, it was the real life experience of the long term effects of rent control and government building projects that had the greatest influence on Hayek's philosophy of economic freedom. He wrote about rent control in 1929, and he returned to the topic in a chapter in, arguably his most important work, *The Constitution of Liberty* (1960).[81] Margaret Thatcher, famously, treated this book as the Conservative Party's manifesto.[82]

I only have room here for the briefest summary of the many unintended negative consequences that resulted from the Viennese socialist government's attempts to address the housing emergency. The lessons learned were only reinforced by very similar outcomes in other major cities, in Europe and America, where rent control regulations were introduced. The biggest negative effect was the eventual decline in available housing units, as tenants held on to their homes, even passing them on as a valuable asset in their wills. This was coupled by a strong lack of financial incentives to build new housing, in large part because of an understandable unwillingness of banks to provide construction loans. Couples held on to large apartments even after their children had married; leaving only very cramped quarters for new families. Furthermore, Vienna had had a large amount of subletting, but this also became far less desirable for tenants. Laws passed to try and address problems such as subtenants paying more than main tenants were unsuccessful and only made matters worse. The result of all these downward pressures on supply, of course, was increased homelessness. For the ten years prior to 1934, an estimated 77,419 people a month were homeless, and another 10,000 lived in makeshift dwellings, such as wagons.[83] A similar lack of supply effected new business property, further depressing the economy. For similar financial reasons, landlords lacked any capital to make necessary repairs and improvements, leading to a general decline in the quality of housing stock. Hayek calls this process "fossilization." He also calls attention to effects on the overall economy that were not so obvious. For example, workers were unwilling to leave their low rent housing to move to areas where there were more work opportunities. As a result, many workers spent more of their time and other assets traveling to work.

Hayek was among the first of many economists, including libertarian critics, to point out that, once they've been enacted, it is very hard to get rid of such laws and regulations as rent control. Those citizens who benefit from such rules become a self-interest group that lobbies, or even bribes, public officials.

New York City's rent control legislation was called the War Emergency Tenant Protection Act. The "War" referred to was World War II. Full disclosure: I benefited from this law in the 1960s, and family and friends enjoyed this financial advantage four decades later. New Yorkers, like the Viennese, held on to such apartments, or passed them to family and friends. Just as in Vienna, the elderly also held on to large apartments, making it harder for young couples with children to find adequate accommodations. It was also well-known, when I lived in New York, that the law encouraged corruption by bribing superintendants or others in order to get one of these valuable prizes. The great Swedish economist Gunnar Myrdal, who, though he shared the Nobel Prize in economics with Hayek, was hardly a libertarian, summarized the consequences: "rent control has in certain western countries constituted, maybe, the worst example of poor planning by governments lacking courage and vision."[84]

With private construction at a standstill, the Social Democratic Party in Vienna tried to deal with these negative effects by building public housing. They rejected the advice of economists like Hayek that they return to the free market, arguing that construction costs and interest rates were too high and would produce rents beyond what workers could afford.[85] There were over 370 such building projects, called "people's palaces," constructed by 1934, with about 200,000 occupants.[86] Not surprisingly, this prescription resulted in its own unintended negative consequences. All this government building, of course, required increased capital, which came from highly progressive taxation, including a luxury tax. Coupled with the big reduction in funds previously collected by landlords, there was far less available investment capital for business expansion. I do not need to enumerate all the social problems that come with public housing projects as they are all too familiar today.[87]

In his 1960 study of housing and government planning, Hayek introduces the economic term, "neighborhood effects" for these social consequences, and points to the obvious fact that these effects are greater with increased population density.[88] Economists today have introduced the terms *positive* and negative *externalities*, since such effects of government actions are not always detrimental to social life. I will return to these concepts later in this chapter. What is more important here is how the Viennese socialist government used public housing as a paternalist tool for controlling the behavior of working-class men and women, including the very nature of marital relationships. For example, there were the many rules imposed by "experts" to ensure that women became good homemakers and mothers. One historian has summed up this "experiment" with the phrase "invasions of the private sphere."[89]

It was his experience of this extreme regulation of every aspect of life by Austrian socialists that allowed Hayek to argue that "in Germany and Italy the Nazis and Fascists did, indeed, not have much to invent. The usages of the new political movements which pervaded all aspects of life had in both countries already been introduced by the socialists."[90] Milton Friedman and his wife Rose point to the origin of the paternalistic welfare state in Otto von Bismarck's German Empire.[91] They note the close relationship of Bismarck's program with aristocracy. As with Franklin Roosevelt, after the Depression, a major motive was to protect capitalism from socialist revolution.[92] The Friedmans add urban renewal, especially in New York City, as another welfare measure that had the consequence of, among other problems, further reducing housing for the poor.[93]

It was during the war years of 1940 to 1943 that Hayek developed his libertarian principles in reaction to the greatest violation of human freedoms then known. In 1944, he published, arguably, the most influential work on the subject, *The Road to Serfdom.* As is so often the case, however, we know from his 1976 Preface, that Hayek did not consider this book that made him famous, his most important work. *The Road to Serfdom* was published first in England, and was a response to debates there about economic planning and the economic and political causes of the rise of totalitarianism. Specifically, it was Hayek's rejoinder to British intellectuals who argued that the rise of fascism was a capitalist reaction to socialism, and, most importantly, that the Soviet model of socialist planning was "scientific" and an advance that should be replicated at home. We have no problem today, recognizing that the idea that a government that controlled the economy would somehow "wither away" was a dangerous delusion. Although there were British socialists, such as H.G. Wells and Bertrand Russell, who had visited Russia and saw through this propaganda, others, such as Sidney and Beatrice Webb were taken in by Lenin and the Communists. What's more, after the Great Depression, and in response to the War, economic planning appeared a necessity. Hayek was able to quote Maynard Keynes's warning about the effect of planning on the growth of central government and the "militarization of our industrial life."[94]In a letter to Hayek, Keynes praised Hayek's work as "a grand book," adding that "we all have the greatest reason to be grateful to you for saying so well what needs so much to be said."[95] But, in a subsequent letter to Hayek, he showed less sympathy and understanding by arguing that Britain could have "safe" and "rightful" planning, if only officials shared Hayek's moral convictions. This ignored Hayek's express warning that a major problem with government planning was that it could not rely on some collective moral code since such ethical rules only exist at the most general level.[96] It was only through the knowledge that comes from the actions of individuals in an open and competitive market that we learn what it is that people desire or value. Hayek summed up his concern by stating that "we have progressively abandoned that freedom in economic affairs without which personal and political freedom has never existed in the past." It was "the individual" who should be "the ultimate judge of his ends," not some state bureaucrats. The ethical beliefs, goals, and desires of individuals far exceed the comprehension of any central planner. Over the next four decades, Hayek expanded on and deepened this analysis, without any major philosophical differences between a late and early Hayek. However, when it comes to economic and political policy, he moved from a classical liberal position, accepting some welfare programs and the taxation to pay for them, to a much more recognizably right libertarian program. He was, no doubt, influenced by his associates, including Ludwig Mises; but, primarily by the tremendous expansion of government services and budgets during the last decades of his long life.[97] Hayek was familiar with the Austrian socialist's claims, which he encountered again in Britain, that their economic ideas were more "scientific."[98]

It is a measure of just how extreme economic divisions were in Britain at this time that socialist planning was generally referred to as "The Middle Way." Fascism was also seen by many academics as a capitalist reaction to socialism; this, despite the strong socialist influences on fascists like Mussolini.[99] As early as 1939 Hayek expressed his concern "that comprehensive economic planning, which is regarded as necessary to organize economic activity on more rational and efficient lines, presupposes a much more complete agreement on the relative importance of the different social ends than actually exists, and that in consequence, in order to plan, the planning authority must impose upon the people the detailed code of values that is lacking."[100] In a 1968 lecture, the title of which is instructive, "Competition as a Discovery Procedure," Hayek deepened and expanded on his other main objection to a planned economy. His arguments for the superiority of competition in an open market as a way of discovering real value are historical, pragmatic, and utilitarian. His approach has been called *methodological individualism.*[101] The scientific methodological influences on Hayek, in this regard, include his friends, Michael Polanyi and Karl Popper, as well as the early work of Joseph Schumpeter.

Polanyi deserves a brief mention, because of his economic ideas, but, especially, for his highly influential concept of tacit knowledge.[102] He wrote with the authority of a highly respected chemist, economist and philosopher. Like Mises and Hayek, Polanyi was an early critic of socialist economic planning. The problem, he asserted, was a lack of the required knowledge:"the central authority, however properly constituted it may be as a government, is in fact ignorant of the desires of its constituents as far as their day-to-day wants are concerned."[103] Polanyi shows how a complex system, such as a market economy, is made up of a number of other complex interactions, none of which are predictable in advance. Clearly his understanding of chemistry was central to his insights about such complex systems. However, like the early Hayek, Polanyi was not a doctrinaire economic libertarian, since he argued that there was a role for government, even beyond protecting against fraud and securing contacts. It was his sophisticated ideas about "spontaneous orders" that gave philosophical weight to libertarian economic arguments. Polanyi was one of the more original critics of the *scientism* that Hayek saw as central to socialist arguments for planning. Like Hayek, Polanyi drew from new insights into the psychology of knowledge and perception. Examples, such as facial recognition or the acquisition of language, demonstrate how *"we can know more than we can tell."*[104] Polanyi notes that one of the most important aspects of interpersonal relations is our tacit knowledge about a person's mood from observing their facial expression and body language. Hayek argued that this view of knowledge explained how an economic market works, but also how abstract rules and an "abstract order" evolves, one that allows for each individual to pursue his or her diverse goals in a pluralistic society. The procedure differs from that of the pure sciences in that it does not lead to the prediction of specific economic transactions or agreed moral principles. But, compared to the omniscience needed by a government planner, and "order created by direct commands," the accumulative knowledge of all the many individuals who participate in a market results, Hayek contends, in a "spontaneous order."

This mechanism, of course, is similar to Adam Smith's concept of the invincible hand.[105] Money and material possessions, in all their forms, are the prime motivator, each person acting in her own self-interest and personal sphere, with knowledge and desires constantly adapting to changing circumstances. Smith's most famous lines cannot be improved on: "It is not from the benevolence of the butcher, the brewer, or the baker that we expect our dinner, but from their own interest. We address ourselves, not to their humanity, but to their self-love, and never talk to them of our necessities but of their advantages."[106]The idea that self-interest was natural was a cornerstone of American Enlightenment thought, as can be seen, for example, in Crèvecoeur's classic *Letters from An American Farmer.*[107]

Hayek argued that this was not greed or selfishness, but simply a natural or biological expression of human desire. Rather than being divisive, it is an expression of our general need to socialize. In an early, remarkably prescient and highly influential essay, "Economic Calculation in the Socialist Commonwealth," Ludwig von Mises summarized many of the deficiencies of a planned economy. He pointed out that money could not perform its usual function in calculating value, as it does in a competitive economy. He adds that "the exclusion of free initiative and individual responsibility, on which the success of private enterprise depend, constitutes the most serious menace to socialist economic enterprise."[108] His comments about the near absence of pressures to perform and improve production, under socialism, as well as his comments about the power relationship between directors and shareholders in large corporations, are strikingly prophetic and prognostic. His comment about the appeal of planning for individuals wishing to be "relieved of the agony of decisions," should have been a profound warning for the coming decades.[109]It is important to note that early libertarians, such as Hayek and Mises, were far from doctrinaire laissez-faire capitalists. In fact, for Hayek, what he called the "Rule of Law" was of paramount importance.

In the *Road to Serfdom,* Hayek was careful to distinguish between his critique of socialist planning and a "dogmatic laissez faire attitude."[110] Hayek, and the best of libertarian thinkers, accepted the need for some rules or laws for the very existence of private property and for a capitalist economic system to even exist. The issue was how to distinguish just laws and how to limit such coercive force to the least amount necessary for the functioning of a free and efficient economy. Hayek had demonstrated that a socialist planned economy had led to the very opposite of the personal autonomy and economic justice it had promised. Now, he needed to show that the spontaneous actions of millions of consumers in a free and open market could lead to order, standards and economic justice; what he styled "order without commands." The way to accomplish this was by updating and expanding on Adam Smith's concept of the "invisible hand."It was in his 1960 masterwork *The Constitution of Liberty* that Hayek fully addressed these key questions. But, Hayek's treatise was not just about economic freedom, but about freedom of choice in all areas of social and political life, including within a person's own home and bedroom.[111]

Hayek admits that, in addition to laws that guarantee property and the sustaining of contracts, there was a role for government as the best provider of, what we call, infrastructure.[112] He goes on to uphold the British tradition that "a man's house is his castle."Laws are necessary to protect this sanctuary, as well as to provide consumers with security against fraud and deception in economic transactions. Hayek even allows that the government will need to engage in taxation, in order to provide for such amenities or public services and for the general security; something that many later libertarians were to question. What keeps these necessary evils from being "coercive," for Hayek, is the nature and the application of the laws involved. Bruce Caldwell offers a succinct summary of what prevents Hayek's "laws of liberty" from being coercive and unjust. They need to be "abstract and impersonal, prospective, known, certain, universal in application, and enforced equally."[113]As I will show in my concluding chapter below, this use of a high level of abstraction can even provide a conception of equality that is acceptable to most libertarians, as well as their opponents. It is the arbitrary or ad hoc nature of laws, and their unjust application, that makes them coercive. It is, also, the monopolistic nature of state planning that leads to the abuse of power. Monopoly in all its forms disrupts the mechanism of free competition that provides the knowledge required for an economy to run smoothly and efficiently. Another libertarian economist, Henry Simons, summed this up: "the great enemy of democracy is monopoly in all its forms: gigantic corporations, trade associations and other agencies for price control, trade-unions, or, in general, organization and concentration of power within functional classes."[114]James Madison had spoken of the need "to break and control the violence of factions," and, especially, that "monopolies are sacrifices of the many to the few."[115]Hayek called them "coalitions of organized interests."[116]

As noted above, Maynard Keynes had admitted that "the central controls necessary to ensure full employment will, of course, involve a large extension of the traditional functions of government."[117] In a small but important work on *Bureaucracy,* Ludwig von Mises painted a much darker picture of this growth in government; what he called "bureaucratism."He asserted that "the capitalist system of production is an economic democracy in which every penny gives a right to vote."[118]At the time that he wrote, Mises had to counter the widely held view that bureaucracy was inconsistent with democracy. He did not attack bureaucracy as such. Nor did he see individual bureaucrats as anything more than victims of the system. Rather, it was the newly developing welfare state, with its consequent expansion of rules and regulations into every aspect of a citizen's life that was the problem.[119]

Like Hayek, Mises understood that capitalism requires laws to operate. But, he contrasted the capitalist system where it was each individual consumer who determined value, with a socialist or planned economy with laws that were meant to "execute the will of the authorities," rather than protect consumers. In his 1949 magnum opus, *Human Action,* Mises shows that the infinite complexity of human beings means that it is impossible to know in advance how much of a given commodity will be needed or will sell, meaning that the price mechanism is the only system that can insure flexibility and adaptability.[120] He makes a highly influential point about the role of prices as information: "in a market economy, prices are not arbitrary, but signal a real, underlying scarcity, and help everyone in the economy adjust his plans in light of reality." This theoretical argument is strongly supported by the history of consumer shortages, or oversupply, in communist countries. The distortion that comes from a lack of this information has played a role in the tremendous increase in medical costs. Because of medical insurance, the consumer rarely knows the true cost of an individual item, such as a bandage, or, even in some cases a whole procedure. The government has had a similar role in the very harmful inflation in the cost of higher education, by injecting huge sums in the form of student grants and loans, thereby, giving colleges and universities the opportunity to go on a spending spree. From an economic viewpoint Mises argued that the welfare state was also inefficient because it severed the connection between revenues and expenditures.[121]

Libertarians would argue that, though we do not have a totally planned economy in America today, we have something close to it, in the "regulatory state." The thousands of regulations enacted since the New Deal coerce businesses in myriad ways, adding to costs and inefficiencies.

What's more, it is a lot easier to add new regulations than it is to get rid of old ones, once they are on the books. This last fact is similar to John Maynard Keynes's major mistake of believing that politicians would eliminate programs used to stimulate a weak economy, and thus reduce budget deficits, once the economy had recovered and was booming.

Hayek was strongly influenced by these arguments. A number of commentators see a shift in Hayek's latest formulation of the rule of law. But, I see a deepening of his lifelong concern with a statist, top-down, "managerial" imposition of controls, and an extension of an evolutionary, spontaneous, bottom-up system, what he calls "grown," as opposed to "made" regulations. Hayek's concept of spontaneity is dynamic, as opposed to the equilibrium theory of other economists. Critics of the classic economic model of equilibrium usually attack its fundamental assumption that actors in the market start with complete knowledge about value. They point to evidence that this kind of knowledge is rarely available. However, the economist Vernon L. Smith, who was awarded a Nobel Prize for his pioneering work, showed experimentally that markets achieve equilibrium even when players do not have the full information that rational choice theory assumes. He also showed how regulations could produce unexpected consequences that disrupted this equilibrium. Most economic transactions appear to function quite well without full information or interference. [122]

A number of commentators have noted that Hayek, who became a British citizen, was clearly influenced by that county's common law tradition. Evolutionary advancement, here, comes from a competition between goals and ideas, as well as goods. It is a different use of evolutionary theory to defend capitalism from the theory of Social Darwinism of an earlier period.

Hayek's last major work of political philosophy, his three volume, *Law, Legislation, and Liberty,* argued that purposely designed organizations or institutions suffered from the same deficiencies as planned economies, and that such "made" organizations would lead to a totalitarian loss of freedoms. From his earliest works to the end of his career, Hayek consistently maintained that the knowledge that we gain from free market competition was not simply which specific products or services are best, but also, which particular companies or professionals we can trust to give us what we need or desire. The results of such a competitive system, of course, meant that there would always be winners and losers; and, that individuals and companies would have to work harder to survive in an always changing marketplace. But, Hayek celebrated such dynamism that he believed only capitalism could create. What's more, it was this competitive system that best expressed the individual's purposes or values. This was an expression of the kind of messy freedom from the bottom up that was the essence of democracy. As Hayek noted, since there weren't any "omniscient men," we need to have the liberty to work together to achieve our ends.[123]

The type of freedom that Hayek and other libertarians promote has been called *negative liberty,* not because it is something bad, but only in order to contrast it with *positive liberty.* Negative liberty is freedom *from* restraint, whereas positive liberty is usually defined as freedom *to* accomplish one's goals. Unlike anarchist libertarians who claimed descent from Mises and Hayek, neither author believed that individuals could have liberty without the protection offered by laws and a state. However, the goal was to reduce the coercion that the government must use to protect and maintain order to a minimum, and make it "impersonal and dependent upon general, abstract laws, whose effects on particular individuals cannot be foreseen at the time they are laid down."[124]The classic analysis of "the permissible limits of coercion" and the differences between negative and positive liberty is the 1958 essay, "Two Concepts of Liberty" by the philosopher and historian of ideas, Isaiah Berlin. The issues surrounding these concepts of liberty are important in this book, and I will return to them in the chapters to follow. As Berlin notes, nothing essential hangs on whether one uses liberty or freedom. Not only is negative freedom something good, but for libertarians, such as Hayek, it is the concept of positive liberty that is suspect, and that can and has led to authoritarianism. The power to do "God's will" has been a major focus of sectarians, from the New England Puritans to the moral majority. The freedom from interference, on the other hand, was a major focus of the America Revolution. Jeremy Bentham famously borrowed the command made by Diogenes to the mighty Alexander the Great "stand out of my sunshine" as his rule for good government.[125] Negative liberty, Berlin argues, is what we normally mean by being free, namely, when "no man or body of men interferes with my activity." This is freedom *from* coercion, which he adds "implies the deliberate interference of other human beings within the area in which I would otherwise act."[126]Hayek, however, warns that we must not confuse the metaphorical use of freedom from, in the sense of "power" or freedom to be able to do something, with this absence of coercion by others. When this is combined with the wide scope of government power, into all aspects of our lives, the danger is readily apparent. Liberalism was largely a reaction to the view of the role of government known as *pastoralism*, the tradition that government should be concerned about the souls, as well as the bodies of its citizens. The popular libertarian, Ayn Rand, clearly expressed the problem, writing that "if a man believes that the good is intrinsic in certain actions, he will not hesitate to force people to perform them." She went on to list four of the worst dictators in history as the direct result.[127] Hayek is less dramatic, but he notes that this confusion of negative with positive freedom comes from substituting *restraint*, with its connotation of inner strength or will power, with coercion from external *constraint*.[128] The "particular obstacle" for Hayek is interference by others, not some internal limitation that prevents self-actualization. As Berlin puts it, "mere incapacity to attain a goal is not lack of political freedom." I will return to this question in the last section of this book.

Hayek and Berlin share, to a large extent, the same concern with what Berlin labels positive liberty or what has been called freedom *to*, in the sense of opportunity or the power to do what one desires. Many people have noted that Jefferson specified the right to the *pursuit* of happiness, the opportunity, rather than a right to actually be happy, the outcome. Note also, that how a person defines happiness is a value that can differ greatly among citizens. But, as one commentator on Hayek notes, "what for one man is a matter of ensuring fair competition by means of a level playing field is for another a restriction of competition and its advantages."[129] Both men are concerned about what is added to freedom, to make it positive, especially the political or moral theory about how one reaches ones full potential; as Berlin puts it, "a particular social and economic theory about the causes of my poverty or weakness," such as Marxism.[130] Such theories leave the door open for imposing a certain ideology or morality, in order to enhance the citizen's full potential. The dangers that can come from the concept of positive liberty and communitarian theories can best be seen in the extreme views of someone like the Massachusetts Puritan, John Winthrop's 1645 "Little Speech on Liberty." [131]For a religious authoritarian like Winthrop, negative liberty, which he called natural liberty, was the freedom of beasts and sinful humans to do what they wished. The opposite of this was "moral or civil liberty," which was acting in accordance with God's precepts.

Hayek understood that the coercive force of law could only be held to a minimum if citizens accepted certain moral principles. But, these social rules could not be imposed from above, and could only evolve spontaneously from habit and custom.[132] This is, especially, true in the pluralistic societies of today. The danger comes from the propensity of moralists to assume that they know what individuals need to reach their full potential. As one interpreter of Isaiah Berlin states, "there are few presumptions in human relations more dangerous than the idea that one knows what another human being needs better than they do themselves."[133]What's more, it is common for individuals to confuse needs with wants. When an adolescent says to his parents, "I need the car tonight," they could point to this common mistake of reasoning.[134] Individuals should be allowed to engage in activities that others would consider self-injurious, just so long as they do not harm others. The classic historical example, most would agree, comes from the sorry consequences of Prohibition in 1920s America.[135] I will return to some differences between the position of Isaiah Berlin and libertarianism in the next chapter. Suffice it to say here that, these differences stem in part from very different interpretations of the history of the effects of the Industrial Revolution that came out of Hayek's collaboration with other libertarians.[136]

In a lecture he delivered in Dublin, in 1945, and later published as "Individualism: True and False," as well as in later works, Hayek outlined a sophisticated theory of another central tenant of libertarian economic and political thought.[137] It is very clear that this work builds upon his central ideas about the Rule of Law that I have just outlined. In this 1945 lecture, Hayek addresses the many misconceptions about the libertarian theory of individualism and, what he calls, "the bogey of the 'economic man'," as well as "the much abused and much misunderstood phrase of 'laissez faire'.[138] Hayek quotes one of his favorite defenders of freedom, Lord Acton: "whenever a single definite object is made the supreme end of the State, be it the advantage of a class, the safety or power of the country, the greatest happiness of the greatest number or the support of any speculative idea, the State becomes for the time inevitably absolute."[139] Hayek praises Acton and Alexis de Tocqueville as the two historians of "true" individualism. Looking to explain how totalitarianism and the "poison of nationalism" had infected Europe, Hayek identified an atomistic and rationalist "false individualism" of "interchangeable units," coming out of the rise of imperial Germany. Hayek contrasts these massive, impersonal relationships with the spontaneous and free interaction of individuals that transpires at a local level.

He traces these ideas to the French rationalists and contemporary positivist faith in experts, science and technocratic control. This rationalism had also led to the belief in an underlying, essential, reality of organic society, over and above the individuals who comprise any group. He was not always careful about his description of the market, which has led some to criticize his views as also essentialist.[140] But, Hayek is clear that the only way we can understand social and market reality is by "understanding of individual actions directed toward other people and guided by their expected behavior."[141] Hayek combines his concept of true individualism with another central principle of libertarianism, a distinction between equality before the law and of the rules of behavior versus efforts to impose equality of status and of opportunity, what he later called *material* equality. It is this latter type of equality that leads to authoritarian rule.[142]Hayek's arguments for protecting the beliefs of minorities, and his statement that minority opinions are sometimes adopted by the majority, has repeatedly been shown to be correct. Hayek dismisses a common misconception about the libertarian emphasis on individualism, that it denies the social nature of human character. Rather, it is this very concept of isolated, atomistic individuals, free of social influence, which he describes as false individualism. Hayek's arguments appear to fit better with recent work in behavioral economics, as opposed to the rationalist assumptions of certain economists.[143]

Hayek's views on the nature of equality are central to all libertarian political thought. He notes that the great line, "all men are born equal" is not literally true, but rather expresses the ideal that every individual should be treated the same, before the law, as well as morally. This cornerstone of liberty, however, conflicts with any effort by the state to make all individuals materially equal. He draws this contrast in the sharpest terms: "the equality before the law which freedom requires leads to material inequality."[144]Unlike some later libertarians, Hayek does not shrink from admitting this consequence of treating every citizen as equal, even when, as he admits, some individuals have benefitted from the morally underserved fortunes of birth, not only what has become known as the genetic lottery, but even the educational and material status of one's parents; all of the advantages that have been called "being born on third base."He simply holds that the level of coercion necessary to bring about material equality is too high a price to pay. He states this boldly in his "Individualism" address: "from the point of view of individualism there would not appear to exist even any justification for making all individuals start on the same level by preventing them from profiting by advantages which they have in no way earned, such as being born to parents who are more intelligent or more conscientious than the average."[145]Hayek acknowledges that, though some who advocate for greater equality are motivated by simple envy many others object to the reality that rewards often do not come from earned merit.  Hayek voices concern with this common association of merit and reward. His subtle, but important, point comes from the disturbing history of the use of the term *merit*, for example by the Social Darwinists, with moral worth, "the moral character of the action and not the value of the achievement."[146] Philosophers today use the phrase *morally neutral* to express Hayek's recognition that an individual's talents or unique qualities are not often the things that she can take credit for, and that reward should come from the specific services or benefits that society receives from her activities. There is, as Hayek reminds us, a danger to freedom that comes from the concept of moral merit. An example, similar to one Hayek gives, would be drug research. All the companies may engage in "meritorious" research, but we correctly reward that company which produces the medically useful drug, with a patent and the economic prize. Remuneration should be tied to the beneficial results for society. We share a natural desire to believe that society and the market reward merit, but in reality, as Hayek notes, luck or chance often plays a major role in success. The concern, as usual for Hayek and libertarians, is that other people, the majority, the state, will determine what behavior individuals should engage in, based on some distribution of rewards. This is the very opposite of freedom. I will return to the central analysis of merit, responsibility, and reward, what is called *distributive justice,* below. But, for now, it is important to note that Hayek embraces the positive goal of seeing that all individuals rise up in their status as a result of an increasingly wealthy economy. Policies that will tend to increase equality may be encouraged, so long as they are not aimed specifically at redistribution of resources, and they do not reduce any individual's personal freedom. In other words, inequality in and of itself is not a sufficient evil to justify any redistributive legal action or preferential treatment by the state.

Hayek's argument depends, in large part, on several underlying propositions: first, as is the case with economic planning, he argued that no government official could possibly comprehend what innate capabilities that individual's might possess. The second proposition is that those individuals with superior abilities will benefit the nation as a whole, and rising national wealth, over a sustained period, Hayek contends, tends to increase everyone's standard of living. The ability to pass on what parents earn to their children, thus providing them with inherited advantages is, he argues, a strong motivating incentive to earn more, thus benefiting the whole society. What is also important for liberty is that egalitarianism or forced equality would require that the government meddle in a wide number of private concerns that convey advantage, including family, ethnic, and cultural traditions. Providing equal opportunity would require a huge increase in the areas that government controls, with a resulting loss in freedom. Think of so-called heritage admissions or scholarships to prestigious universities.

As I noted earlier, Hayek, for most of his career and unlike some contemporary libertarians, accepted an obligation by the state to care for the "weak or infirm," and for the protection of citizens against certain of life's risks. However, he argued that "the common provision of some services is no justification for anyone claiming as a right a share in all the benefits."[147]The use of the concept of *right* here will prove important in what follows. But, in light of recent events in Europe and America, it is interesting to note his pragmatic argument against such a right, namely, that it would probably lead to a battle over immigration, since many will wish to come to an egalitarian state to benefit from its welfare provisions. Hayek, also, put forward an influential critique of a progressive tax system in *The Constitution of Liberty.*[148] It should not be surprising that he would criticize any sort of economic policy that was championed by socialists and had been introduced into Europe by Marx and Engels in their *Communist Manifesto.*[149] Even though Hayek begins by expressing some hesitation about criticizing such a popular policy, his position would be considered too supportive by libertarians today, many of whom reject all taxation as a form of theft. Hayek accepts that some amount of graduation of income taxes is justified in order to reduce the burden of other taxes, such as the sales tax, on people with low incomes. He does quote John Stuart Mill's statement that progressive taxation is "a mild form of robbery."[150] Mill objected to imposing "a penalty on people for having worked harder and saved more than their neighbors."[151]Hayek begins by noting that, when a progressive tax is first introduced, the rates are very low, but soon increase to major proportions. He adds that, though the negative effects of this form of taxation on incentives is a real concern which is often noted, there are other economic consequences that are equally troubling. Investors are understandably more risk adverse. The necessary knowledge about the value of resources is disturbed. There are serious dampening effects on saving, further reducing capital for investment. In general, the market mechanism that assures that such investment in resources, time, and energy is correlated with social benefits is disrupted. This is, especially, true for the self-employed and small business owners. His warnings against the ways that such taxation favors large corporations and "quasi-monopolies" are quite prescient in light of recent history. Hayek puts forward a very different set of criticisms of progressive taxation as a policy for achieving greater economic equality. In fact, his first line of attack is directed at the idea that progressive taxation is more socially just. He notes that such taxation has the unjust effect of a majority, in his day the middle class, coercing a minority, with little benefit accruing to the poor.

But before turning to these moral and political concerns, a line of critique that he later wrote a whole book about, I will first address another of his purely economic arguments attacking the defense of this form of taxation, a critique based on the law of decreasing marginal utility of successive acts of consumption. Despite the technical jargon, the principle behind this economic law can be stated simply and it is quite intuitive. It is based in a reality of human nature that has been known since ancient times, namely, that successive acts of satisfying a particular desire lead inevitably to the satiation of that desire.[152] If you are very thirsty, your desire for the first bottle of water will be considerably more than for the second or successive bottles. The amount of benefit derived from $20 to someone who is starving is considerably more than what $20 provides to a millionaire. The application to the graduated income tax is easy to see: the benefits in social welfare that accrue to a citizen with a low income far exceed the pain felt by the citizen who is wealthy.

Hayek contends that a policy that is meant to promote social justice and reduce inequality by enhancing the welfare of the poor ends up violating the one principle of equality he recognizes, namely, equality before the law. "An even more paradoxical and socially grave effect of progressive taxation," he asserts, "is that, though intended to reduce inequality, it in fact helps to perpetuate existing inequalities and eliminates the most important compensation for that inequality which is inevitable in a free-enterprise society."[153] His argument here is again quite prescient in that he points to an economic rigidity, lack of social mobility, and the concentration of capital in the hands of an ever smaller coterie of financiers, who have not previously held property or incurred the risks of small businessmen or developers. In the words of Justice Louis Brandeis, the bankers "control the people through the people's own money."[154] Hayek was wrestling with issues that are still central to concerns about inequality and distributive justice today: is the issue the distance between the best and the worse off in society, or should government concentrate resources to help the worse off, whether or not this reduces the separation.[155] The central contrast is between libertarianism, with its commitment to individual rights, pluralism, and the promotion of diverse viewpoints, "letting a thousand flowers bloom," and a dangerous worldview that seeks to promote or enhance some agreed upon common interest of social justice or the public good. The former view is classical liberalism, which is contrasted with a communitarian or classically republican political outlook. This use of the term is contrasted with authoritarianism, and it is used to designate the British political thinkers who influenced the American founders.[156] "Libertarians," as Jonathan Haidt notes, "are the direct descendants of the eighteenth-century and nineteenth-century Enlightenment reformers who fought to free people and markets from the control of kings and clergy."[157]

An excellent study of authoritarian social psychology uses libertarian in this contrasting way.[158]Hayek argues that any political system that aims to encourage or discourage the conduct of private citizens in support of some social or public good can easily become a threat to individual freedom. These contrasting political systems have been at the center of the American political dialogue, at least since the Federalists and anti-Federalist debate over ratification of the *U. S. Constitution.* The anti-Federalist fear of consolidated power, which takes control further from the local people and encourages the denial of individual rights, mirrors in many ways Hayek's concerns about collectivism and monopoly. Their concern that, for example, excessive taxation would result from a centralized government, because the representatives would be far removed from the local people who would be adversely effected, sounds like Hayek and other modern libertarians. The pluralist interpretation of our political system agrees with Hayek in asserting that, though we should all be treated equally, we are all different, which allows for some inherent inequality. It is this wide diversity of backgrounds and interests that balances one faction against another, thereby protecting against the empowerment of one dominant interest group.

Even the title of the second volume of his 1976 magnum opus, *The Mirage of Social Justice*, gives a strong indication of Hayek's final position on these issues of equality. Hayek always comes back to the central difference between designed organizations, where there is a set of specific, agreed upon, goals that each individual member is expected to work to achieve, and spontaneous orders, where each member is given the freedom to achieve his or her own aims within a framework of generally accepted, abstract rules. He argues that in a large, pluralistic, multiethnic society, such as the modern United States, only the latter form of organization contributes to true liberty. The argument can be generalized, since any complex society is made up of unique individuals with their own experiences, traditions, beliefs, and capabilities, all of which contributes to developing their own personal interests and aims. Hayek believed that history demonstrated that a well ordered and functioning government, what he called a "Great Society," did not have to be designed, with top-down authority and a hierarchy of prescribed aims. However, as I have shown, Hayek was far from being an anarchist. He believed that government had an important role to play in setting abstract, non-arbitrary, rules that would facilitate the functioning of free but organized institutions, including a free market, and in protecting individuals and organizations in the competitive process of promoting individual or group self-interest.

Much of Hayek's mature political philosophy, in this specific area, is reminiscent of James Madison's justly famous analysis of, what he called, factions, and how "a well-constructed Union" can "break and control the violence of faction."[159] The major difference here is instructive. It comes from Hayek's use of evolutionary theory, which is to say, a natural, unplanned, ordering, based on the survival of the best rule, as determined by a spontaneous and recurrent competition of ideas and laws. I will conclude my all-too brief presentation of Hayek's contribution to libertarian thought with an equally cursory analysis of his highly influential critique of the concepts of *social* and *economic* justice.[160]The addition of the adjectives social and economic, Hayek argues, is an abuse of the concept of justice brought about by a "primitive" tendency to "anthropomorphic" thinking. In fact, Hayek argues that these adjectives add no real meaning to the concept of justice, hence the use of "mirage" in his title. We are unable to see that anything short of an act of conscious planning, or certain acts of will by planners, as opposed to an impersonal process, could possibly lead more successfully to the satisfaction of our individual or collective desires.

This was not simply a conceptual or terminological dispute for Hayek. Rather, it was a confused mode of thinking that had led inevitably to serious negative consequences by encouraging coercive government interventions to achieve a morally prescribed just social order. Until the end of his long career, Hayek mounted a crusade against the use of the term *social*. He included a section "Our Poisonous Language," in one of his last works, he which he called this term a "weasel word."[161]In a 1979 lecture, that he delivered in Sidney, Australia, Hayek made it clear why he felt this phrase was a meaningless and even a dangerous one. He argues that "rules of just conduct are as indispensable to the preservation of a peaceful society of free men as endeavors to realize 'social' justice are incompatible with it."[162]It was not the concept of "justice", or even "social," that was the target of his concern, but rather the fact that the phrase "social justice" was being used as a substitute for what really troubled him, the belief that there was a need for "distributive justice" in order to maintain order and achieve the goal of a just society. The false idea of a just distribution of goods and services presupposes an omniscience that is illusory and a control that would be corrosive of freedom. In a society that is free, where individuals are allowed to pursue their own goals and interests, whatever distribution of goods that results must be natural and not artificially imposed from above. Moreover, individuals can only be held morally responsible for actions freely chosen, not those imposed from without. Finally, market competition must be allowed to function without interference, and, Hayek admits, such a free market will not produce some preconceived just distribution of goods and resources. Hayek finds only one general formula of social justice that most individuals agree upon, and that is "equal pay for equal work"; but, this rule is allowed because it is produced by free market competition for employees.

Hayek feels the need to explain why it is that most individuals feel that justice requires some equal distribution of goods; and, as he so often does, he turns to evolutionary ideas about primitive man in small, closed communities where this kind of sharing would be efficient and even necessary. In this late lecture, and elsewhere, Hayek contrasts this primitive cooperation with a market economy. He compares the latter with a competitive game, with rules, challenges that award and advance skills, and a "common pool from which each will win an uncertain share."[163] Hayek sees the progressive development of a different, market, morality that resembles the morality of abiding by the rules of a competitive game. He goes on to describe Adam Smith's views about laws of property and contract. His modification of Smith's famous concept of the division of labor is to argue that the most important division is between different companies, each bringing its own resources and expertise to the greater economy. It is only this competition between companies, as well as the price system, an impersonal mechanism, that provides the knowledge that is needed to make an efficient economy function. It is only when governments interfere with the operation of this impersonal system, by redistributing resources to help those groups considered most deserving that the information necessary for a smooth running economy is no longer available. This is the only game, Hayek argues, that has led to the general improvement of living standards and well-being, and, unless someone can be shown to be cheating, all who benefit must accept the rules of competition and his or her particular outcome. Hayek readily admits that the results of this game "will necessarily be that many have much more than their fellows think they deserve, and even more will have much less than their fellows think they deserve."[164] Free competition and the information that comes from price are the mechanism that creates wealth. Any effort to force a redistribution in order to help those who are disadvantaged or losing, though understandable, ends up destroying the mechanism, shrinking the pie, leaving less wealth for everyone. It is like weighing the meat for some with the metal hook.

The appeal to social justice, Hayek objected, had become a way to sanction the use of government power. The locus of just behavior had moved from being a moral requirement of the individual citizen to a duty to submit to government authorities. More and more special interest groups have learned to use this formula as a way to extract resources from the general coffers. This process, of course, has led to a massive increase in government agencies, and their arbitrary powers, and, therefore, in the overall size of all branches, but especially the executive. What Madison wrote of the state legislatures in his day could be applied with even greater truth to the federal executive branch today, namely that, "power is of an encroaching nature" and "the legislative department is everywhere extending the sphere of its activity, and drawing all power into its imperious vortex."[165] The process brings ever more groups within society under the dependence and control of government bureaucrats. Hayek acknowledges the feelings of sympathy we have at the injustice that "befalls" many groups, families, and individuals in society; calamities for which there is no discernible culprit. "Some succeed brilliantly," while others fail despite their "meritorious efforts."[166]Hayek believes that when the market is allowed to function as it should, within broad "rules about the conduct of the players," but without specific government interference, the idea of assigning responsibility or blame for outcomes is an example of anthropomorphic thinking. The values or rewards that the market gives to an individual's work or goods often fails to correspond to the individual's needs and is just as often beyond her control. Hayek felt that the ethic promoted by the Social Darwinists and by pop culture figures such as Horatio Alger contributed to this misunderstanding of the relationship between personal effort or merit and reward. Another factor is the belief that certain services and goods are of greater or lesser value to society as a whole. But, Hayek contends that such a determination can only come from the impersonal price mechanism and not from some government fiat. Hayek's argues that it does not make sense to assign moral judgments, such as that an action is just, to outcomes that were not the result of intent. This is an issue I will examine further in the next chapter. Meanwhile, I will finish my discussion of Hayek's positive contribution by briefly noting some common misrepresentations of his views.[167]

Hayek's political positions were more nuanced than either his supporters or his critics appreciated. I have shown that Hayek was not simply a free market fundamentalist, since he maintained that both a healthy functioning market economy, as well as the freedom of the citizens of a republic required the legal structure and protections afforded by government and the rule of law.[168] He even supported the desirability of some government assistance for citizens in dire distress, as well as the importance of some regulation of the economy. His greatest concern was with any form of redistribution of resources based on some set of social ideals imposed by government or governmental bureaucrats. This form of "manipulation," he argued, can only lead to a distortion of the spontaneous order needed for a well-functioning and vibrant economy. But, it is important to note that, at this time, there were German libertarians who accepted an even more active state than Hayek ever accepted.[169] Hayek presented a realist position of class differences, based on such arbitrary benefits as health, native aptitude, good parenting, and economic and educational advantages. Efforts to control or transform these inherited factors by government will lead, inevitably to a loss of liberty by imposing some uniform set of values, inimical to a pluralist and free society. It is important to note that Hayek's target was one that is shared by both libertarian and non-libertarian defenders of democracy. For example, Joseph Schumpeter, writing about the dangers to democracy from the use of concepts such as the common good and the will of the people, wrote that "there is, first, no such thing as a uniquely determined common good that all people could agree on or be made to agree on by the force of rational argument."[170] Hayek summed up the danger here in one of his last works: "to act on the belief that we possess the knowledge and the power which enables us to shape the processes of society entirely to our liking, knowledge which we in fact do *not* possess, is likely to make us do much harm."[171]

Hayek's influence on the development of modern libertarianism went far beyond his writings and teaching; it was also politically practical. He was able to utilize the fame that came from the huge success of *The Road to Serfdom* in order to organize a ten day conference of 36 international academics, most of them economists, who met at a mountain hotel overlooking Lake Geneva, Switzerland in April of 1947, that became known as the Mont Pèlerin Conference. This was to be the first meeting of the Mont Pèlerin Society, which has met annually and then biannually since that date. It is noteworthy that four of the original members, including Hayek and Milton Friedman later became recipients of the Nobel Prize in Economics. Other prominent attendees of the first meeting included Ludwig Erhard, who is usually credited with Germany's postwar economic recovery; as well as the leading philosopher and Hayek friend, Karl Popper. The Conference was partly modeled on a similar one named for the popular American journalist and author, Walter Lippmann, who had published ideas similar to Hayek's in his widely read 1937 book, *The Good Society*. The Pèlerin Society became the model for what came to be called "think tanks;" institutions which have become a powerful tool for the spread of libertarian ideas and influence. Among other tools meant to promote libertarian ideas were journals, foundations, and endowed academic chairs. Topics discussed at this first meeting included: European federation, taxation, wage policy, trade unions, even liberalism and Christianity. The aims of the Conference and the Society were to restore the "belief in private property and the competitive market; for without diffused power and the initiative associated with these institutions it is difficult to imagine a society in which freedom may be effectively preserved."[172]Hayek and the other participants consciously understood that they were engaged in a "long-run effort" to actively influence both academic and public opinion and thereby effect political change.[173] As late as 1980 when one of the world's wealthiest individuals David Koch ran as its Vice Presidential candidate, the Libertarian Party was barely able to muster one percent of the vote.[174] But, this long view effort was to culminate in the elections of the Margaret Thatcher and Ronald Reagan governments more than three decades after the Society's founding.[175] They had gone from a belittled minority to become what the definitive history of their triumph calls the, *Masters of the Universe.*[176] The ideas that came out of the first conference show a strong imprint from Hayek, as well as from economists of the University of Chicago and the University of Manchester in England. However, Mises forcefully objected to these more moderate libertarian views, and even "stormed out" of one session, accusing some participants of being socialists or communists.[177]

Hayek argued that intellectuals had played a key role in the spread of socialist and "collectivist" ideas.[178] He and other Mont Pèlerin members believed that historians of the rise of capitalism and the Industrial Revolution had strongly promoted a negative attitude about capitalism. This prevailing intellectual "bias" was based on the argument that history had shown that political freedom was not possible without state intervention to secure economic freedom.

Of course, the standard historical indictment came from Engel's work on the early factory workers in Manchester, England; but, many more historians had followed Engel's lead. A number of revisionist historical papers were delivered at the 1951 meeting of the Society, and three years later they were published as *Capitalism and the Historians*, with Hayek as editor. This was the beginning of what has become known as the standard-of-living controversy by historians of the British Industrial Revolution, with T.S. Ashton from this 1951 book as the leading representative of the libertarian or "optimist" side, and E.P. Thompson as the socialist or "pessimist's" champion. I will not litigate the historical debate here, except to note that Hayek and the other authors defended a historical reading that countered the prevailing view that the living conditions of workers had deteriorated; that "the weakest elements of society" had suffered with the rise of capitalism. The libertarian revisionists argued that this "false" view had been based on "one-sided data."[179]The historians in this little volume showed that, contrary to this influential reading, the lifestyle of industrial workers had actually improved significantly under capitalism. Although this is still the subject of debate by economic historians, it is generally accepted that between 1860 and 1890, the real wages of workers increased by about fifty percent; with a comparable increase in life expectancy and good nutrition.[180]

The other "myths" addressed in this slim volume were that the eventual increase in the living standards of the working class only came from political agitation, such as the labor movement, and that the increase in wealth only came from exploitation of non-European peoples. At the very least, these libertarian historians must be credited with introducing new data and complicating an oversimplified interpretation of the rise of European capitalism. Hayek argued in this work and elsewhere that the appeal of the "mythological" history of capitalism was based largely on the "scientism" of intellectuals, who wished to impose "a design theory of social institutions."[181]This misplaced use of science and the imposition of rationality onto spontaneous individual actions was the underlying basis for social and economic reform. Hayek emphasized individual actions and intentions, but noted that they were not totally rational since they often lead to unintended consequences.

It is easy for champions of a more activist role for government to dismiss these concerted efforts to change public opinion as conspiratorial. This can be seen in the reaction to the famous, or, depending on one's view, infamous "Powell Memorandum" of 1971. This document was a call to arms sent by Lewis Powell to the U.S. Chamber of Commerce, just before he went from being a corporate attorney to being sworn in as a United States Supreme Court Justice. Lending support to conspiracy theories is the fact that it was not available to the public during his confirmation hearings. But a careful reading of Powell's memo, now easily available on the internet, shows that it was the promoters of free enterprise who had a good reason to feel under attack by the critics of capitalism. Powell presents a detailed case for how schools, the media, and other elite groups were dominated by such critics, and how such an overwhelming control of the message had transformed public opinion and, thereby, politics. What's more he shows how business and finance had been more than complicit in this gradual takeover, against their own interest and, he argued, the interests of the economy, by funding the very individuals and groups that attacked them. It is the "sweeping, coordinated and long-term effort to spread conservative ideas on campuses, in academic journals, and in the news media" that has made this such an important historic document. It involved financing of think tanks, speaker's bureaus, textbooks, political consultants, and reporters and news outlets, all in a concerted effort to gradually transform public opinion to reduce government control of the economy. Powell argued that "the very survival of the free enterprise system" depended on such a concerted counteroffensive. He pointed to what he saw as the negative influence coming from the popularity of such alleged enemies of a free economy as the German refugee philosopher, Herbert Marcuse. Marcuse had been an important member of the Frankfurt School of philosophers, sociologists and political scientists who were highly critical of modern capitalist society. He had become a remarkable celebrity in American colleges and universities, spreading what Powell saw as a "socialist" political, economic, and social agenda. Marcuse was one of the founders of the unique, European style, graduate department at Brandeis University where I had the pleasure of studying. However, Karl Popper, Hayek's friend and Mont Pèlerin Society member, had also been a Visiting Professor in the same program.

One highly influential intellectual Powell put forward as an example of someone the business community should be supporting was the libertarian economist, friend of Hayek, and member of the Mont Pèlerin Society, Milton Friedman. The United States Defense Secretary, Donald Rumsfeld called Friedman "the embodiment of the truth that 'ideas have consequences.'"[182]In an introduction he wrote for a collection of essays on Hayek's moral and intellectual support of a free society that had been presented at the 1975 meeting of the Society, Friedman notes that his own libertarian ideas came from his association with the University of Chicago economists and predated his reading of Hayek.[183] Even economists who oppose Friedman's policies and politics respect his technical contributions to economics. Friedman's 1976 Nobel Prize in economics reflected his contributions to monetary theory, but he is also known for advancing the classical view of man as a rational maximiser of self-interest or what economists call utility.

In his early works, where he uses the European term neoliberalism, Friedman accepts the need for a more active role for government in the economy. Government was necessary not only to maintain contracts, but to help promote and protect competition in all sectors, including among workers and consumers. At least until the decade of the 70s, Friedman was sometimes critical of laissez-faire and even saw a role for the state in helping the poorest and most distressed citizens. Like Hayek and others, he was highly critical of government planning, and shared fully in the concern that an activist state represented a serious threat to individual freedom. Friedman had worked in government and, therefore, had practical experience of its limitations and inefficiencies. At this early stage of his career, Friedman argued that "there were some functions that the price system could not perform," and he even borrowed the Keynesian phrase "middle road" for his own economic ideas.[184]Friedman agreed that the limitations in knowledge that Hayek and others pointed to led to the failures of "collectivism" and "nationalism," but the state still had a significant role to play in maintaining a vibrant and humane economy.

Friedman never lost his desire to help those at the bottom, but he also maintained his emphasis on doing so without harming the general economy. In an early essay, reprinted in his 1953 volume of technical papers, *Essays in Positive Economics,* Friedman asserts that in addition to political freedom and economic efficiency, "equality of economic power" and a reduction in "inequality" should be such a central objective for any society that additional "fiscal measures," beyond purely market measures should be employed.[185]At this stage of his career, Friedman even advocated for "transfer payments," such as "social security" and "unemployment payments," as well as for a "progressive income tax." Even at this early date, Friedman was concerned about "the inflationary effects of abnormally high government expenditures," as well as the need to maintain the flexibility of prices.[186]All of this shows the strong influence of his University of Chicago colleague, Henry Simons.

Friedman delivered a series of lectures in 1956 that six years later became the work that has been called the American *The Road to Serfdom*, his enormously influential *Capitalism and Freedom*. It was the notoriety from this book that propelled Friedman into becoming a leading public intellectual for the rest of his long life.[187] Through his frequent appearances on the new medium of television, Friedman became the chief promoter of libertarian economic and political ideas. Very many of his presentations are still available on the newer medium of youtube. By 1987, even so unlikely an economist as John Kenneth Galbraith could call it "the age of Friedman."[188] Critics of Friedman and other libertarians like to question the motives behind a move toward advocating economic policies that benefitted the wealthy businessmen who commissioned and funded the publication of works, such as *Capitalism and Freedom*.[189] This is a complex issue that I will address in the next chapter.

The influence of Hayek can be seen throughout this important work, especially in Friedman's embrace of the need for the rule of law and his rejection of anarchism. Like Hayek and the other early libertarians, Friedman tended to equate state intervention with socialism and ultimately with serfdom. Friedman is even stronger about this, asserting that "however attractive anarchy may be as a philosophy, it is not feasible in a world of imperfect men."[190] He later adds, for further emphasis, that "the consistent liberal is not an anarchist."[191]

However, Friedman was able to draw strength from the growing libertarian network described earlier, and would push libertarian ideas well beyond Hayek. In fact, Friedman would become a controversial figure in politics, and, despite the Nobel Prize he received for his important technical work, also in economics. The well-written introduction to the published lectures summarizes much of his position with this assertion: "government is necessary to preserve our freedom, it is an instrument through which we can exercise our freedom; yet by concentrating power in political hands, it is also a threat to freedom."[192] He uses the same analogy with sports, noting that government is necessary to set "the rules of the game" and act as "umpire." However, he finishes the first chapter of *Capitalism and Freedom,* with a long list of areas where government only causes more problems by getting involved. Along with the already familiar areas of regulation of transportation and rent control, he adds the still contentious interventions of the minimum wage, banking regulation, and programs such as social security. But, arguably, the most controversial objection is to licensing requirements for professionals, such as physicians.

Although he saw the need for laws to combat monopoly, like any libertarian, Friedman saw such tools as antitrust laws as, at best, necessary evils. His position was to harden late in his career, leading him to an almost complete rejection of antitrust legislation. Here he relates the story of arguably the best example of such laws, namely, the rise of railroads and of government regulation of all public transportation. Railroads went through almost every permutation of control, from complete laissez-faire to full government regulation. Friedman asserts that government regulation is the worst way to achieve this necessary evil, in part because it is the most resistant to making the needed updates that come from invention.[193] The target of Friedman's critique is the Interstate Commerce Commission, the oldest such governmental regulatory agency. Law professor, Paul Stephen Dempsey gives an excellent summary of the prior history that justified antitrust regulations: "ruinous rate wars, often of a predatory nature, designed to drive competitors out of business, were interspersed with price fixing and pooling agreements, whereby carriers in competitive markets would agree to raise prices and pool revenue and freight, whereupon rates soared."[194]

Governmental regulation of businesses has been justified by a number of different concerns, including, protection of consumers from predatory practices; encouraging the smooth operation of a particular type of industry, such as railroads, for example, by preventing monopoly; some alleged higher social goals; protecting health; and, increasingly, protection of the environment. Of course, none of these reasons is exclusive and several overlap. Friedman introduces a counterfactual argument that, if the ICC had never existed and transportation had not been subject to government regulation, competition alone would have prevented monopolies from forming, leading to the development of a more efficient system for transporting goods. The same argument would be applied to the regulation of other sectors of the economy requiring a national infrastructure, such as energy and communications. Instead, what happened, Friedman argues, is that the ICC was manipulated by the railroads to prevent competition from other forms of transportation, such as trucking.[195] This illustrates a general problem with government regulation, namely, that it is subject to undue influence from powerful lobbying groups, interested only in their own financial gain or advantage. Libertarians argue with justification that active state liberalism leads to regulations that benefit the wealthiest and the biggest companies. After all, the resources to get their self-interests enacted into law are available to the largest corporations and trade groups. The irony is that this leads to monopolistic outcomes that are the antithesis of free competition.

The period following the Great Depression, when faith in laissez-faire was at its lowest, saw a blossoming of regulatory agencies, with the model being the ICC. These New Deal agencies were, at least theoretically, consciously designed to be as free as possible from direct manipulation by the Executive Branch.[196] The traditional doctrine on monopolies by classical free market economists was best expressed by one of Friedman's leading economics professors at the University of Chicago, Henry Simons, when he described monopoly "in all its forms," including "corporations" as "the great enemy of democracy."[197] In fact, for Simons and the early libertarians, including the early Friedman, "any concentration of power" was a supreme danger to freedom. For example, in 1947 Friedman put forward specific proposals to mitigate concerns over consolidations and mergers that were creating larger corporations.[198] In one of his first studies, Friedman and Simon Kuznets showed how physicians had been successful in raising their salaries through the use of monopolistic governmental licensure practices.[199]

But, by the time he came to write *Capitalism and Freedom,* Friedman claimed that it was a historical fact that almost all monopoly came from government intervention designed to shore up a particular industry or other interest group, such as a particular trade or its workers. Allowed to operate without interference, free market competition and trade would eventually break up all such collusion and monopoly. He uses the example of the United States Postal Service, where there was no real technological reason for a government monopoly; an argument which has been subsequently shown to have been correct. Friedman was also correct in his analysis and predictions regarding the important relationship between inflation, wages, and unemployment.

Because we live in a highly complex society, Friedman does recognize a government role in regulating what he calls "neighborhood effects." This phrase is used, with a different meaning by sociologists today, and so Friedman's other term, *externalities,* is now more common with economists. Like many economic terms, this is a fancy word for a rather simple concept. It refers to the consequences, costs or benefits, of market transactions to individuals who are not direct participants or customers in those transactions. Friedman also refers to them as "third parties" to a market transaction. As I mentioned earlier in this chapter, these side effects can be positive or negative. Friedman's favorite example of negative externalities, namely pollution effects, has, of course, taken on much greater importance since he wrote. The utility companies, he used as examples of imposing social or monetary costs without our direct consent, have been joined by countless other polluters with much more extreme consequences. In fact, today the "neighborhood" is often the entire globe. Friedman acknowledges that such effects are failures in the ideal market mechanism. But, he is at pains to demonstrate that turning to government solutions will, almost inevitably, lead to adding other negative results. Friedman has little difficulty coming up with a number of good examples where government solutions to negative externalities led to even more disastrous unintended consequences. An example of a positive externality might be improvements my neighbor makes to his property that have an unintended third party effect of increasing the value of my home. It is clear that this economic concept goes beyond the individualist core of liberalism, and that defining what are considered positive and negative is an intrinsically social affair. There is, also, often a difficulty, as Friedman acknowledges, in determining which company or industry is directly responsible for these negative effects. The same difficulty, however, has a similar adverse effect on any government attempt to regulate pollution. But, the main problem with government solutions to negative externalities, such as pollution, is its urge to create new, huge, highly costly, bureaucratic, agencies, all the various alphabet soup we have become all too familiar with today.

The only other reason that Friedman can see for government directly intervening in people's lives, besides addressing positive or negative externalities, is paternalistic concern. This latter form of meddling, he argues, can only be justified where there is a legitimate question of the individual's capacity to be responsible, in other words, autonomy. This paternalistic concern, therefore, only applies with young children and those with profound mental deficits. Friedman's genius can be seen in the market-based solutions he devised for dealing with negative externalities like pollution. In his ten-part 1980 TV series, and the accompanying book that he wrote with his economist wife, Rose, he describes this market-based solution as an "effluent tax," what today has become the widely employed carbon tax on emissions.[200]

Another area where Friedman has had a lasting influence is around the role that government has in education. He distinguishes between two different areas of concern: "general education for citizenship and specialized vocational education," with very different justifications for direct government involvement.[201] At this stage in his career, Friedman was trying to balance two very different political principles. On the one hand, he accepted the traditional view that a "certain minimum of schooling of a specified kind" was necessary for "promoting a stable and democratic society." Friedman is unclear, at this stage, about the content of this education of a "specified kind" for citizenship and, and the "common set of values," that would promote democracy. One element he mentions is "literacy." Later, I will briefly examine Friedman's controversial views on social values and the responsibility of businesses. It is interesting that he saw the need for education reform in market terms as a positive externality, since the individual citizens who benefit, and the value to the economy or the amount we all gain, cannot be identified and, therefore, charged.

This very individualistic understanding of society is very characteristic of libertarianism, but, in this case, the individual is not the autonomous individual but the family "unit." Friedman's other major concern, of course, is to limit the role of government, especially any requirement for taxation or subsidy. He first proposed his creative approach to these issues, the voucher system, in an article in 1955.[202] Friedman acknowledges that parents with substantial wealth have always had an advantage when it comes to school choice for their children. They are not only in a position to move to a better school district, but they could always send their children to private schools. Friedman acknowledges that concerns about parochial or religious schools instilling different social values have some justification, but this would violate parental freedom and is not enough to justify government administration.[203] Free market competition, he believes, will create newer institutions and take care of any concern about democratic values. He acknowledges that government subsidies may be the only way to guarantee the minimum, mostly elementary, education justified by the externalities argument. Surprisingly for an economist, he does not believe that subsidizing vocational education has any social value.

His biggest concern, however, is what he calls the "nationalization" of education, that is, the role of government in administering the system. The use of this term may have been because the immensely popular writer Edward Bellamy had used it instead of socialist in his best-selling novel, *Looking Backward*. Bellamy inspired the rise of Nationalist Clubs throughout late nineteenth century America. A major goal of Friedman's voucher plan is to allow for subsidy without such government control. Initially, Friedman accepted another role for government in setting "minimum standards" for "approved" institutions, comparing this to the government cleanliness standards for restaurants. He would not only include private institutions, but even private for-profit on the accepted list. Friedman acknowledges that his model was the highly successful G.I. Bill that subsidized higher education for returning World War II veterans at approved colleges and universities.

In light of the history of the outcome of voucher plans, it is particularly interesting to note that Friedman was sanguine about any negative effects it might have on social stratification. He acknowledges the concern, but argues, quite correctly, that schools already tended to be divided by class based on residential divisions. One of his primary arguments, both in his 1955 article and in *Capitalism and Freedom*, is that parents who choose to send their children to private schools are required to pay twice, first in taxes and then for costs of private education. Libertarian concerns about the effects of government bureaucracy have a good example in the more recent movement for mainstreaming special-needs children. Without getting into the intense debate about the merits of inclusion, it cannot be denied that the Education for All Handicapped Children Act of 1975 added substantial red tape and paper work, as well as other duties onto teachers, contributing to their historic low morale. Examples could be multiplied of other government regulations, often with excellent social purposes, like the school lunch program, that have had unintended negative consequences. Many times the negative results come from adding additional valuable purposes, such as not calling attention to poorer children, onto existing programs. Government has added ever more "social" goals to the role of education, increasing the need for more personnel and greater tax revenue. Friedman often points to studies that show that bureaucratic work and funding tends to expand with less and less real or measurable output or value. Friedman, also, argued that market competition would have the effect of increasing teacher salaries. It certainly cannot be denied that one of his expressed concerns has been born out, namely, that an increase in administrators, with their high salaries, would result from increased governmental regulation. However, the same increase in administrators and costs has occurred in all educational institutions, including private schools, especially in higher education.

In their 1980 TV series and best-selling book, *Free to Choose*, Milton and Rose Friedman focus their comments on educational reform, especially on the deterioration of inner city public schools. A major area of concern throughout this work is on the increasing power of so-called experts, in this case, professional educators, in our "over-governed" society. This critique harkens back to Hayek's analysis of the "scientism" of government planners and bureaucrats in Europe. The Friedman's question the lofty motivations of Horace Mann and other early reformers, noting their "self-interest" in having more secure employment and greater control from government run education.[204]They acknowledge that a motivation of increased government control was to achieve greater "equality of opportunity." The recent increase in funding and control by the federal government has had the effect of lessening direct parental influence over their own children. Local governments must be more responsive to their citizens or risk removal or declining revenues. The failure of government to provide good education, as well as legal protection, to inner city poor families has been well-documented, and is an indictment of active state liberalism. The Friedmans present examples, mostly from New York City, for example Harlem Prep, where a combination of very limited private charity and direct parental control was successfully used to achieve more positive outcomes. They argue that giving parents direct funding, through their voucher plan, would achieve much wider successes of a similar nature. With incredible optimism, they assert that "let schools specialize, as private schools would, and common interest would overcome bias of color and lead to more integration than now occurs."[205]

In *Free to Choose*, Milton and Rose Friedman have some interesting observations to make about equality and its relationship to liberty; ideas that will be of importance in the rest of this book. They borrow the concept of *personal* equality, or what they call "equality before God and the law."[206]The type of inequality that America's Founders were most in revolt against was hereditary advantage. When Thomas Jefferson coined his most famous phrase, he spoke in terms of rights that could not be alienated. As everyone knows, the full realization of these rights has required a great deal of struggle, and has been closely tied to our expanding notions of liberty. This is the libertarian belief that every individual has a right to self-rule, to control his or her own actions and choice of projects, just so long as they do not interfere with the liberty of others. The Friedmans note that this concept came to be associated with a related form of equality, namely, equality of opportunity. People are born with very different talents or capacities and external opportunities, but they should not be held back by "arbitrary" or "irrelevant" obstacles, such as "birth, nationality, color, religion, sex."[207] They argue that there can be no true liberty without these first two types of equality. Not surprisingly, they see the fullest expression of this liberty in the right of each person to pursue his or her own financial livelihood. They contrast some of the active government measures, such as Alexander Hamilton's introduction of protective tariffs as ways of denying real equality of opportunity. These measures grow out of the opposite of liberty that they maintain comes from a third conception of equality, what they call equality of *outcome*. They amusingly define this problematic concept with a quotation from *Alice in Wonderland,* where the Dodo bird tells Alice, "everybody has won, and *all* must have prizes," a view that has captured our public schools. The whole idea that each individual should get a "fair share" is quite fungible, and they compare it to a line from another classic work, George Orwell's *Animal Farm,* that is, the idea that "all animals are equal, but some animals are more equal than others."

I will return to their arguments about the dangers of this type of equality in the next chapter. Also in the next chapter I will come back to the ways in which the Friedmans and other libertarians equate humans, in this case children and parents, with capital and consumer products in their arguments about government's role. The story is one of a conflict between different economic interest units, on the one side the family unit, on the other the individual administrator, with power over the child hanging in the balance. To some extent, this use of family unit runs counter to the libertarian emphasis on the individual. The next chapter will also examine one of the other major policy recommendations put forward by Milton Friedman, namely, privatization of social security. But, before leaving my brief discussion of his highly influential analysis, I also need to briefly look at his controversial theory about the social responsibility of businesses, because the issues he raises will play an important role in the rest of this book.

Friedman first addressed these issues in *Capitalism and Freedom*, in his discussion of monopoly. He states boldly that, in a nation with capitalist markets, "there is one and only one social responsibility of business [namely] to use its resources and engage in activities designed to increase its profits so long as it stays within the rules of the game, which is to say, engages in open and free competition, without deception or fraud."[208]However, it is his expanded presentation of these ideas, in a September 13, 1970 New York Times Magazine article, with the revealing title, "The Social Responsibility of Business is to Increase its Profits" that has generated a huge amount of interest and controversy. Friedman's first and perhaps main concern was to establish that it is only individuals, in this case mostly chief executives, who can have agency and responsibility; there is no such agent as *business*. Business, like society, is only a collection of distinct individual agents. Hayek, as noted earlier in this chapter, put forth a similar argument for his asocial liberal individualism. Methodological individualism was firmly established by the great German sociologist, Max Weber. Arguments similar to Friedman's can, also, be found in William Graham Sumner's essay, "The State as an 'Ethical

Person'."[209]Friedman argues that the chief executive of a corporation has a responsibility to the owner or shareholders of that company. To act on his or her own, to use any portion of the company's funds for some "social" end, no matter how important he believes the end to be, is tantamount to imposing a tax on the company and its shareholders. For the State to impose regulations, including corporate tax laws that are meant to serve some higher "social" end is also a form of coercion. Friedman argues, in a more positive way, that it is free market competition, with every company pursuing its own maximum profits that generates social progress. This can be seen, arguably, in the medical and transportation fields. Less than a year before he died, Friedman took part in a debate about his business ethic in another journal. The cover picture of Friedman has the caption: "Is this a face only a stockholder can love?"[210]A friendly critic in this debate was John Mackey, one of the founders of the Whole Foods Market chain. Friedman acknowledges that a company, especially a small one in a local community, might find it advantageous for its profits to make charitable contributions. But, he argues against the view that individual executives, anymore than government bureaucrats, are in any position to know what society needs or how best to engage in charity; that they should not use other people's resources even if they did have such knowledge; and, that they are being hypocritical in calling their motivation some sort of social responsibility. It is important to humanize shareholders here, as they often include individuals who themselves contribute to the economy and social progress. Many citizens, no doubt, benefit from increased corporate profits in their retirement and other investments. After expressing deep admiration for Friedman, and accepting that any charitable giving must be totally voluntary, while also asserting that capitalism has led to great advances in life, Mackey argues that profits are not the only thing a company should value, and shareholders are not the only people who should benefit from a company's goals.

Ever since the publication of his masterwork, *Anarchy, State, and Utopia* in 1974, the philosopher Robert Nozick has been considered by the academic community as the most sophisticated modern champion of libertarian political theory. The book, which won the National Book Award, is generally considered one of the two or three most important contemporary works in political philosophy. It has spawned a small cottage industry of commentary and critique, and I only have room here to touch on a few of Nozick's most important arguments in defense of libertarian ideas. Among his most important and creative contributions are his critical use of Locke's idea of private property and rights; his analysis of the coercive nature of taxation; his argument about self-ownership; and, his most famous thought experiment about compensation for celebrities.

It is useful to note that Nozick started out to counter the anarchist ideas of Anarcho-capitalists, like Murray Rothbard, and ended up with the most important defense of the view that "a minimal state, limited to the narrow functions of protection against force, theft, fraud, enforcement of contracts, and so on, is justified; that any more extensive state will violate person's rights not to be forced to do certain things, and is unjustified; and that the minimal state is inspiring as well as right."[211] What is unique about Nozick is not this standard libertarian viewpoint, but the creative and sophisticated, sometimes amusing, arguments he puts forward to defend it. He accepts the methodological individualism of Hayek and Friedman, that there is no "social entity," with its own motives over and above the individuals that live in a society. He adds that there is no generally acceptable rule, or what he calls a "pattern" of just distribution of resources. An extreme example of such a pattern would be the egalitarian principle that each person should receive the same share; but, even a modified rule, for example that the spread in wealth between those at the top and those at the bottom must only be a certain percentage, also violates Locke's principle of liberty that human beings are born with inviolable rights to life, liberty, and property. Nozick thus basis his argument on a strong principle of natural rights, stating that "individuals have rights, and there are things no person or group may do to them" without violating their rights.[212] He adds a powerful Kantian argument that individuals should always be treated as ends and never as means to achieve some collective goal or value. When active state liberals defend a social goal, Nozick argues, they are disguising the fact that this involves interfering with the individual citizen; "something is done" to that citizen "for the sake of others." Individual human beings are separate moral agents, each with her "own life to lead," and should not be treated as a single entity with a common purpose or set of interests. Using a person can also involve imposing some financial lose or other obligation on her against her explicit consent.

This will be recognized as the negative liberty that I described early in this chapter. We have a right to do what we wish without fear of interference from others or from the government, so long as our actions do not interfere with the rights of other individuals. It follows that the state should not redistribute wealth, mold or guide individual morals, or protect individuals from the supposed negative consequences of their own actions. Charitable giving is morally laudable, because voluntary. Given our strong commitment to individualism, Americans have always been more willing to accept some degree of "natural" inequality, just so long as it was not too severe. The one type of equality that has been generally accepted has been a formal or legal equality of opportunity. Individuals should have equal access to such social advantages as education, training, and choice of career. The American creed held that an individual who works hard and plays fair can succeed in rising up the social ladder. Nozick would add that we should not penalize the individual who has this gumption simply because she began with certain advantages. America was also founded on a strong belief in the virtues of individual ownership, especially, ownership of land. The distribution of land was accepted as a means to promote responsibility, respectability, and good citizenship.

I will postpone till the end of this chapter addressing Nozick's powerful arguments for a minimalist state based on the concept of self-ownership; the idea that we are all autonomous individuals responsible only to ourselves. I will first examine Nozick's influential and highly creative arguments for what he calls an *entitlement theory* of just distribution. Nozick argues that "redistributionists," his prime target is John Rawls, wish to have it both ways: on the one hand, they wish to promote individual autonomy, personal dignity, self-respect, and choice, while at the same time asserting that these individuals are not totally responsible for developing their talents or the choices they make because they suffer from some external social obstacles.[213] It is one thing to point to the morally arbitrary aspect of the natural lottery of advantages at birth, for example, such accidental factors as wealthy parents, intelligence, and other talents, but a full story, like the famous parable, needs to include the personal choices the individual makes to develop or neglect such gifts. Liberals who wish to promote personal autonomy ought to include personal responsibility if they wish to give a complete understanding of economic and social achievement. Nozick also argues that the fact that a person's natural talents and capacities were unearned or arbitrary does not establish that the person does not deserve them and the resources that "flow from them."[214]Most importantly, it certainly does not give the government the right to redistribute these assets to achieve equality, even equality of opportunity, without the explicit permission of the person who earned them.

It has become a common ritual for economists to report 'tax freedom day': the time in the year when we stop working to pay our taxes, and start working purely for ourselves. This period is often four or more months into a year. This holiday may not have originated with Nozick, but it fits his view that taxes are a form of "forced labor."[215]He concedes that taxation is not exactly slavery, because an individual who values leisure over luxury could stop working before he reaches a taxable level of earnings. However, it is still the case that the government, in effect, coerces the individual citizen into working a certain number of hours in order to provide goods for people she does not personally know. As with earlier libertarians, Nozick argues that the state not only lacks any real authority to redistribute, it also lacks the information and ability to plan and control an efficient economy. While socialists and other egalitarians contend that property is theft, Nozick and other libertarians contend that taxation is a way of taking their hard earned money against a citizen's will.

Nozick's defense of private property has three parts: the first is that an owner must have had an original entitlement or a "just" right to acquire the property; the second possibility is that the new owner has acquired the property from that original owner through a just transfer; and, the third possibility is that an individual owns the property through some repetition of these first two actions. Nozick's *entitlement theory* of the acquisition of property is meant to establish the legitimate ownership and transfer of resources, such as land. It is clear that the most problematic of these historical processes is the first, or the justification of original acquisition. Nozick acknowledges that there are examples of unjust acquisition. As I noted early in this book, clarity about legal ownership of property, though essential, is not a simple matter. It is always possible that material goods were acquired by theft, and some of the historical injustices may have even occurred with the assistance of government; think of native lands in America and Australia. We may even feel a moral obligation to voluntarily compensate living descendants for such historical theft. Like earlier libertarians, Nozick also worries about monopolies; admitting that we may question the justice of someone acquiring a life-saving substance, such as water in a desert, and either not sharing it or selling it at an exorbitant rate. He also gives a clever argument against Locke's justification of the right to property based on our self-ownership. Locke was concerned to justify the private ownership of property, given his religious view that God had "given the world to man in common."[216]His way out of this dilemma was to argue that it is through our ownership of ourselves, and the mixing of our personal labor with the property, for example gathering acorns, digging up ore, or plowing a field, that we establish entitlement to the material resource. It is by this mixing of our labor, Locke holds, that we remove things from their "natural state." No other person, Locke holds, has a right to my body or my labor. Modern libertarians would argue, and most of us would agree, you cannot appropriate another person's body part, without that person's consent, even to save another person's life or give another full functioning. The well-known children's parable of the little red hen provides an amusing example of property rights that come from mixing one's labor. The hen finds some grains of wheat and asks three other animals if they would help her plant, thresh, harvest, and bring the flour to the baker to be made into bread. Each time the animals demur, saying that they are too busy. But, when the bread has been baked, they are all-too-willing to share it with the hen. The hen, of course, turns them down, and shares it with her chicks and maybe the baker. Locke added the important proviso that we need to leave enough resources behind to meet the needs of other individuals. It is interesting, in light of our environmental concerns today, that Locke added that we should not allow natural resources to "spoil." Nozick accepts the idea that we have an ownership in ourselves and our body as an essential component of our natural rights. However, he amusingly complicates Locke's labor theory of ownership by asking, rhetorically, do I own the ocean if I mix it with my personal can of tomato juice?

Nozick grounds his theory on a foundation of individual rights, which, as I noted above, he announces as the very first sentence of the book. A number of commentators have noted that providing protection from the violation of negative rights can actually require more government action than providing positive rights. I will look at this issue, along with Nozick's example of private protection agencies, in the next chapter. Here, I will turn my discussion of Nozick to his most famous Wilt Chamberlain thought experiment.

A full examination of this example would require an examination of John Rawls political philosophy. But, the libertarian use of this example can be stated simply. Nothing is lost by substituting any very popular celebrity and any amounts of income for Nozick's use of the great basketball player. Fans of the celebrity will, no doubt, show a willingness to pay an extra amount for a ticket to see him or her perform. Nozick simplifies, for the sake of his argument, by stating that the fans pay this extra amount directly to the celebrity by depositing it into a separate box whenever they purchase a ticket. This extra amount, which could be quite sizeable for a popular athlete or performer, would be paid directly to the particular celebrity. What is important here, for Nozick and other libertarians, is that these payments have been made voluntarily by fans, that they understood the amount would go directly to the celebrity, and that any rule or pattern that would prevent this from happening is an interference with the free market in entertainment. A patterned interference would be to repeatedly "forbid capitalist acts between consenting adults."[217]

In the last section of Nozick's masterwork he shows how the key libertarian principle of freedom to do what one desires could lead to the growth of many voluntary communities or associations of like-minded individuals. This section of the book has been largely neglected perhaps because he calls these various communities "utopias." However, his defense of this idea of a pluralism of utopias has the virtue of demonstrating how libertarianism can work to foster a liberal acceptance of the pluralism that has become so important to modern democracies.

In his brilliant and highly popular book and Harvard University and television lectures on *Justice; What's the Right Thing to Do?* Michael Sandel demonstrates why Nozick's arguments for the concept of self-ownership have been so difficult to refute by non-libertarians like himself. As I noted earlier, this idea comes out of John Locke's concept of property and natural rights, concepts that strongly influenced the Founders of our

American system of government. There are certain things that the government should not be allowed to do to its citizens, even in the interest of some supposed social good, because such actions violate these basic or natural rights. One such basic right is that we have ownership of our body and person, including our specific life goals or projects. Sandel points out that even those who would strenuously object to Nozick's use of the self-ownership concept to attack such interventions as taxation use very similar arguments to defend a woman's right to choose to have an abortion and by those who wish to defend what goes on in a person's bedroom from any interference by the state. Sandel presents five different arguments that have been used to attack this libertarian central concept, and he finds that at least four of them can be rejected. Arguments about the sale of body parts and assisted suicide raise difficult issues for some libertarians. But, the most difficulty comes with his fifth argument which raises the issue of the natural lottery of skills and other birth advantages, as well as the issue of luck, none of which can be counted as based on merit or a person's moral right. I will examine this issue further at the end of this book.

I will conclude this all-too-brief examination of the positive contribution of libertarian/neoliberal political theory with the following summary points:

> Individuals should be free to do what they want with their life, actions, and property, without the interference of others, just so long as what they do does not interfere with the same freedom for others.

> Politics attracts people who are addicted to power; it also has the widest scope of direct influence on citizens in their

daily lives; therefore, government represents the greatest threat to individual freedom.

➤ Organic or *social* theories of government, such as Rousseau's *general will*, or Hegel's *State*, tend to represent an even greater threat to individual freedom, and should be suspect.

➤ It is government, therefore, that has the burden of proof to demonstrate that its authority to coerce its citizens is legitimate.

➤ Government can have a strong negative effect on a person's development and experience. Welfare programs can foster a habit or culture of dependence that saps initiative and is hard to break.

➤ Every individual should be treated as an end and never used as a means to someone else's end, without their explicit consent.

➤ The free market capitalist economic system has greatly improved the health, technical innovation, and standard of living wherever it has been instituted.

➤ Free trade and globalization have led to much lower prices for many commodities, including food. It has also brought a cornucopia of new products, including produce in the winter that was previously unavailable out of season. In a remarkably prescient passage in his classic *Wealth of Nations* (Book 5, Ch. 2, Article 2, p. 800), Adam Smith warned that new forms of wealth such as stock, unlike land, would mean that individuals could avoid "burdensome taxation" by moving their wealth to another nation, "where he could either carry on his business, or enjoy his fortune more at ease." The end result of thus driving wealth away would be a loss of revenue for any particular country. What Smith could not foresee was that technology would allow large corporations and whole industries to also transfer their operations to countries with more favorable tax, regulatory, and wage policies. Some libertarians argue that Americans should welcome this process of globalization, even though it has contributed to our extreme inequality, not only because it has reduced consumer prices, but it has also led to the creation of a middle class in countries such as India and China. I will return to this argument below. But, it is useful to call attention here to Adam Smith's famous parable of the Chinese earthquake. Smith tells the story in his less well known, masterpiece *The Theory of Moral Sentiments*. Smith asks us to imagine that a man of humanistic sentiments learns that the vast country of China has been devastated by an earthquake that swallowed all its millions of inhabitants. He imagines the first reaction of this good man would be great sorrow at this massive loss of life, "he would make many melancholy reflections upon the precariousness of human life, and the vanity of all the labors of man, which could thus be annihilated in a moment." He might expand his concern to the negative effects on the economy of Europe. After all these moral sentiments, Smith imagines, this man would go about his own business and pleasurable activities, "with the same ease and tranquility, as if no such accident had happened." But, if this same man were to learn that he was going to lose his little finger the next day, he would not be able to sleep that night. Assuming that he never saw the Chinese victims and had no strong ties to them, "he will snore with the most profound security over the ruin of a hundred millions of his brethren, and the destruction of that immense multitude seems plainly an object less interesting to him, than this paltry misfortune of his own." (1790/1979, III.3.4, pp.136 137). This natural lack of moral imagination and empathy for things distant ensures that Americans who lose their jobs will not likely be impressed by the creation of middle class Indians and Chinese.

➢ Planned economies have proven to be less efficient, innovative, and more intrusive on individual freedom. Venezuela is a recent, dramatic example. Prior to the election of Hugo Chávez in 1998 as President, Venezuela was perhaps the richest country in Latin America, attracting immigrants from all over the world. Although its wealth was based largely on its vast oil reserves, and there was the same kind of inequality seen throughout the region, Venezuela had a relatively large middle class. Chávez instituted his socialist reforms, his so-called "socialism for the 21$^{st}$ century" in 1999 with devastating unintended negative consequences. He nationalized oil and other major industries, and proceeded to redistribute income to the poor.

An early result was that the rich and middle class fled the country in huge numbers, leading to gross inefficiency in oil production and other key industries. Government deficits soared, leading to astronomical inflation. Inflation has risen to levels never before seen. In recent years, an estimated 30,000 Venezuelans have fled to nearby countries, often using expensive and highly dangerous means to get away from starvation, crime, and misery.

➤ Government bureaucratic institutions tend to provide fewer incentives for efficiency, adaptability, and innovation. They are often staffed by political appointees, who it is very difficult to get rid of, even when incompetent or nonproductive. Public unions also tend to make it very difficult to terminate such individuals.

➤ Government regulations and laws often have unintended negative consequences. Prohibition, of course, is the classic example. Although the Eighteenth Amendment led to a marked decline in deaths from cirrhosis of the liver, it had serious unintended negative effects in society. The Twenty-First Amendment was the only Constitutional Amendment to repeal a prior one. It is also a good example of why government paternalism is questionable.

➤ There is evidence that, at least for some individuals, a culture of dependency, or what Oscar Lewis called a "culture of poverty," can result from the concept of a right to welfare assistance. Alexis de Tocqueville was probably the first to point to this phenomenon in his 1837 analysis of the results of the British Poor Laws, *Memoir on Pauperism.* He described it as an unintended negative consequence of well intentioned "legal charity," which came into conflict with certain aspects of human nature. The argument that a life on welfare can discourage initiative and personally responsible behavior is an important contribution to the debate.

➤ America's military interventionism abroad, since The Truman Doctrine and the Cold War has fostered the development of a culture of dependence, among European and other free world countries; and, it has led to the development of a military-industrial complex that threatens our economy. Despite President Eisenhower's warning against the military/industrial complex, we now live in a country with the largest and most expensive military in the world. This behemoth encourages numerous wars and coercive interventions abroad, and now spies on its own citizens at home in ways that would amaze George Orwell. This development not only threatens lives and busts budgets it also threatens the very survival of our democratic rights.

➤ Libertarian principles tend to give support to the pluralistic values of today's modern urban democracies. For example, libertarians have pioneered the concept that the government has no place imposing moral judgments about relationships, including those in the LGBTQ community.

Chapter Two

## CON

We must make our choice. We may have democracy, or we may have wealth concentrated in the hands of a few, but we can't have both.
—Justice Louis Brandeis

Freedom for the pike is death for the minnows.
—R.H. Tawney

The end of law is not to abolish or restrain, but to preserve and enlarge freedom. For in all the states of created beings, capable of laws, where there is no law there is no freedom.
—John Locke

The law, in its majestic equality, forbids the rich as well as the poor to sleep under bridges, to beg in the streets, and to steel bread.
—Anatole France

Actually, there's been class warfare going on for the last twenty years, and my class has won.
—Warren Buffett, 2011

What do the following examples have in common?

(1) The income disparity in the United States, as of 2014, had become so large that one tenth of one percent of the working population earned 184 times what the bottom ninety percent earned, over six million dollars; the top one percent earned

thirty-eight times what the bottom ninety percent earned, an average of $448, 489; the top ten percent earned nearly nine percent more than bottom ninety percent, $295, 845 to the bottom ninety percent's $33, 068. There is a much higher disparity when it comes to overall wealth, as opposed to just income (see below). These extreme rates of inequality have not been seen since just before the Great Depression.[218]

(2) Also, in the United States, white, middle age, men and women, ages 45–54, have seen a wide disparity in mortality rates from 1990 through 2010; especially when compared to other industrial countries. Men in the high income brackets, listed above have seen an increase, and they can now expect to live, on average, to 88.8 years of age, while men in the lowest income brackets have seen a decline in life expectancy to 76.1 years. The difference for women is even greater, with the highest earners now expected to live to the ripe old age of 91.9 years, and the lowest group seeing a decline to 78.3 years. A major reason for this decline can be seen in the changes in reasons for mortality. Lung cancer deaths, which used to be the single greatest reason for deaths has now been eclipsed, among middle age whites by drug and alcohol poisoning; which has gone from near zero to thirty for every 100,000 deaths. Suicides and alcohol associated liver damage have also become one of the highest causes of death. According to the American Psychiatric Association there has been a similar spike in the amount of chronic stress and related disorders. Finally, studies of white males who have dropped out of the work force, an

estimated 20 million between the ages of 25 and 55, has shown that a remarkable forty-five percent report chronic stress, and over three quarters of these men are taking prescribed pain medication. As someone with over forty years experience working in substance abuse, and with a number of honors in that field, I can attest from personal experience that a large percentage of these individuals are the unwitting victims of over prescription and related addiction.[219]

(3) Libertarians, correctly, rail against government bureaucracy and inefficiency, but tend to ignore the much more dangerous increase in economic corruption. Not since the high point of government corruption during the Gilded Age has there been so much direct manipulation of our political institutions in order to promote financial interest. The methods are less direct: arguably not as much direct bribery, but rather use of loopholes in lobbying laws to garner favors for corporations, unions, and individuals. The revolving door between government and lobbying agencies allows former politicians to earn many times what they did working in the public sector; a surprising number of laws and regulations are directly written by giant financial and corporate institutions and their representatives; and, lobbying agencies raise the funds necessary to win elections by such means as campaign events at expensive restaurants. The newly elected President of the United States campaigned, implausibly, with rhetoric about curbing the power of big money in Washington. But he has moved quickly to bring key lobbyists into his administration to oversee the various

industries they recently championed. With more and more foxes in charge, many will, no doubt, wonder how all the chickens disappeared.  Prior to his election, he was more open about the changes in the tax code that he wished to make; changes that, among other consequences, will allow the wealthiest to pass on more of their fortunes to their offspring; thus creating the kind of aristocracy our Founders most dreaded. The euphemism for this proposed process is *dynastic* wealth. Whatever it is called, it is the creation of an entrenched privileged class with permanent advantages over others. The libertarian position that this is an argument for market self-regulation was shattered by the realty of the Great Recession of 2007. Even some leading libertarians had to admit that self-regulation was a contributing factor in the mistakes that led to this devastating outcome.[220] The corrupting influence of what has been called *dark money* has been well-documented by Jane Mayer and others.[221] A more recent means of buying interest can be seen in the lobbying, including wining and dining of secretaries of state by organizations such as the tobacco industry, the National Rifle Association, and fossil fuel interests, like the Koch brothers. The motivation behind this little known effort is to directly influence how state voter petitions are worded, to ensure outcomes favorable to industry. The end result of all this corporate expenditure is the same as with the first Gilded Age: a government committed to promoting the interests of financial elites, and supplanting democratic values.[222]

(4) Just as Adam Smith and the libertarians predicted, international free trade has brought the world great benefits. Among these have been a far greater variety of goods, often at lower costs, and a rising middle class in some former developing countries. However, since the wealth created by this trade has mostly gone into the pockets of the very wealthy individuals and largest corporations, at the cost of lost jobs, lower wages, and profound insecurity among workers in America and Europe, there has been increasing political resistance, and even violence in reaction to the increased economic inequality created by global treaties. The gains of the international super-rich and corporations have come, largely, through what economists call rent-seeking, namely, the use of political power to obtain a greater than deserved share of assets. Moreover, forced austerity policies, imposed by agencies, such as the International Monetary Fund has devastated the workers and economies of some countries, greatly increasing political instability.[223]

(5) Years of bad behavior by the wealthiest plutocrats of the Gilded Age, including violence toward workers, led to a growing move to enact income taxes, culminating in ratification of the Sixteenth Amendment to the U.S. Constitution in 1913. Theodore Roosevelt argued that "the man of great wealth owes a peculiar obligation to the State, because he derives special advantages from the mere existence of government." Among the ways the wealthiest should express their obligation, Roosevelt added, is by paying for the protection the State gives him."[224] Even Andrew Carnegie supported the enactment of an

inheritance tax. Significantly, the Amendment called for taxation of income "from whatever sources derived." Progressive income taxation was mainly responsible for reducing the extreme inequality that existed in the nineteenth century.[225] However, tax policies that were originally designed to have the wealthiest Americans pay for their advantages have been manipulated by those in the one percent. These wealthiest individuals have found ways to avoid paying their fair share, or even, in many cases anything at all; while everyone else, the poor, the middle class, and even many close to the top, are forced to contribute. This outrageous system has gotten so bad that a declared billionaire, who has become America's current President, is able to, not only, get away with not sharing his tax returns, but can even brag that he has not paid taxes because he is so smart. Libertarians who argue that taxation is a form of theft often add that private charity will provide for social needs. Unfortunately, the evidence is all the other way. Of course, many individuals are encouraged to contribute to various charities because they can then take a deduction on their taxes. On an international scale, the economist and economic historian, Thomas Piketty, in the most important work on economic inequality, has a great deal of importance to say about the positive and negative effects of taxation.[226]Piketty has also had an important role to play in showing how vital a role financial transparency, especially regarding corporate wealth plays in ensuring freedom and true prosperity. He has also played an essential role in demonstrating the need for restoring political economy to his profession. The economic profession has been complicit in the rise of dangerous inequality by turning away from the essential contribution of historical and political insights, because of its erroneous view of science and mathematics.[227] Finally, Piketty's demonstration that both positive and negative consequences, what he calls *convergences* and *divergences,* are built into capitalism, rather than being the result of market imperfections, moves our understanding beyond partisan argument and ideology.

(6) These are perilous times for civil liberties and democratic institutions in America and Europe. Surveys of voters in the United States find that the vast majority believe that their vote no longer matters, because their political institutions are controlled by corporate interests. I will examine the effect of mistrust and political legitimacy in the last section of this book. But, one very apparent result is that there has been a rise in nationalism, nativism, xenophobia, attacks on dissent, free speech and other liberal values, along with an increase in violence and bullying in America and Europe. Not coincidentally, this level of right-wing populism has not been seen, like the levels of inequality, since the 1920s. It also should be no surprise that a number of authoritarian figures have taken advantage of the anxiety noted above, as well as the anger and other negative passions directed at the establishment in order to gain political prominence and power.

(7) America's prison population increased from between 200,000 and 300,000 in the 1970s to 2,220,300 in 2013; almost twenty-

five percent of prisoners in the world, despite the fact that America has only about five percent of the world's population.[228] One result of this mass incarceration is that we now have an estimated 20 million men, many of them blacks, who are saddled with felony records that make it almost impossible to find employment. Because of the tremendous increase in the prison population in the 1990s, the Federal Bureau of Prisons decided to contract with three private, for profit, corrections companies to open prisons to house some federal inmates. The racial aspects of the so-called war on drugs, and the unprecedented number of inmates of color have led to comparisons with Jim Crow legislation in the South. The abusive use of inmates to make clothing and other products for large corporations has been compared to slave labor. Independent investigative journalists, examining many thousands of pages of documents, under the Freedom of Information Act; and, in one case, even getting a job as a guard, documented inhumane and deplorable conditions compared to facilities operated directly by government. Many of the violations involved neglect or mistreatment of medical conditions, by the grossly unqualified staff hired by these private for-profit companies. The Federal agency eventually decided to phase out these private contracts. The abuses could be directly traced to the desire to increase profits. Government accounting studies showed that this privatization measure did not reduce government costs, as originally hoped. In a separate case, a state judge was convicted of taking kick backs for sending inmates, many of them adolescents, to a state penitentiary. In many cases, the youth were convicted of minor school offenses that have been common in all schools for many years. Related investigations have shown that inmates and prisoners in work release facilities have been forced to work for large corporations, including, allegedly, Victoria Secret, JC Penny and Walmart, for near slave wages in one case as low as twelve cents an hour. There have been many similar issues with the for-profit higher educational institutions. In one of his popular lectures on justice, Michael Sandel tells the true story of a local private fire department. Homeowners pay a monthly fee and, if their house catches on fire, the company will send out its trucks. They will also rescue your neighbor's house, but only if the neighbor has signed up and is paying the company. One of their customers had his house catch fire, and they sent out the trucks. But, they learned that he had not made a couple of monthly payments, so they stood by while his house burnt to the ground. The homeowner attempted to make the late payments on the spot. But the company said, sorry, but we cannot run our company that way. They added, you cannot decide to pay your car insurance after you've had an accident. After the 2008 Great Recession, elderly citizens and other Americans shivered at the thought of what would have happened to their retirement savings if the George W. Bush administration had been successful in their prior effort to privatize Social Security. Two exhaustive studies of the explosion in incarceration since the 1970s, and its relationship to political economy and ideology demonstrate a strong and direct correlation between the highest rates and libertarian/neoliberal ideas and policies. The buildup has largely been among the poorest citizens, and especially African Americans. Since most of this incarceration takes place at the state and local level, it is important to note that both the countries and the states which have adopted libertarian politics are the ones with the highest incarceration rates.[229]

(8) Recently released documents show that two, highly influential Harvard University scientists were paid a huge sum of money by the sugar industry association to write review articles downplaying the negative role of sugar in coronary heart disease. The industry blatantly made it clear that their goal was to counter evidence in the 1960s showing a correlation between sugar consumption and heart disease, and they were allowed to approve drafts before they were published in one of the nation's most prestigious medical journals. Internal documents show that this was part of a larger campaign to shape public opinion that included industry funded research, propaganda, and government lobbying. Nutritionists and other scientists state now that these articles had a detrimental effect for decades in drawing up nutritional guidelines and in the whole debate about the role of obesity in disease. Separate revelations show similar campaigns by the sugary drink and candy industries. In one case, a study funded by the candy industry supposedly showed that children who eat candy weigh less than those who abstain. The so-called Sugar Trust was one of the most powerful monopolies and lobbying associations in the Gilded Age and, it was actually

successful in getting the government to promote the alleged health benefits of sugar. The industry continues to wield enormous power today. The history of similar research and lobbying activities by the tobacco industry are too well known to need repeating here. The history of the battle over the use of pesticides illustrates an important point about self-interest. The issues with pesticides, such as D.D.T., initially pitted chemical scientists, especially those who worked for companies that produced these agents, against biological and other natural scientists. It is important not to assume crude manipulation on the part of all these chemists. Rather, the effects of self-interest are often subtle and may involve as much self-deception as they do conscious falsehoods. Also, the issue is not just health and the environment, but the erosion of trust in the objectivity of science. This history also shows how there can be unintended negative consequences from industry, just as there can be from government regulations.

(9) According to the National Bureau of Economic Research, an institution trusted to tell us when we are in a recession, the top tenth of one percent of the United States population, 160,000 families, owned 22 percent of the nation's wealth in 2012, almost the same amount as 90 percent of the rest, some 144 million citizens. One family, the Walmart Waltons alone owns as much as 42 percent of other American families. Meanwhile, the top one percent has earned some 99 percent of the recovery from the Great Recession. The inequality can be seen in worker's wages. From the end of the 1970s to 2013, middle

income workers saw a largely flat increase of six percent, with much of that increase coming during a brief period in the late 1990s. The lowest income workers actually experienced a decline of five percent over the 80s, 90s, up to the present. Meanwhile, the highest earners saw their wages increase by forty-one percent. Even more dramatically, the top one percent saw an increase of 138 percent over this period, compared to fifteen percent for everyone else. Looked at another way, there has been a decline of more than half in the amount that workers receive from productivity gains over this period; as compared to the years up till the late 1970s, while the share of the productivity gains going to the top one percent has increased by 138 percent. Another way to present this fact is to note that productivity, adjusted for inflation, has increased by 147 percent since 1973, while the adjusted hourly compensation of workers has only increased by nineteen percent over that same period. What's more, the growth in the inequality of wealth has been far greater: first, because the total compensation packages of top executives include much more than income. But, also, because huge amount of new wealth, in the form of other assets such as stock, is hidden in secret accounts in tax havens, and is not captured in government data. The trend has been for this concentration of wealth to go to an even smaller group, ever smaller fractions of the one percent. Finally, the reason for this large discrepancy can be seen, in part, when one examines the increased gap between the compensation for top executives, now 300, often 400 times more than their workers. This gap is far higher than the average twenty percent gap that existed in earlier generations. As for children, the most innocent victims of inequality, in 2012 the United States ranked 30th out of the 35 countries in the International Organization for Economic Cooperation and Development; it had three times more child poverty than Norway or the Netherlands.[230] Inequality of this spectacular degree has hardly been seen since the Gilded Age. Similar disparities can be seen in Britain and some other Western nations. This decline in the income and wealth of workers has come at a time of marked increases in healthcare costs, while also seeing a decline in medical benefits to most employees.[231] What's more, the American healthcare outcomes, measured by all the categories of health, including life expectancy, are comparable to those in third world countries, despite much higher costs. These differences are mirrored by similar disparities between states; with those states that have adopted libertarian policies producing poorer outcomes in education, health, and other social measures. Often such states, Louisiana is a good example, end up with much higher government deficits, contrary to their fiscally conservative rhetoric.

(10)    The percentage of workers who belong to a union declined by almost half between 1973 and 2008. The sharpest decline has been in the private sector. The minimum wage, adjusted for inflation, declined by 25 percent during the 1980s. Twenty-one percent of children in the United States now live in poverty. A remarkable thirty-seven percent of young black males who have

dropped out of high school, are now incarcerated; a rate that is more than three times what it was in 1980.[232] In contrast, periods of history in which wages are high, for example, in Britain just before the birth of the Industrial Revolution, have been followed by a renaissance of innovation and commercial expansion.[233]

(11)    The huge inequality in wealth, or what libertarians call outcome, is matched, not surprisingly, by a similar divide in equality of opportunity. People of my generation grew up during a period of relative equality of wealth, but also of greater opportunity and upward mobility. We could believe in the American dream because we and those we knew lived it. In the familiar phrases, if you worked hard and played by the rules, you could get ahead of your parents. The ideal that in America opportunity should not be denied because of such morally arbitrary obstacles as heredity, race, or religion has been lost. This ideal has always made it harder to recognize and acknowledge class differences; and, it has also led citizens struggling economically to vote for those political leaders who inspire hope in their upward mobility. In an address before Congress in 1861, Abraham Lincoln stated that the main purpose of our democratic government should be "to elevate the condition of men—to lift artificial weights from all shoulders … to afford all, an unfettered start, and a fair chance, in the race of life."[234] The fact is that income mobility has declined in recent decades, not only as compared with prior generations, but also when America is compared with other developed nations. It

is well established fact that income status and education play a critical role in mobility, so one example from education will serve here as illustration. Compared with other developed countries, American educational achievement is quite dismal. But, when you compare reading scores from American schools with less than ten percent poor students, American students actually lead the world. The evidence is conclusive, opportunity, as well as achievement, depend more on a child's family status than at any time since the Gilded Age. What's more, today's enormous wealth gap has led to a corresponding social gap, as well as such isolation that the rich no longer need to even see or interact with the poor. The key questions are: how did we get to this level of severe economic inequality? Why should citizens who are well-off or reasonably comfortable be very concerned about it? And, once they are concerned, what can they do about it?

(12)     Arguably no libertarian propaganda campaign has been more successful and more damaging than the deliberate misinformation about the negative or corrupting effects of government assistance on the poor and society. The best economic analysis of why this propaganda has been so influential on public opinion points the finger squarely on America's pervasive racial prejudice.[235] The highly influential reports by libertarians, such as Charles Murray, are a quintessential example of confirmation bias: focusing on a small percentage of examples, such as the notorious "welfare queen," rather than the full sample or data. The best data shows

that of the 46.5 million Americans who live below the poverty line, some 16.4 million are children. Some 57 percent of the poor are either employed or live with someone who is working. Poverty is substantially higher in states with the lowest wages. It is estimated that almost 62 percent of Americans would live in poverty if it were not for social security. Almost half of all Americans will experience poverty, at least once, before they reach the age of 65.[236] These misleading methods used by some libertarians also commit other logical and statistical fallacies of argument.[237] The misuse of science here is similar to that of the Social Darwinists, as well as Charles Murray's other work on IQ and race.[238] The facts are that the actual number of welfare recipients who are "welfare chiselers" is quite small; best estimates are two percent. There is no solid evidence that receiving welfare encourages illegitimacy and discourages recipients from seeking work. The evidence is that most recipients do not become dependent on assistance. In fact, forty percent of those receiving welfare do so for one or two years.[239] Although my personal experience is anecdotal, unlike the data referred to here, I can attest that no one I worked with in over forty years as a social worker, including two years working for the City welfare office in the Bronx, New York, wanted to do anything but get off welfare and move up economically. What has become known as the 1996 welfare reform act was legislation enacted by the Republican Party but signed into law by Democratic President Bill Clinton. Republicans had issued a libertarian "contract with America," and Clinton had pledged to "end welfare as we have come to know it." This law is still having profound, mostly negative, effects on inequality and the health of America's poorest citizens. Even more germane to my position here, the so-called reform act had a quite negative effect on the educational attainment of children,[240]

(13)    The comments of the Democratic Senator from North Dakota, Byron Dorgan, in the spring of 1999 about the negative consequences of repealing the Glass-Steagall Act (1933) were farsighted in light of the effects that action had in contributing to the Great Recession of 2007/2008. Dorgan warned that the banking problems leading to the Great Depression would return within "10 years." The factors contributing to the Great Recession, as also with the Great Depression, were very complex, involving among other things, global pressures on financial institutions, the creation of hybrid private/public agencies with dual social and profit goals, the corruption of government by business, and just plain greed. But, that the repeal of Glass-Steagall and the relaxation of regulatory oversight played an important role cannot be denied.

(14)    Libertarians have had huge resources and many years to perfect their ability to manipulate public opinion through the art of persuasion. For example, one propaganda technique, which has been called the *ad nauseam*, namely the deliberate, prolonged, repetition of a falsehood or misleading statement by design by people in authority, has been shown by cognitive psychologists to be very effective. A good example is the repeated assertion that the number of federal employees has

been increasing. The facts are that the percentage of federal employees in relationship to all nonfarm laborers has actually decreased since just after World War II.[241] Of course, one can repeat a truth *ad nauseam* as well. There is a moral psychology, as well as a cognitive psychology intrinsic to rhetoric or the art of persuasion.

(15)    There has been a recent spread of right-wing, authoritarian, populist movements in America and Europe, with strong nationalist, racist, and nativist platforms that, like the fascist movements of the 1920s and 30s, have similar causes and pose a similar threat to the survival of democracy. As I write these words, my country is facing the greatest threat to its freedom in my lifetime, with a radical authoritarian and extreme right wing nationalist as the President of United States of America. The significant role that America's extreme inequality played in his election cannot be denied. With some 45 million people living in poverty, and an elite that has shown very little, if any, empathy for their plight, citizens threw the dice, hoping for some positive change in their life. Emblematic of this lack of empathy were the comments of one CEO of a large company. He lamented that middle class workers in America demanded much higher salaries than workers in developing countries, adding "if you are going to demand ten times the paycheck, you need to deliver ten times the value. It sounds harsh, but maybe people in the middle class need to decide to take a pay cut."[242] Jonathan Haidt, in his excellent book on why Americans have become so politically polarized, *The Righteous Mind: Why*

*Good People Are Divided by Politics and Religion*, describes research that shows how a key factor is that people differ, often sharply, on the moral dispositions of Care, Fairness, and Liberty. Libertarians, not surprisingly rate high on the liberty part of his moral matrix. Haidt notes his own sympathy with libertarian ideas as described in David Boaz's book, *Libertarianism: a Primer*. But, he also describes massive survey research that shows libertarians score low on his Care matrix.[243] I will return to the issue of values in the last section of this chapter.

The answer to my question concerning what these issues have in common, as well as the answer to many related issues will come in the remainder of this chapter under the sub-headings of *Inequality*; *Dark Arts*; and *Values*. However, this is a good place to mention that libertarian economics suffers from at least five myths;

(1) The myth of the perfect market.

(2) The myth that unfettered markets are always more efficient than government entities.

(3) The myth that deregulation inevitably leads to increased market competition.

(4) The myth that only governments and not private corporations, live beyond their means.

(5) The myth that any degree of inflation is always bad.

(6) The myth of asocial individuality.

(7) The myth of the rational consumer and investor.

(8) The myth that great wealth is usually the result of more effort and superior merit.

(9) The myth that so-called market forces will take care of the rights of consumers, while ensuring their well-being and flourishing.

(10)  And, the myth of trickle-down economics.

Another concept, known as the trade-off thesis, is only partly correct. This is the thesis that inequality is just the price we have to pay for a more productive market, because it is incentivizing. This belief comes with the added provision that we will all benefit from the resulting increased productivity.[244]

These mythical concepts at the heart of libertarian economic and political theory can only be maintained by ignoring the vast amount of historical and empirical evidence that is disconfirming, while concentrating on the very real failures of government. Sometimes the effort involved in this psychological process of ignoring the evidence seems so Herculean, as after the Great Recession of 2008, that the only charitable explanation is rationalization to buttress self-interest. Other citizens have been the victim of a long campaign of propaganda. New "methods of persuasion" have been developed" that are "subtle, insidious, sugarcoated, focus-grouped, and market-tested —and comparable in their effectiveness to anything served up by despots and demagogues of the past."[245]Our Founders, John Dewey, and many others have recognized the central role that public education plays in a democracy. Just as young girls should be taught to recognize the early controlling behaviors that are a sign of possible domestic violence, so too, should all young people be taught to recognize when they are being lied to, seduced, and manipulated for a motive of self-interest by people in positions of power. Citizens who can recognize when people of power are acting selflessly, in the national interest, and to promote individual well-being are the only safeguard for democracy. Moreover, the libertarian propaganda effort involved the rewriting of the history of the Great Depression, mentioned in Chapter One above, and even what happened to cause the recent Great Recession, in order to blame these massive market failures on government, while ignoring the overwhelming evidence of private sector causes. This kind of alteration of past reality is a frequent tool of those with power.[246] A major problem is that we now have several generations that were raised on advertising. Orwell understood the negative effect of advertising on citizenship when he called it "the rattling of a stick inside a swill bucket." Power brokers, like advertisers, know how to use framing, reference points, and other psychological factors to influence our political decisions. The explosion in technology and social media has only increased their ability to manipulate citizens, and has exacerbated this undermining of democratic habits.

I noted in the last chapter that Adam Smith has been considered a founding father for libertarians. However, Smith's position in the libertarian pantheon has been promoted by a highly selective reading of his work; not only by ignoring his moral writings, but by ignoring key passages and ideas in his *Wealth of Nations*. Smith wrote a great deal about the importance of taxation. A declaration such as the following is hard to reconcile with the doctrine that taxation is theft: "every tax is to the person who pays it a badge, not of slavery but of liberty."[247] Any careful reading of his position on taxation will show that he was not only concerned with its fairness, but also that taxes must be equitable and progressive, with those who benefit most from a nation's economy paying more. He argued strongly against taxes and rules that favor the wealthiest and hurt laborers and the middle class, such as, what we would call sales taxes. Smith was greatly concerned with the danger inequality poses for a free society. He noted that "whenever the legislature attempts to regulate the differences between masters and their workmen, its counselors are always the masters;" whereas when "regulation … is in favor of the workmen, it is always just and equitable."[248] What's more, Smith maintained a view totally antithetical to the libertarian thesis about the economic benefits of inequality. Instead, Smith maintains that it is those nations that encourage equality that are most likely to have a robust economy. "No society can surely be flourishing and happy," he declared, "of which the far greater part of the members are poor and miserable." Smith argues that maintaining higher wages gives a worker "the comforting hope of bettering his condition." Where there is this motivation, "we shall always find the workmen more active, diligent and expeditious, than where they are low." The whole society benefits from their resulting increased productivity.[249] If this pragmatic motivation is not sufficient, Smith adds an argument based on justice and morality. "It is but equity, besides," he asserts, "that they who feed, clothe, and lodge the whole body of the people, should have such a share of the produce of their own labor as to be themselves tolerably well fed, clothed and lodged."[250] Smith is legitimately seen as a founding theorist of libertarian political economy in that he argued that equality could be achieved through a less regulated market, which would bring "universal opulence." [251]However, as one of his greatest students, Dugald Stewart, summarized Smith's goal for government, it was "to make as equitable a distribution as possible, among all different members of a community, of the advantages arising from the political union."[252] I will return later in this chapter to Adam Smith's philosophy, specifically to aspects of his moral theory; his interesting argument about the clash between three self-interest groups or factions; and, his characterization of the values of merchants and large capitalists.

Few economists today really believe in the automatic efficiency of self-regulating or self-policing financial markets. Even some of those who consider themselves libertarians, speak of unregulated markets as an ideal to be aimed at. One does not have to look hard or far back in history to find countless examples of the pathology of "exuberance" leading to financial crisis. Just in recent decades we have seen the savings-and-loan crisis, the commercial real estate bubble, the tech bubble, crises with bond markets, and, of course, the Great Recession that we are still recovering from. Charles Kindleberger's classic book, *Manias, Panics, and Crashes: A History of Financial Crises* contains many examples, and he has had to update the book a number of times (my copy is the fourth edition).[253]The most interesting aspect of this history, I believe, is that even when economists and others can see that the financial bubble is heading for disaster, self-interest, power, and politics, as well as libertarian ideology most often blocks preventive action. A prime example is the Federal Reserve Chairman, Alan Greenspan, who had to eventually admit that he had been blinded by his own libertarian philosophy.[254]

When combined with other major problems with libertarian economic precepts, such as austerity policies; general problems relating to different rates of growth between capital in the form of stock or other financial securities, on the one hand, and income from wages, on the other; the much greater gains from globalization on wealth from capital versus wealth from wages; the tremendous power of international corporations as opposed to labor unions; and, the effects of technology, the result has been the kind of extreme inequality, and related problems, that I have enumerated above. The most serious price which we all pay for extreme inequality and which should most concern all freedom-loving people, including the wealthiest citizens, is its threat to the continuation of democratic rights. Extreme economic inequality as the most serious of dangers is, therefore, the subject of the next section of this chapter. The rest of the chapter addresses the issues of power and values which I argue can help us move beyond ideology to a new synthesis that combines the best ideas of minimal state and active state liberal political views and policies..

But before turning to my critique, it is important to realize that all these difficulties, over more than thirty years, have been the result of deliberate, and specific political action and inaction based in power and self-interest. Inaction can preserve and even enhance special privileges and inequality. These specific acts and deliberate failures to act were based on the economic and political agenda of Mont Pélerin and the Powell Memorandum. Prime Minister Margaret Thatcher gave this agenda a pro-libertarian spin when she, supposedly, said "first you win the argument, then you win the vote."[255] Referring to this decades- long libertarian effort to transform public opinion, the French social theorist Pierre Bourdieu cynically noted that "it takes time for something false to become self-evident."[256] This kind of negative view would be conspiratorial and perhaps unfair, and it would give the title of this chapter a different meaning from the one I intended. Of course, there have been significant reasons for inequality that are the result of causes other than political maneuvering. I hope that by the end of this chapter the reader will understand why it is that the major role played by technological change and globalization in creating inequality is also an outcome of political actions and deliberate inactions. The important role played by an individual's perception of relative social status in how he or she reacts to inequality is something I thoroughly covered in my book, *Love of Having.* Adam Smith understood that individuals can both underestimate their wealth, as well as overestimate their material well-being.[257] In a remarkable passage, Friedrich Hayek laments the fact that most people mistakenly believe that the free market system "regularly rewards the deserving." He muses whether we are doing a disservice to the young by encouraging them to believe "that when they really try they will succeed." He wonders whether we should let them know instead "that inevitably some unworthy will succeed and some worthy fail."[258] As I noted in the last chapter, classical economic and some moderate libertarian theorists hold that economic transactions should conform to rules or regulations. A system where powerful self-interest groups of any kind are allowed to make special deals with government is opposed as contrary to how free market economics should work. Just as with the justice of rewards based on merit, economic reality differs considerably from theory.

The problem of economic inequality in America, of course, is very old. Michael Harrington's highly influential 1962 best seller, *The Other America* was followed ten years later by a book that described a tax system that was "a welfare program" for the "super-rich."[259] However, the period from the end of World War II through most of the 1970s was one of strong economic gains by workers and the growth of an increasingly vibrant middle class. The deliberate political agenda of the libertarians has had the negative effect of bringing about our current level of extreme inequality, which was far from inevitable, nor was it their implicit intent. The specific actions included changes to our democratic institutions that make it much more difficult to bring about inequality reform: such as, legal and media measures that have greatly increased the need for huge sums of money to accomplish such reform; more sophisticated gerrymandering of congressional districts; mass incarceration, especially of people of color; changes in voting procedures that are aimed at suppressing minority voting, and various other forms of elite manipulation. Lower voter turnout by poor people is more of a problem because of the decline in union membership, as unions used to work precincts to get their supporters to the polls.[260]

I will mention just one other interesting example of this process here, because it is far less apparent or well-known. There has been a pattern of self-fulfilling prophecy, where programs are under-funded to such an extent that they cannot function as originally mandated; and, then the inefficiencies caused by this emasculation are used in order to argue that these programs or agencies are dysfunctional. An equally common variation of this maneuver is to insert amendments to legislation that introduce similar problems in functioning, and then point to these problems as justification for totally eliminating the program. I leave it as an open question whether or not such manipulation is totally conscious, since the practical results remain the same. The final outcome of this decimation is that it provides ammunition in order to advocate doing away with the program or agency entirely. This has been a very effective propaganda tool for libertarian policies. It shows the effectiveness of taking a long range, methodical approach to power. A similar, though shorter, example of long range maneuvering was the highly successful plan to control gerrymandering of Congressional Districts for Republican Representatives by first gaining control over state legislatures that draw such districts. Before returning to these and other specific examples, however, it is important to make it clear why inequality threatens not only individual health, but also the health of our democratic institutions and governance.

## Inequality

The founders of the American republic made it very clear that they were very concerned about the possible development of political parties in the United States. In a letter to Jonathan Jackson of 2 October 1780, John Adams wrote "there is nothing which I dread so much as a division of the republic into two parties."[261] In a letter written from Paris on 13 March 1789, Jefferson was even stronger, stating "if I could not go to heaven but with a party, I would not go there at all."[262]Of course the founders did not mean exactly what we do by parties; rather something closer to Madison's factions. Yet the question remains how is it possible that these same individuals developed their own political parties, only four years after George Washington warned about "the baneful effects of the Spirit of Party" in his 1796 *Farewell Address*.[263] The answer is that the founders were even more concerned about the dangerous effects of inequality. The political ideology of the American revolutionaries was classical republicanism, with its central tenet that the primary guarantee of liberty was the maintenance of a large, civic-minded, and vibrant middle class.[264]

This understanding about the dangers of severe inequality to freedom was based on literally thousands of years of historical example. Plato had Socrates assert that states which had such a division of wealth were divided and "just as an unhealthy body requires but a slight impulse from outside to fall into sickness," and "the man is one internal war," in such a risky condition the state will "become diseased and wage war with itself," and "even apart from any external impulse faction arises."[265] In an important section of Book 8 of *The Republic*, Plato gives his analysis of the defective forms of government, and how they dissolve into tyrannies. His warnings are clearly based on his own substantial experience, as well as his knowledge of human nature and history. Of particular importance is the understanding of the insatiable character of human appetites, including greed and the lust for power and the corruption and strife this causes in any form of government. I have examined the negative role that the appetite for more and more plays in generating conflict in another book. This role is no less important for democratic government.[266] The fact that Plato was not a believer in our ideal of democracy should not be allowed to take away from these insights, especially in light of the fact that it is economic conflict between the rich and poor and the appetite for more and more that Plato believes is a chief defect of democratic rule. This conflict leads to the rise of a demagogue who "hints at the abolition of debts and the partition of lands," thus winning over the poor.[267]

Aristotle was even more alarmist about the dangers of inequality and the importance of a strong middle class of moderate wealth for freedom. It is in his discussion of the best state, coming directly after his discussion of tyranny and dictatorship in his *Politics*, that he gives these dire warnings. After noting how difficult it is to maintain a democratic government, he states unequivocally that "the true friend of the people should see that they are not too poor, for extreme poverty lowers the character of the democracy, measures therefore should be taken to give them lasting prosperity, as this is equally the interest of all classes." He goes on to recommend some distribution of public funds, sufficient to start a little farm or business.[268] He argues further that the state must provide a flourishing economy for all, and that this requires construction and maintenance of all roads, bridges and other infrastructure. It is important to point out that, for Aristotle, the issue is not only the best state, but even more critically, the "best life for most" of us.[269] It is also important to note that Aristotle presents a form of government that is practical and based on human nature as it is, not on some unattainable utopian ideal. He argues that "it will clearly be best [if most citizens] possess the gifts of fortune in moderation; for in that condition of life men are most ready to follow rational principle." Aristotle is following Plato here, in noting that people who are too poor are so weakened by the daily fight for survival that they are not able to fully participate in government.[270] I would take issue with his statement that those who are poor will turn to "violent and great criminals", while the wealthy will turn into "rogues and petty rascals"; today these roles have often been reversed. But Aristotle's contention that "the middle class is least likely to shrink from [authority] or to be over-ambitious for it; both of which are injuries to the state" has usually been born out by subsequent history. He goes on to assert that citizens who have too much wealth most often are not willing to submit to authority, because in their parenting and education they have not learned "the habit of obedience."Instead of being spoiled, he argues, the poorest citizens have been too demeaned and debilitated. Aristotle's assertion that "the one class cannot obey, and can only rule despotically; the other knows not how to command and must be ruled like slaves" has been justly condemned. But, his conclusion that economic inequality in a state leads to the opposite of friendship and civic virtue has only been repeatedly confirmed by the history of republican forms of government.

It is important to point out that neither Aristotle, or, for that matter, any of the other political thinkers I discuss here were socialists or promoters of redistribution; not only because they tended to be wealthy themselves, but because they argued that such state intervention also threatened political stability and justice. Aristotle asserted that if either of the opposite groups, the rich or the poor, gained control of political power, they would use it to advance their own, very different, self-interests. He realized that each group would use different means to increase their hold on power and to subvert the general interest; with the rich tending to use subtler means of power. Centuries of history, including very recent events, have only confirmed this observation.

In his great epistolary debate with Thomas Jefferson, John Adams put forth a position very similar to Aristotle's.[271] In a series of letters between 1813 and 1814, Adams, who had arguably done the most extensive research on the history of republican governments of any of the Founders, added some important insights about this more subtle use of power by the rich to advance their selfish interests. After noting that "birth and wealth together have prevailed over virtue and talents in all ages," he adds that the lower classes have only acknowledged the wealthy and high born as the "*aristoi* [best]." He called the methods used by the rich to gain and hold on to power, "a subtle venom that diffuses itself unseen." He notes that economic conditions can adversely affect political functioning. One of his greatest insights is that "mischief may be done negatively as well as positively." He notes that "so long as the idea of property exists, it will accumulate in individuals and families." He calls this "wealth another monster to be subdued." Adams makes some related observations about political parties that I will return to below. In a letter to James Sullivan, dated May 26, 1776, Adams expands on this insight, noting that "the balance of power in a society accompanies the balance of property in a land." It is essential to make "the acquisition of land easy to every member of property," such that the power that comes from ownership is spread very broadly, in order to equalize "liberty and public virtue."[272] Suffice it to note here that Adams conflict with Jefferson centers on the latter man's Enlightenment faith in progress toward the perfectibility of man. Adams had, what I would call, a more realistic view of human nature, which directly informed his equally more realistic understanding of political power.

Aristotle firmly criticized the pure communism of Phaleas as a danger to political order.[273] I will return to Aristotle's influential views on the role of character and values in the last section of this chapter. Needless to say, none of the ancient writers mentioned here, least of all Aristotle, shared our modern inclusive values of citizenship, and, it would be highly anachronistic to expect that they would. However, this fact should not, in any way, discount their deep understanding of political ideas based on history and human nature. Suffice it to note here that in his *Discourses on Livy*, Machiavelli expands considerably on ancient ideas about the relationship between certain essential aspects of character and the stability of states. He needs to be studied for his understanding of the ways that republics are lost, for the insatiable nature of the lust for power, for the subtle ways that the people can be manipulated and conspired against, and not for his dangerous prescriptions. He can be added to the chorus of great political thinkers who warned about the danger to the preservation of liberty that comes from economic inequality.[274]

Not surprisingly, an even greater influence on the Founders of the American Republic came from the late seventeenth and early eighteenth century Commonwealth Men.[275] Especially influential were *The Commonwealth of Oceana* and *A System of Politics* by James Harrington. Harrington asserted that "where there is inequality of estates, there must be inequality of power, and where there is inequality of power, there can be no commonwealth."[276]He generalized this insight in a manner that has proven historically prescient by noting that "equality of estates causes equality of power, and equality of power is the liberty not only of the commonwealth, but of every man."[277] Another influential Commonwealth Man, especially so for Jefferson and Adams, was Algernon Sidney, who in his *Discourses on Government,* pointed to the corrupting effects of the value system associated with the accumulation of great wealth as the death knell of republics.[278]

The key distinction for these classical, Renaissance, and Enlightenment authors was between a healthy competitive spirit and the kind that leads to social conflict.[279]The issue was, in large part, independence of will and agency that came from owning enough wealth to be directly involved in political life. This central belief has been called *The Jeffersonian Persuasion*. A balancing of interests, but also a significant "identity of interests" connecting elected officials with citizens.[280]

The influence of *Cato's Letters* on the American revolutionaries cannot be exaggerated. Like so many works that expand on the liberties of individuals, this series of letters from 1720s Britain were inspired by a financial crisis and panic; namely, the South Sea Bubble. The two authors, John Trenchard and Thomas Gordon, put forth the belief that our "natural equality" is often destroyed by lack of opportunity, which is directly related to the inequality in the distribution of wealth. They shared the belief that concentrated wealth threatened the security and stability of any republic. They asserted, in Letter 35, from 1721, that "when men's riches are become immeasurably or surprisingly great, a people, who regard their own security, ought to make a strict enquiry how they came by them, and oblige them to take down their own size, for fear of terrifying the community or mastering it."[281] They go on, in this same Letter and elsewhere, to note the "divisive effect" of wealth on the Roman and other republics. They add, in Letter 85, that "an equality of estate will give an equality of power; and an equality of power is a commonwealth, or democracy." Although they prescribe laws that bring about "a suitable disposition of property," they, like Madison and the other Founders, were hardly socialists or economic egalitarians.[282] Rather, it is Madison's balance of ambitions and interests that best expresses their concerns. However, like the other authors mentioned here, they are, also, concerned about the fact that the very pursuit of wealth tends to focus a person's interests on themselves, and away from the common good. This concern was more than just the aristocratic distain for commerce, although it was partly that, but rather a general appreciation that the money-making value system can corrupt other values.[283] It was the need for a certain level of independence from want, which would allow citizens to be self-reliant and to look beyond their own narrow self-interest.

The need for freedom from want is closely related to individual autonomy and independence, as well as control over one's desires and judgment. Those without these virtues of character are easily manipulated by the powerful. For these and other reasons, a nation that is composed mostly of a middle class is the "best political community," and most "secure." Such a nation is "most likely to be well-administered, in which the middle class is large, and stronger if possible than both the other classes, or at any rate than either singly; for the addition of the middle class turns the scale, and prevents either of the extremes from being dominant." Many books and articles, by academics and others, "quote" the ancient biographer and philosopher, Plutarch's saying: "an imbalance between rich and poor is the oldest and most fatal ailment of all republics." Despite the fact that he, almost definitely, did not write these exact words, nonetheless they are a succinct summary of the historical record.[284]

The great Irish and Irish/American political leader, scientist, and polymath, Dr. William James Macneven walked around Switzerland in 1802 and 1803, shortly after his release from four years in captivity for efforts to free Ireland from English oppression. He wrote a magnificent book about his experiences: part travel diary, part political, social and cultural history, but mostly a very important political treatise.[285] Macneven entered Switzerland at a time of great political, military, and economic turmoil. The years 1798 through 1803 saw the so-called Helvetic Revolution, the Second Coalition War (fought largely on Swiss soil), with two separate occupations of large sections of the country by French troops, a Civil War, fanned in large part by the French technique of providing military resources to local oligarchs; and, finally, it was the period of Napoleon's "Mediation."[286] Macneven approached his walking tour with his usual scientific and rationalist style, preparing by studying all the constitutions of the various Cantons, as well as reading their histories and interrogating their citizens. His conclusions are highly relevant to the role of economic inequality and the preservation of liberty. He found that republics that had been corrupted by wide divisions in wealth, and were now controlled by oligarchs, were politically corrupt, had miserable citizens, and were the ones that submitted to French intervention without much opposition. Cantons that remained relatively free, and where there was a large middle class, were prosperous, happy, and resisted outside force. Macneven called the first type of Cantons "demi-republics," where the people were purposely kept in ignorance, where French patronage corrupted the leaders, and where the people had no sense of patriotism or reason to fight the French. Macneven lived a long life, in Ireland, Prague, Vienna, France, and for his last 35 years in America. He knew many languages and read an enormous amount; and, from all this experience, he maintained until his dying day that only liberty brought prosperity and only widely shared prosperity ensured the survival of liberty. Macneven sums this up clearly in his book on Switzerland, advocating for:

> Representative government; that happy discovery, which fairly and honestly established would terminate the eternal warfare that has hitherto existed between the rich and the poor, under all the governments of Europe, ancient and modern. The poor should surely enjoy complete protection; the rich will always be ambitious of honors. A fair representation reconciles these interests.[287]

It should not be surprising that Macneven joined the party of Thomas Jefferson when he arrived in the new nation of representative government, in that he argued for the importance of the role of land ownership in promoting patriotism and preserving liberty:

> When the roof that shelters a man, and the field from which he eats, are not at the disposal of another, but are permanently his own, he already possesses great independence of person and actions. Practically, he enjoys a great share of freedom, who, in things so essentially connected with human happiness, is his own master. He

imagines [his property] with cheerfulness as far as he
knows how, and it is easy to give him a taste for
improvements: for when he invests his labor or capital in
the soil, he knows that he is hoarding for his children.

In a remarkable letter, written toward the end of his life, Jefferson
looked back at the defining ideas that motivated the American Revolution
he had helped lead. Key among these was the extreme economic inequality
that had been fostered by the "kings, nobles, and priests" of Europe. The
methods of oppressive power he enumerates were well known to
Macneven and the vast Catholic majority of Ireland. They maintained
power, Jefferson asserted, by keeping the people "down by hard labor,
poverty, and ignorance," and by exploiting their "unremitting labor" that
provided the masses only with a "sufficient surplus barely to sustain a
scanty and miserable life." He added that "the inequalities" the rulers
"produced, exposed liberty to sufferance."[288] In a remarkably insightful
passage in *Democracy in America,* Alexis de Tocqueville argues that "the
mass of the citizens, sincerely wish to promote the welfare of the country;
nay, more, I even grant that the lower classes mix fewer considerations of
personal interest with their patriotism than the higher orders; but it is
always more or less difficult for them to discern the best means of attaining
the end which they sincerely desire." He goes on to note how wealthy elites
and those in power, even in a republic, are able to mislead the people to
satisfy their own self-interests. The dangerous result is that "the lower
orders are agitated by the chance of success, they are irritated by its
uncertainty, and they pass from the enthusiasm of pursuit to the exhaustion
of ill success, and lastly to the acrimony of disappointment."[289]

The Roman historian, Polybius, gives some fascinating detail about
what can happen to those accustomed to liberty who forget the history of

oligarchic tyranny: "but when a new generation arises and the democracy falls into the hands of the grandchildren of its founders, they have become so accustomed to freedom and equality that they no longer value them, and begin to aim at preeminence, and it is chiefly those of ample fortune who fall into this error; democracy in its turn is abolished and changes into a rule of force and violence."[290] Alexis de Tocqueville, made some similar observations about the stabilizing effects of the "innumerable multitude of men" in a middle class between extremes of rich or poor, with "sufficient property to desire the maintenance of order, yet not enough to execute envy." He added that "such men are the natural enemies of violent commotions," thus assuring "the balance of the fabric of society."[291]In his discussion of the negative effects of most revolutions, Tocqueville notes their cause is to "consolidate or destroy social inequality." If you look beyond the immediate trigger of revolution, "you will almost always find the principle of inequality at the bottom. Either the poor have attempted to plunder the rich, or the rich to enslave the poor."[292]To a large extent, all of his great work on *Democracy in America* is a development of these ideas. He was perhaps the first to define the American dream, noting that "I never met in America with any citizen so poor as not to cast a glance of hope and envy on the enjoyments of the rich, or whose imagination did not possess itself by anticipation of those good things which fate still obstinately withheld from him."[293] Tocqueville believed that there was less of a threat to democracy from inequality in America, however, because without an aristocracy "great fortunes should not remain in the same hands," so that there may be "rich men, but they do not form a class."[294] This would only be true, however, if there were major inheritance taxes, and it ignores the tremendous advantages that come from being born into wealth, even without any aristocracy.[295]

Based on his experience of the Dutch Republic and his study of the ancients and the Venetian Republic, the great pioneer of democratic liberalism, Benedict de Spinoza promoted equality and reason as essential to the preservation of freedom. Spinoza put forth a positive view of liberty, and argued that "all men have one and the same nature; it is power and culture which mislead us."[296]Like the other theorists I've discussed, Spinoza rejected the extreme view of a contemporary leveler, but argued that the possession of property by all citizens was the only guarantee of personal freedom and independence and national stability.[297]

In their grand historic overview of *Why Nations Fail?* Daron Acemoglu and James Robinson tell a cautionary tale about how corruption of political institutions can negatively impact economic institutions and vice versa.[298]Historical analysis on their sweeping scale has long been suspect in academic circles, because experts can always question the details on any one example. However, the recent return of historical works that advance broad generalizations should be welcomed for many reasons. History never repeats itself, except as rhyme or pattern. Most relevant for political theory is the fact that the transformation of democratic governance into autocracy has been repeated many times and with certain common features. These similar patterns should not be surprising given the common aspects of human nature and the common behaviors and reactions seen in human relationships. Nor should the differences be surprising, given the specifics of environment and culture, as well as the complexities of human nature.

The usually slow process of undermining free institutions is most often hard to discern while it is happening. One common pattern is for republican institutions to be gradually hijacked, first by becoming more and more dysfunctional, leading to a right wing populist revolt. These periods of xenophobia, anti-immigrant and racial fears and sentiments have occurred repeatedly in America and Europe. This is the pattern, one that took at least thirty years to ripen, that is unfolding in Western countries today. Also, any brief summary of *Why Nations Fail* will, necessarily, not do justice to this large book. I will only focus here on the very relevant example of the decline of the Venetian Republic; but, a few key concepts must be mentioned in order to set the stage.

The authors present two contrasting types of economic and political institutions that they call *inclusive* vs. *extractive* as contrasting "engines of prosperity."[299] They provide plenty of examples of the overwhelming superiority of a free market capitalist economic system for generating national prosperity. The types of institutions that make up this system are already familiar from my analysis in the Pro chapter of this book. These inclusive economic institutions foster and nourish "participation by the great mass of the people in economic activities that make best use of their talents and skills and that enable individuals to make the choices they wish."[300] The authors emphasize that any capitalist economy requires the legal mechanisms and "public services" of the state, for all the reasons that I have enumerated, and that all but the most utopian libertarians acknowledge. Although they agree that some services can be privatized, they maintain that in any modern economy and society, the "degree of coordination necessary" to provide these tools on "a grand scale" requires a much more substantial government apparatus than most libertarians are willing to continence. Inclusive institutions provide both these legal protections and "a level playing field," which encourages innovation and the entrepreneurial striving for advancement. Extractive economic and political institutions are ones in which a relatively small elite gain control of resources and political institutions in order to exploit them for their own personal advantage. Acemoglu and Robinson argue that there is a "strong synergy" between inclusive and extractive economic and political institutions. Their analysis has the great virtue of emphasizing the importance of power, and its use in extracting political advantage, as well as wealth. Much of *Why Nations Fail* is devoted to the mechanisms by which nations are transformed from one type of structure to the other; what the authors call *institutional drift* and *critical junctures.* I will briefly examine these processes in the next subsection of this chapter. For my purposes here, the example of the history of how the Venetian Republic moved from a more inclusive and free government to one which was both economically and political extractive will make the connection to economic and political inequality clearer.

Acemoglu and Robinson introduce their brief discussion under the felicitous title of "How Venice became a Museum."[301] They describe the synergy that slowly developed during the Middle Ages between newly created inclusive economic institutions and more democratic political structures. New political institutions brought a growing number of Venetians into the political decision making process. The Venetian economic system, in turn, welcomed new entrepreneurs and expanded trade. These economic freedoms led, in turn, to both increased prosperity for Venice and upward social mobility and greater economic equality for Venetians. Adam Smith's argument that greater political freedom and openness leads to increased national wealth is fully illustrated by this historic example.[302]By the Fourteenth Century Venice was the richest city in Europe.[303] So, what went wrong? By now, you should not be surprised to learn that the newly established elite took steps to consolidate their wealth and power, creating political changes that in 1297 resulted in the, appropriately named, institution known as *La Serrata* ("The Closure"). This was followed by the creation of a hereditary aristocracy and new nobility. These new extractive institutions led eventually to economic decline, and thus Venice went "from economic powerhouse to museum."[304]The pattern is clear: those elites that benefit from an inclusive economic system will, if given the opportunity, institute extractive political institutions and policies that conserve their privileges and powers.

The Founders of the new American Republic knew this history of what had caused the demise of prior republics, and they took the threat very seriously. The topic came up repeatedly during the debates at the constitutional convention in Philadelphia, as well as during the struggle over ratification of the resulting document. Also, a disagreement about the extent of the danger of economic inequality to democracy was, as I noted earlier, at the center of the conflict that led to the development of political parties, despite the almost unanimous opposition to such institutions which were seen as one form of monopoly of power.

James Madison was, arguably, the strongest voice warning of the danger of inequality at the Convention. On June 6, 1787 Madison gave an important speech on the nature of faction, in which he asserted that no matter what size, every government will be divided between "different sects, factions, and interests," consisting of rich and poor, debtors and

creditors, the landed and manufacturing or commercial interest," etc.[305]
Drawing on examples from ancient and recent history, Madison argued for
the necessity of balancing these differing class interests to protect freedom.
His clearest, most influential, and boldest comments came in a speech on
Tuesday, June 26, 1787. Again drawing on examples from history, he
asserts that the proper goal of liberal government should be, "first to
protect the people against their rulers; second, to protect the people against
the transient impressions into which they themselves might be led." After
noting that democratic governments were historically "unsteady" and
impulsive when economically unequal, and subject to political conflict
over differences in self-interest; he goes on to state that "the man who is
possessed of wealth, who lolls on his sofa and rolls in his carriage, cannot
judge the wants or feelings of the day-laborer." To make it even clearer
what his concerns were, he immediately adds that "the government we
mean to erect is intended to last for ages."[306]

Negatively influenced by Shay's Rebellion, as all the Founders
were, Madison goes on to make it clear that he is just as concerned, if not
more so, to protect the "opulent" against those day-laborers. But, it is the
instability and danger that comes from any concentration of wealth and the
need for a buy-in to the general interest by some possession of property
which is Madison's central warning.

In a remarkable letter from Thomas Jefferson to Madison, written
from Fontainebleau, France on October 26, 1785, Jefferson begins by
noting that total economic equality is not a practical thing. But, at the other
extreme, "enormous inequality" causes such "misery to the bulk of
mankind [that] legislators cannot invent too many devices for subdividing
property." One such device to lessen inequality that Jefferson suggests is a

progressive tax system, namely, to "exempt all from taxation below a certain point, and to tax the higher portions of property in geometrical progression as they rise."[307] Jefferson's goal was, in part, to lessen misery by providing wide "employment," and thus, to increase political stability. It is generally well-known that Jefferson felt that the agrarian life and the small farmer were the only secure basis of political stability in a republic. Jefferson voiced pride in the relative economic equality in America in a letter to Dr. Thomas Cooper in 1814. Jefferson observed that, in contrast with Britain and France, America lacked a "pauper" class. The poorest Americans were laborers, and most of them possessed some land. Moreover, these people employed "dexterity" and "the acutest resources of the mind" in their pursuit of necessities of life, as well as happiness. What's even more important is that these poor laborers are able "to exact from the rich" high enough prices to have families and "to be fed abundantly, clothed above mere decency," and have "all the comforts and decencies of life." America's rich, Jefferson added, "possess [only] moderate wealth," and they "know nothing of what the Europeans call luxury." Jefferson sums up this happy picture of his country with the rhetorical question, "can any condition of society be more desirable than this?"[308] Jefferson, like the other Founders, clearly saw a relatively egalitarian citizenry to be a political strength, and a unique feature of America's more democratic economy. For Jefferson, living in an agrarian period, it was the ownership of land that would ensure patriotism. Some historians have tended to dismiss the concerns of the Virginia Founders as simply snobbery directed at the newly emerging class of merchants and professionals. Although there certainly was some of that prejudice among the landed gentry, especially in Europe, it ignores the central fact that

Madison, Jefferson, and most of the other Founders were anxious about extremes of wealth no matter what the form of property.

Madison's most famous and greatest work is generally felt to be his *Federalist Paper 10.*[309] Many people, over the years, have asserted that this paper anticipated Karl Marx and his theory of economic determinism. It would take me too far afield to completely demonstrate that this is, not only, not a correct reading of Madison, but, in my opinion, lessens the full brilliance of Madison's argument. Suffice it to say here that what Madison meant by his key term, *factions,* is something much broader than economic self-interest, and more like our *self-interest group.* I should also reiterate that, like the other authors here, Madison was far from being a leveler; in fact, he directly argued against economic egalitarianism. That being said, he could not have been clearer that it was above all economic conflicts that he saw as the most important of "the mortal diseases under which popular governments have every where perished." He elaborates:

> The most common and durable source of factions has been the various and unequal distribution of property. Those who hold, and those who are without property, have ever formed distinct interest in society. Those who are creditors, those who are debtors, fall under a like discrimination. A landed interest, a manufacturing interest, a mercantile interest, a monied interest with many lesser interests, grow up a necessity in civilized nations, and divide them into different classes, actuated by different sentiments and views.[310]

One of the so-called "other" supporters of the new Constitution, Noah Webster, writing from Philadelphia on the October 17, 1787 as "A Citizen of America," drew the same lesson from history. Webster calls attention to the new commercial or capitalist form of economy, with its own, different, set of values; a transformation I covered in my previous book, *Love of Having.* He notes the positive effects that this change has brought, in spreading wealth to a much broader class of citizens. However, he expresses his concern that "wherever we cast our eyes, we see this truth, that *property* is the basis of *power*; and this, being established as a cardinal point, directs us to the preservation of freedom." He goes on to assert the need for laws to ensure the just distribution of property, so that each citizen "will possess each his share of property and power, and thus the balance of wealth and power will continue where it is, in the *body of the people.*" He adds for emphasis that "*a general and tolerably equal distribution of landed property is the whole basis of national freedom.*"[311]

It is interesting to note that Madison anticipated that there would be an increase in manufacturing and commerce in America. It is useful to know that other Founders, besides Alexander Hamilton, had this insight. However, it remains true that Hamilton was the most sanguine about this great economic transformation, and that he did the most to make it happen. The founding generation lived at a much simpler time, one that could not fully imagine the power that would be wielded by captains of industry, like Carnegie or Rockefeller. As early as 1771, Abigail Adams could celebrate America's relative "equality of circumstances" compared to European countries, with "none so immensely rich as to lord it over us, neither any so abjectly poor as to suffer for the necessities of life."[312] Tocqueville remarked on the same remarkable level of economic equality over six decades later.

It was certainly not very long after the founding of the new nation that it suffered its first financial bubble and panic. Hamilton became the first Secretary of the Treasury in 1791, tasked with placing the highly stressed economy on a firm foundation, after years of war and borrowing.

As his Assistant Secretary, Hamilton unfortunately picked William Duer, a man from a family that had become wealthy from the West India trade. Duer, himself, had made a lot of money on profits from the American Revolution. He was a man who seems to have combined all the worst characteristics of the unscrupulous speculator.[313] Space here does not allow for an account of all the machinations surrounding the credit bubble of 1791 and the financial panic of 1792; the pattern is all too familiar, with run-away speculation, artificially inflated stock prices, vast fortunes earned, followed by falling stock prices, panic and crash, huge debts, and a well-orchestrated bailout by Hamilton.[314] Duer was to end up spending his remaining years in debtor's prison. Of interest here is the effect all this had on the Founders, and on the development of the first American political parties. Not surprisingly, these events only reinforced the views of Madison, Jefferson, and Adams about the dangers to free government from banking, speculation, and inflated wealth. Madison gave a speech in Congress on February 2, 1791 opposing Hamilton's National Bank.[315] In a letter to Jefferson dated August 8, 1791, Madison predicted that because of "the daring depravity of the times, the stockjobbers will become the praetorian band of the Government, at once its tool, and tyrant; bribed by its largesse, and overawing it, by clamors and combinations." As early as 1790, speculators who knew about Hamilton's plan to "assume" the debt of the states into the new Federal Government had bought up, at great discount, the state instruments, much of it from revolutionary soldiers. Both Jefferson and Madison reacted with horror to this wild market. Jefferson commented that "it is impossible to say where the appetite for gambling will stop."[316] The disagreements between Madison and Jefferson, on the one hand, and Hamilton and others concerning the dangers of inequality were a major contributing factor in the formation of the first political parties; a development that the Founders claimed would itself threaten liberty. I can only touch very briefly here on the most relevant part of that history. This heightening of partisan politics was caused by the first glimmers of a new commercial economy through the enactment of Hamilton's fiscal program.

In his excellent book on Madison's political philosophy, *The Sacred Fire of Liberty,* Lance Banning includes an analysis and generous quotations from a series of essays that Madison published, during this period, in Philip Freneau's *National Gazette.*[317] This series of essays provide a very important elaboration and commentary on Madison's justly famous *Federalist Papers.* But, they also help to explain why it is that Madison felt so strongly about the dangers to liberty posed by aspects of Hamilton's economic plan that he was willing to engage in the worrisome practices of political parties. For my purposes here, Madison's elaboration of the ideas contained in his *Federalist Papers* numbers 10 and 51, and, especially, his arguments against economic inequality and the need for a large, vibrant, middle class, should be widely known. Madison was, particularly, concerned about any economic laws that give "artificial" powers to financial speculators and commercial interests, thereby "withholding *unnecessary* opportunities from a few to increase the inequality of property by an immoderate, and especially unmerited accumulation of riches." What was required, instead, was "the silent operation of laws which, without violating the rights of property, reduce extreme wealth toward a state of mediocrity and raise extreme indigence towards a state of comfort."[318] Madison would prohibit laws that favor the self-interest of powerful commercial and financial players, while balancing one such interest group against the ambitions of other such groups. A government which preserves liberty must aim for an equilibrium or balance between the many factions and interests, especially, in a modern commercial society. What's more, Madison presciently argued for the necessity of government promotion of the "branches of manufacturing and mechanical industry" that serve to enhance the health, vigor, and happiness of the general population. He was concerned about the promotion of industry and employment that would provide for the independence and a comfortable living for the mass of citizens. By providing for these essential interests, a representative government engages the patriotic commitment of citizens, just as Macneven was to note in his observations about the Swiss Cantons. In order to maintain this freedom and commitment, government would need to discourage, rather than "pamper" the "spirit of speculation." It bears repeating that Madison, much more than Jefferson, recognized the positive and essential role of banking and capital in the enhancement of commerce. But, he was equally aware of the dangers of unregulated financial speculation on the preservation of the general liberties and the survival of democratic government.

As the great American historian, Sean Wilentz, notes, in his important work on *The Rise of American Democracy,* Madison had to admit, in one of these *National Gazette* essays that, instead of the many differing factions he had prescribed in *Federalist 10,* only two political parties had developed in the new republic.[319] There were multiple ironies in this development: it is Jefferson and Madison who are, rightly, associated with minimal state liberalism and Hamilton with the active state proposals. Even more ironic, as Wilentz shows in his recent, *The Politicians and the Egalitarians,* the slaveholding Democratic Republicans were motivated by their fear of economic inequality, and the need for a wide distribution, at a time when Southern plantation owners owned the most extreme wealth.[320]But, the greatest irony of all, and the one most central to my concerns in this chapter, is that Hamilton, the founder justly famous for his promotion of a strong commercial republic, not only appreciated the negative effects of domestic and international commerce, but wrote some of the most critical attacks on "utopian" political views of, what today, would be considered capitalist or neoliberal arguments and values. One place where this can be seen most directly is in his *Federalist Paper no. 6.* Hamilton begins that work with some strong realist comments about human nature as "ambitious, vindictive, and rapacious."[321]He goes on to demolish the notion that commerce and republics will tend to be more pacific, noting that anyone with "a tolerable knowledge of human nature," and of the "accumulated experience of the ages" will recognize the "utopian" nature of this position. He notes that it is often merchants who promote aggression between states and nations, in their desire to extract their resources and trade. Of course, we have many subsequent examples of this process that confirm his insight.[322] He goes on to give some historical examples, and then turns to recent events, asserting that "if Shays had not been a *desperate debtor* it is much to be doubted whether Massachusetts would have been plunged into a civil war."[323]The "spirit of commerce," "avarice," and "desires of unjust acquisition" are equally strong in republics. Hamilton's views on political economy, as seen in his great *Report on the Subject of Manufactures,* of December 13, 1791, are far from libertarian, although he does note the bad effects of excessive debt and extreme taxation.[324]In a speech at the Constitutional Convention, Hamilton stated his belief that "in every community where industry is encouraged, there will be a division of it into the few and the many. Hence separate interests will arise. There will be debtors and creditors, etc. Give all power to the many, they will oppress the few. Give all power to the few, they will oppress the many." He went on to argue that there was a need to have separate branches to protect and be "the guardians of the poorer orders;" while the other branch protected the property and the interests of the wealthy.[325] In his excellent book on the role of economic inequality in the founding of America, Clement Fatovic shows that, though he was not the most concerned Founder, Hamilton did promote active political measures to help elevate, protect, and relieve the suffering of America's poorest citizens, and provide the balance necessary to sustain liberty.[326]

Since I have already written at length on the economic turmoil and battles over inequality during Andrew Jackson's era, in my chapters on the *Bank War* and *Social Reformer* in *Irish Rebel, American Patriot,* I will turn here to a very brief look at Abraham Lincoln's views on economic justice.

Most Americans are well aware of Lincoln's role in saving the union and freeing the slaves, but very few know about his seminal role in the development of active state liberalism, and his efforts to promote economic justice. Lincoln built on ideas and actions based on federally funded, domestic economic improvements which had been central to the so-called American System of the Whig Party. The Whigs were known for their strong pro business sympathies, which were combined with an active government, internal improvements program, unlike anything that had been seen on this scale before.[327] As I will show below, this combination has proven much more effective in reducing extremes of economic inequality and boosting economies than has the current libertarian austerity approach. In their excellent book on this important topic, *A Just and Generous*

*Nation: Abraham Lincoln and the Fight for American Opportunity,* the leading Lincoln historian, Harold Holzer, and the celebrated economist, Norton Garfinkle, let Lincoln's beautiful prose document much of their case. In one passage, Lincoln summarized his political economy by noting that "the legitimate object of government is to do for a community of people, whatever they need to have done, but cannot do, at all, or cannot, so well do, for themselves in their separate, and individual capacities."[328]Lincoln was quite clear about his belief that the government had to play a central role in several key areas, including providing for "internal improvements," what we call today, infrastructure, but, also, "schools" "orphanages," and other "charities." This is not the place to discuss the long list of federal programs that Lincoln and the Republican led Congress enacted during his tenure; but one, the Morrill, or Land-Grant Act of 1862 is significant for the thesis of this book. This law eventually became the basis for our current state system of higher education. It represents an active state intervention that has had immense impact in improving the lives of ordinary Americans, while also contributing substantially to America's rise to the greatest capitalist economy.

Many Lincoln experts have pointed to the phrase "for the people," in Lincoln's most famous address, as a reference to his active state liberalism. These authors, along with others, like Sean Wilentz, note the central importance for Lincoln of the marked difference between the economies of the Northern and Southern states.[329]The Northern economy was remarkable for its relatively large middle class and upward mobility; whereas, the Southern economy, with its reliance on slave labor, had extreme inequality, even within the white population. Lincoln feared that the spread of slavery, therefore, would threaten our democracy, not only because slavery itself was inimical to democratic values, but, also, because the political economy of slavery produced marked economic inequality. In the first of his famous debates with Stephen Douglas in 1858, Lincoln said that the slave had a "right to eat the bread, without leave of anybody else, which his own hand earns."[330]

Lincoln, like almost all the political thinkers examined here, libertarians as well as most of their critics, were all influenced by John Locke's ideas about property, as put forth in Locke's *Two Treatises on Government.* Those libertarians who are economists have tended to interpret Locke's use of the term *property* in the narrow, common sense, meaning; whereas, most philosopher's and Locke specialists have pointed to its much broader meaning at his time. It was this understanding of the term that the American Founders used in the *Declaration* and the *Constitution.*[331] Madison made this clear in his short, but highly important article on *Property,* in the *National* Gazette, dated March 29, 1792, when he stated that "in its larger and juster meaning, [property] embraces everything to which a man may attach a value and have a right; and *which leaves to everyone else the like advantage.*"[332] Madison is most concerned that democratic government needs to protect the equal property that citizens have in their own ideas, capabilities, and other freedoms, including religious beliefs and practices. We are not used to thinking of these as property, but rather as personal rights. Madison sums up this connection in a famous line, "as a man is said to have a right to his property, he may be equally said to have a property in his rights." He goes so far as to argue that "conscience is the most sacred of all property … more sacred than his castle." A brief passage about taxation sounds superficially like it was written by a modern libertarian. But, Madison's emphasis is squarely on just and equal, as well as the right amount of taxation to encourage, rather than discourage labor and enrichment. Individuals should have the right to, as Lincoln would put it, the fruits of their labor, and enough wealth to thrive. In a key passage, he states that an overly powerful government threatens all these kinds of property; but, also, that "where there is an excess of liberty, the effect is the same, though from an opposite cause." What is primary here is Madison's general philosophy of the balance of power centers, as well as his stress, reminiscent of Aristotle, on moderation.

At the end of his section on this topic, in his *Second Treatise on Government,* Locke had made a similar comment about justice when he noted that in his concept "what portion man carved to himself was easily seen, and it was useless, as well as dishonest, to carve himself too much or take more than he needed."[333] As I noted in my discussion of property above, the meaning of this term has to include the idea of laws or exclusionary rules. Locke, famously, started from the religious idea that *men* (the gender is deliberate) were given the earth by God. He was, therefore, faced with justifying legal exclusion and unequal distribution. His answer, which brings me back to Lincoln, was his famous argument that we all have ownership in our own person, and we come to have ownership in external property by mixing the labor of our body to the land. These ideas were central to Madison and most of the Founders. The appeal of these principles to someone opposing slavery, such as Lincoln, should be obvious.

In his own short passage on slavery, Locke specifically opposes the negative type of liberty that has come to be associated with libertarians, "a liberty for everyone to do what he lists, to live as he pleases, and not to be tied by any laws." Rather, his prescription for freedom was a government of laws, "a liberty to follow my own will in all things where the rule prescribes not, and not to be subject to the inconstant, unknown, and arbitrary will of another man."[334] But, this is not the place to go into Locke's evolving ideas about slavery and resistance to government. What Lincoln made of these moral ideas about property, free labor, and the need for a large, vibrant, middle class is the key to understanding his policies. The rights to the fruits of one's labor, rights of self-ownership, including of one's faculties, opinions, and practices, and a government that actively promotes the general welfare, apply to Blacks as well as Whites, and the extension of these rights were what the Civil War was fought for. Lincoln accepted the idea of self-government, that individual's should have the right to do what they please; but, he wished to extend this right to all groups and the community at large; although he was never able to extend his reasoning completely to Blacks.[335] To the libertarian principle that every individual has a right to do what he pleases, he not only adds with "the fruit of his labor," but, he also, extended the principle to "the general government" and "that general class of things that does concern the whole."[336] Locke's analysis is both political and moral, and has become one of the foundations of both minimal state and active state liberalism.

When Locke wrote that "the preservation of property was the end of government," and that "the great end of [mankind's] entering into society" is "the enjoyment of their properties in peace and safety," he started a chain of ideas that led to Lincoln's rejection of the old doctrine of property that held that the protection and freedom of property allowed for the enslavement of other people.[337]The misleading term, *human capital,* used by economists today, unfortunately applied literally to the American South in the time of Lincoln's debate with Douglas. Treating the terms of this debate as economic ignores the essential moral importance of the issues involved. One scholar, John Burt, writing about the position of Stephen Douglas, puts it starkly, "to treat the slavery issue in economic terms is to concede that it is essentially an issue about property, and to treat the slavery issue as an issue about property is to concede almost everything to the slaveholders."[338] In a speech at Edwardsville, Illinois on September 11, 1858, Lincoln warned his audience that "accustomed to trample on the rights of those around you, you have lost the genius of your own independence, and become the fit subjects of the first cunning tyrant who rises."[339] In his fascinating and important book on the moral conflicts of Lincoln's time, John Burt compares the insights of this speech with the deep human conflict of the master and slave, which, as I have noted elsewhere, was known to Irish leaders like Dr. William James Macneven and Theobald Wolfe Tone long before it was made famous by the philosophers Hegel and Sartre.[340] Burt also notes that Lincoln was opposing economic and social ideas similar to those that would become prominent under the heading of Social Darwinism; ideas similar to those of some early libertarians.[341] One adherent of this biological determinism summarized the dilemma of the poor by stating "that we are born well, or born badly, and that whoever is ushered into existence at the bottom of the scale can never rise to the top because the weight of the universe is upon him."[342]

Lincoln's active state government led to a booming economy, from which all classes of Americans benefitted. Some argue that, since his Party had control of Congress, and he was not as actively involved with economic matters, the Congress deserves more of the credit.[343] There were, no doubt, a number of reasons for this boom; but, the improvements and actions set the basis for the expansion of industry in the last half of the nineteenth century. What is of importance for my purposes here is that Lincoln was strongly committed to innovation, education, technological, individual labor over other forms of capital, and economic improvements largely because they would raise the standard of living of all Americans and lead to greater economic equality, liberty and stability. All of these elements appear in an informal address he gave to at an agricultural fair on September 30, 1859.[344] His was a much more optimistic and egalitarian view than that of Sen. John C. Calhoun of South Carolina. Calhoun argued that as nations became richer and more populated, "the difference between the rich and the poor will become more strongly marked," as would the percentage of "ignorant and dependent" people.[345] To some extent, this was a self-fulfilling prophecy for the South. Efforts were made, during the Reconstruction period, to address the extreme inequality in the South. Among the methods was to introduce public schools and to expand access to all classes and to the newly freed slaves.[346]

Sean Wilentz shows how the same concerns about the corrosive and destabilizing effects of economic inequality on America's democratic institutions was a strong motivating factor in the abolitionist movement, the Civil War, and Reconstruction period. Racial inequality and economic inequality have been strongly intertwined concerns throughout American history.[347] The eventual end to Northern efforts to ensure civil rights to the newly freed slaves came with the withdrawal of the Federal protections of the Reconstruction period. This change was the result of an economic recession, with resulting financial stress, but also of increased Northern racism. The same reformers who worked to gain basic rights for the newly freed slaves, also worried about the corruption of government by the wealthy few; what was called the "self and pelf" or spoils system, where favors were rewards "to interest groups that wanted government power used on their behalf."[348] It was in the subsequent period known as Jim Crow when, not only the hard power aspects of this connection were apparent, but also some of the more subtle, psychological and social, soft power features can be seen. These soft power aspects have been repeated throughout our history as well, and since they are, unfortunately, very much influencing our politics today, I need to take a brief look at them here.

In his Address at the Conclusion of the Selma to Montgomery March, on March 25, 1965, Dr. Martin Luther King, Jr., always the superb teacher, enlightened his audience and the American people about some of the economic and psychological causes behind the Jim Crow political movement. Drawing on the classic work of the great historian of the Jim Crow South, C. Van Woodward, King described "the political stratagem" of plantation and mill owners to suppress the wages of white workers by threatening to replace them with free slave labor, who would be paid even lower rates.[349] This divide and control manipulation was enhanced by propaganda, use of fear, revival of traditional racist ideology, as well as by a universal tendency for suppressed people to wish to have a group over which they can feel superior. This latter, psychosocial phenomenon has been described by members of the Frankfurt Institute for Social Research, who drew from direct experience in Fascist Europe.[350] These last studies are especially relevant today, as we struggle to understand how "the masses can be won over to a politics which conflicts with their own rational interests."[351] Whether it is authoritarian political leaders, elite business interests, or domestic violence, some of the same psychological techniques can be identified. I will go more into this dynamic in the next section.

The Civil War and the Reconstruction period saw a tremendous expansion of railroads, especially west of the Mississippi.[352] The horrible working conditions for nineteenth century laborers, including women and children, are too well known to need recounting here. Tens of thousands died each year, and many times that were injured just from work-related conditions.[353] The period of American history known, after the title of the novel by Mark Twain and Charles Dudley Warner, as the *Gilded Age*, roughly 1878 till 1900, was when the "winner take all economy" really came into its own in a big way. The great historian, Vernon L. Parrington, coined a fittingly American title for this feeding frenzy, calling it "the Great Barbecue."[354] The political economy of this period echoes laissez-faire, minimal state, libertarian ideas, and President Grover Cleveland's summary is quoted approvingly by one contemporary libertarian. In vetoing a bill that would have reduced the fee for riding New York's elevated trains, dated February 16, 1887, Cleveland asserted, "I do not believe that the power and duty of the general government ought to be extended to the relief of individual suffering which is in no manner properly related to the public service or benefit." President Cleveland added for emphasis that" a prevalent tendency to disregard the limited mission of this power and duty should, I think, be steadfastly resisted, to the end that the lesson should constantly be enforced that though people support the Government the Government should not support the people."[355]His pithy formula for the people was "a fair field and no favor."[356] Early in his meteoric political career, however, Cleveland had spoken about protecting "the laboring classes" when their rights were "endangered by aggregated capital" and of "improving the condition of the workingman."[357] However, like the other presidents of the Gilded Age, Cleveland's prohibition against aid did not extend to big business, especially the railroads. By 1894, Cleveland could countenance sending federal troops to put down the Pullman Strike, leading to arguably the greatest loss of life in all the many anti-union attacks of the Gilded Age. In a political maneuver that is all too familiar today, the decline in government activity during this period tracks the increase in inequality, with a steady decline in the number of bills passed by Congress to a low of just seven percent. Corporate leaders, their lawyers, and other associates filled the Cabinets and other major powerful positions in the executive administrations and legislatures of the Gilded Age. Libertarian apologists for this infamous period of history draw a distinction between these political capitalists and other, private capitalists, but it is a distinction without a difference. The fact is that, with corporate power at an all-time high, and legislative action at an all-time low, local, state, and federal government ballooned in size, largely due to government patronage to assuage corporate interests and other forms of political corruption. It was a time when great fortunes could be made, "where great waste is permitted for great accomplishment," but also, "where [there were] many temptations and few restraints imposed."[358] In one of the best recent histories of the Gilded Age, *Age of Betrayal: The Triumph of Money in America, 1865-1900*, Jack Beatty calls attention to the sharp contrast between views of Cleveland and other presidents of this period, and the generous and just political economy of Abraham Lincoln.[359] Beatty raises the question that still puzzles political scientists today, namely, why did American citizens vote for governments that systematically opposed their economic interests, supporting big business elites who used government power to amass fortunes. The short answer, too short of course, is race. The evidence for this particular example of stoking and exploiting of prejudice for economic and political gain is overwhelming.[360]

The most interesting aspect of the Gilded Age, for my purposes comes from the use of a specific ideology to garner and command political power. The steel magnate, Andrew Carnegie, certainly not the worst of the Robber Barons, gave a clear expression of this new ideology. Writing in the June, 1889 issue of the *North American Review*, Carnegie argued that "while the law of competition may be sometimes hard for the individual, it is best for the race, because it ensures the survival of the fittest in every department." Americans should "accept as inevitable," he asserted, the "great inequality of environment, the concentration of business, industrial and commercial, in the hands of a few," because they would not only benefit economically, but this outcome was "essential for the survival of the race."[361] This pseudo-scientific ideology of Social Darwinism, with its inherent racism, was, arguably, the nadir of libertarian and neoliberal social theory. Inequality could now be seen as inevitable, a law of nature like gravitation; as Carnegie asserted that "we cannot avoid it." But, as I noted, Carnegie was far from being the worst of the industrial giants, not only because of his great philanthropy, but because he spoke out against "the sin of having made beggars."[362] The religious terminology here, like the frequent reference to the race and the fittest to survive, shows how easily the newly scientistic ideas fit with the old Calvinist doctrines about the just.[363] More relevant to my concerns here was the, equally easy fit, between Social Darwinism and the libertarian commitment to negative liberty, as opposed to a rights-based conception, and laissez-faire economics. This ready mix of ideas was largely imported to the new world with the wildly popular British evolutionary science, filtered through the sociology of Herbert Spencer, and his American disciple, William Graham Sumner. Spencer was even more popular in his native land, and it was his version of Darwin that had the greatest influence; it was Spencer, after all, who first used the phrase "survival of the fittest." The analogy was drawn between the competitive economic struggle in the unfettered marketplace which, it was argued, mirrored the same struggle to survive in nature that Darwin saw at the heart of evolution. This analogy got mixed together with American ideals of progress, always a loose concept, and the self-made man (gender specific). White males, specifically those of northern European stock, would inevitably triumph in this competitive struggle, just so long as government got out of the way. The government could also interfere with this *natural* process by propping up the weakest members of the species, thereby allowing them to reproduce; nature should be allowed to take its course if the species as a whole was to advance. For this reason and others, Spencer opposed state assistance and most regulations, including sanitation and housing laws, and laws protecting patients from medical quacks.[364] Regulation of the economy, Spencer argued, was especially bad, since it ended up penalizing superior individuals and stifling commercial progress. Active state liberal policies, Spencer warned, would interfere with evolutionary laws and lead to "the artificial preservation of those least able to take care of themselves." In Europe, these Social Darwinist and extreme economic liberal concepts were later combined with a "tribal nationalism" to provide the foundations for fascism, the very antithesis of Spencer's views on freedom and his libertarian individualism.[365] This use of libertarian economic liberalism and authoritarian politics is far from unique. One prominent example was Milton Friedman's assistance to the Chilean dictatorship of General Augusto Pinochet.[366] I will very briefly examine this shameful involvement later in this book.

William Graham Sumner was a very popular and influential spokesman for the Gilded Age. In essays and books with titles such as *What Classes Owe to Each Other*; *The Absurd Effort to Make the World Over*; *The Concentration of Wealth: its Economic Justification*; and *Laissez-Faire*, he publicized ideas very similar to the libertarian views described in the last chapter.[367] Sumner is something of a hero to libertarians, but he is usually dismissed by simplistic comments by active state liberals. For example, his ideas in *What Classes Owe Each Other* are often dismissed with the blithe summary: "absolutely nothing." But, Sumner's ideas, though ultimately dangerous, deserve to be treated with more respectful commentary given their continued influence. Like Hayek, Friedman, and others, he anticipated arguments against the concept that the state is a separate entity with a "conscience, power, and will" as a dangerous view for liberty. The state, he wrote, is "only All-of-us," a group of individuals exercising their own will. Active state liberalism really comes down to the question "what ought All-of-us to do for Some-of-us." It also comes down to the question of whether one group or class in society has an obligation to relieve the suffering of any other group or class; individuals who are not "capable of satisfying their own desires"? He puts forth the familiar libertarian formula "that every effort to realize equality necessitates a sacrifice of liberty." Rights come into play, for Sumner, only when some individuals in a society are forced to help some other group in a society. A poor man who cannot work is "a burden," Sumner makes it clear, and "on no sound political theory ought such a person to share in the political process."They are a subject for voluntary charity, but as "dead weight" on economic progress, and hold back the more industrious members of society.

Spencer had written that "the whole effort of nature is to get rid of such, to clear the world of them, and make room for better."[368] They simply lack "the essential powers" required for life's struggle. Sumner groups the poor together with "the weak, the negligent, shiftless, silly, inefficient, and imprudent," basically the dregs that hold a society and economy from flourishing. His view of the state's functioning is also the negative one already familiar from more recent libertarians. In fact, Sumner has rightly been embraced by contemporary libertarians, who are anxious to rescue him from the ignominy into which he has fallen. He expresses their same horror of any tampering with market forces. But, instead of the idea that some vague market equilibrium would keep monopoly in check, Sumner and other Social Darwinists pointed to the scientific mechanism of "natural selection." However, Sumner's particular version of minimal state economic liberalism was one of a harsher view of the struggle for survival, one of an economic reality that was "cold, and matter-of-fact." It made for a relationship that lasted "only for so long as the reason for it endures." Modern capitalist relations are different from the "sentimental relations" of former times. For Sumner, economics is a zero-sum process: every dollar given to a shiftless or worthless poor person is one less dollar that could have gone to promote economic growth. "The advantage of some is won by an equivalent loss of others." He is careful not to condemn all charity. Efforts to support family or friends are part of the sentimental relationships. However, anyone who accepts charity is "demeaned" and "under obligation" and those who give are, by the very act, patronizing and asserting their "superiority."[369]

Sumner was criticized by some for his claim that the only choices were "liberty, inequality, survival of the fittest," on the one hand; and, "not-liberty, equality, and" the opposite "the survival of the unfittest." "The former," he added, "carries society forward and favors all its best members; the latter caries society downwards and favors all its worst members."[370] He, eventually, dropped the phrase altogether as it had been confused with the moralistic belief in "survival of the best." Lords of industry, like John D. Rockefeller, were, understandably, flattered by this moralistic reading. Rockefeller asserted that "the growth of a large business is merely the survival of the fittest …it is merely the working-out of a law of nature and a law of God."[371] Sumner was also careful to distinguish between *plutocracy*, which he condemned, and what he called "the power of capital."[372] His argument here is an important one, in that he expressed concern that democracy was endangered by plutocrats, who used their wealth to subvert democratic institutions by the use of lobbyists and the corruption of legislators to gain monopolistic advantages. Sumner argued that this process of corruption needed to be attacked in its early stages in order to preserve democracy. Sumner's libertarianism held that economic gain would come from unfettered market forces, and he worried that "there is no form of political power which is so ill-fitted to cope with plutocracy as democracy."[373]

Sumner explicitly rejected criticism that his views were moralistic, since after all, they were based on *science*. It may be obvious to us today that, not only were his views based on a misinterpretation of Darwin, but that the assumptions of this former Episcopal Priest were largely shaped by the Protestant ethic. The worthy could be known from their success, and the worthless from their lowly status. This can be seen very clearly in one of his most famous and most libertarian essays, "The Forgotten Man."[374] The title character of this civic drama is the "honest," "industrious," "hard-working" *man*, who only wishes to enjoy the benefits of his labor and provide for his family. It is this worthy individual who "is the victim of the reformer, social speculator, and philanthropist." It is he, not some abstract entity called "society" that is oppressed by government taxation, in order to pay for government services, but also for "the vicious, the idle, and the shiftless." It is a message that appeals to populist discontent, to all those who feel that government does not feel their pain. Whether knowingly or not President Donald Trump echoed Sumner when during his campaign he pledged, however implausibly, to work for "all the forgotten men and women of America."

The virtue of reading someone like Sumner, or Ayn Rand, is to encounter libertarian ideas in their starkest reduction. Sumner proclaimed that we should let nature, red in tooth and claw, take care of those he considers degenerates, by imposing "its most frightful penalties." He realizes that his prescriptions "may shock" his readers, but "it will do you very good to" to have to think about them. For example, "a drunkard in the gutter is just where he ought to be. Nature is working away at him to get him out of the way, just as she sets up her processes of dissolution to remove whatever is a failure in its line." He goes on to give a familiar list of other "vices" that ought to be dealt with in a similar hard manner, rather than to require that the industrious among us are unnecessarily burdened.

Reform policies, what many libertarians today like to call do-gooder interference, Sumner warns, only get in the way of Nature's, admittedly, harsh remedies and protections. He goes on to give familiar libertarian arguments against government regulations, including sanitary laws, dwelling conditions, and the safety of factories. His concern is similar to his fears about interference with nature, in that he believes that such laws prevent a natural process of education in freedom, and, thereby, promote dependency. Tocqueville and others have argued that the habit of being free helps to develop more freedom. But, Sumner's views are moralistic and naturalistic. He asserts that there are two basic problems with the regulatory bureaucracy that social reformers wish to impose: first, the tyrannized forgotten man has to pay for it; but, even more important, "boards, commissioners, and inspectors" relieve "negligent people of the consequences of their negligence," thereby "leaving them to continue negligent without correction." Employees, tenants, and others need to learn to take care of themselves, and not become dependent on the assistance of others in society who have not been so foolish as to get into such bad situations. The forgotten men, who have been "careful and prudent" should not be required to rescue the negligent. The same kind of argument holds for the criminal. We should not be spending good money, Sumner argues, to reform him. Punishment is "God and Nature's" true method of reform. The concern here was made even clearer by another Social Darwinist, when he said that the reformers might convince "the drunkard, gambler or a libertine" that he was "a victim, more than a sinner; that there is no very loud call on him to be a man so long as there are opportunities of being a brute."[375] Especially in light of subsequent world history, it is very difficult for us today to believe in this Social Darwinist correlation between the worthiest and the strongest individuals.

Another reason why this is an important essay is that Sumner presents here some interesting arguments about liberty or freedom. He begins by painting a dark, Hobbesian, picture of life as a history of men and classes struggling for power over others in order to enjoy the fruits of the earth. This war of all against all is universal, and not confined to any particular class. The goal is to shift life's burden onto the shoulders of others. The political ideal should be to live in a society of laws, similar to Hayek's, where the individual citizen is guaranteed "the exclusive employment of all his own powers for his own welfare." He rejects at least one formulation of the negative liberty promoted by most libertarians, namely, that "a man may do what he has a mind to do." He points out that freedom of this type has never really existed and is unrealizable. He, also, rejects a rights-based view of liberty that is not tied directly to a corresponding duty or obligation. There is no free lunch; we all must work for our individual happiness. We have the right to pursue happiness, but not *to* happiness. Sumner's conception of liberty suffers from the same defects that have been the basis of common criticisms of Nozick's entitlement theory. First, it does not take into consideration the fact that individuals start life with very different advantages or disadvantages. For Sumner this is just the way God and Nature intended things. In a 1902 essay on "The Concentration of Wealth: Its Economic Justification," Sumner goes so far as to state that extreme inequality, whether caused by inheritance or created by legislative privileges, is just part of natural selection.[376]Sumner recognizes that someone else's freedom can directly interfere with my own freedom; but, unless this happens because of government regulation, it is an aspect of the natural order. Finally, Sumner's conception of freedom, like that of most libertarians including

Nozick, is too atomistic. In this last respect, it is interesting to contrast Sumner with more recent discoveries in evolutionary theory that emphasize that it was social bonds and cooperation that gave homo sapiens their advantage in life's struggles. Sumner would have been better off deriving his views on political economy from his anthropological discoveries in his pioneering book, *Folkways*, than from his religious views. If so, he might have discovered that individual freedom cannot be secured without social cooperation.

It is highly instructive to briefly examine how these pseudo-scientific ideas influenced one contemporary economist who expressed concern about the threat of extreme inequality to America's democratic institutions. Willford King published the results of his detailed analysis of the unequal distribution of income and wealth in 1915. Using the best data available, King showed that the income and wealth of the country was now concentrated in the hands of "a few of the very rich."[377]He was, especially, concerned about the decline of America's middle class, and the likelihood that this degree of inequality would result in the same kind of political upheaval that extreme inequality brought to Europe, and that it would erode what had made the United States such a free nation. He, correctly, noted the evidence that such extremes of wealth were the result of "the laws governing industry."[378]However, when it came to solutions for this serious problem, he strongly rejected those proposed by the early progressive reformers, especially any form of government redistribution. He even voiced concern about the use of private charity. His concerns with these methods were right out of the Social Darwinist playbook. He expressed horror at any such action that, he argued, would only lead to "the multiplication of the lowest and least desirable classes." He referred to the new *science* of eugenics, which had shown "the absurd folly of breading great troops of paupers, defectives, and criminals to be a burden upon organized society."[379] The early birth control movement suffered from these same racist views, as can be seen in this 1919 statement of purpose: "more children from the fit, less from the unfit — that is the chief issue of birth control."[380] He blamed the ancestors of the poorest class, who had been "incompetent, ignorant, and unwilling to restrain their animal passions," by bringing this horde into existence. He expressed the worst nativist passions, by also condemning the "rapid influx of ignorant and unprogressive" European immigrants as a burden on the United States.[381]

It is important to note that the eugenics movement was hardly confined to social theorists with libertarian leanings, but was embraced as well by progressive reformers of the first decades of the twentieth century, including such leaders as President Theodore Roosevelt. Such groups as The American Breeder's Association and The National Conference on Race Betterment included many scientists and other professionals concerned about the preservation of the "racial stock" from groups supposedly determined to become poor, mentally defective, or criminal. These latter were almost always defined as those unfortunate enough not to have been born to relatives from northern European nations.[382] It hardly needs mentioning that these ideas spawned the racial purity theories that reached their dark apotheosis in 1930s Germany.

Social scientists and eugenicists, such as Edward Alsworth Ross, pronounced that the wealthiest Americans were committing "race suicide," because of a lower birth rate, and increased immigration of Chinese and Japanese workers. Ross opposed economic regulations and assistance programs that would lead, in his view, to a decline in individual self-control, acceptance of sin, and a breeding of "moral weaklings." He expressed concern, for example, that those with an appetite for liquor would only breed "ill-constituted offspring" with a similar "weakness."[383]

President Woodrow Wilson offered a very different prescription for the relationship between the individual and the state, one that I will build upon in the remainder of this book. In his 1918 book on *The State*, Wilson asserted that "the case for society stands thus: the individual must be assured the best means, the best and fullest opportunities, for complete self-development."[384] Wilson's chief economic advisor was Louis Brandeis until his appointment to the Supreme Court in 1916.

Justice Louis Brandeis's warning about the corrosive effects of great wealth on democracy, quoted at the beginning of this chapter, is a succinct and stark reminder of this danger. We cannot have plutocracy and democracy. "The [American] ideal which we have," he warned, "can be obtained only if side by side with political democracy comes industrial democracy."[385] Like John Dewey and other reformers, Brandeis knew that true liberty involved struggle between countervailing powers. "Those who wield a large amount of power," Brandeis asserted, "always shall feel the check of power. The very principle on which the nation exists is that no person shall rise above power."[386] Only another power can balance out an already established power, through the legal process of negotiation and contract. President Woodrow Wilson was strongly influenced by Brandeis. Wilson expressed the same concern about the dangers of plutocracy to democracy. "No nation can remain free," Wilson warned, "in which a small group determines the industrial development; and by determining the industrial development, determines the political policy."[387]Power, and the concentration of power, as I will show in the next section below, is the real problem for the preservation of democratic liberties.

Jefferson and Madison, like Brandeis, and like the best of the early libertarians, were all concerned with monopoly and large collective power. Brandeis was just as active in curbing government power whenever it infringed on the rights of individuals. Libertarians today focus on the very real inefficiencies that come from big government. But Brandeis understood and warned against the same bureaucratic inefficiencies that can be found in big business. Brandeis and other trust-busting reformers wished to preserve the innovation and efficiency that comes from competition between small businesses. Unlike President Theodore Roosevelt, Brandeis was skeptical about government regulations. He declared "that no methods of regulation ever have been or can be devised to remove the menace inherent in private monopoly and overweening commercial power."[388] Laws and regulations that allow large corporations to play by different rules, while imposing burdensome costs on small business owners and employees do not benefit the economy or the nation, besides being unjust. Regulations should always prevent harm and help promote efficiency. It would solve some of the confusion if we would substitute the term *protections*, since that is what good regulations are meant to be. When I served as the chief executive of a large agency, I would start the new fiscal year by having my employees look at our procedures and regulations to see whether or not they still serve useful functions; and, if not, we got rid of them. The employees liked this process.

Concern about the corrupting influence of money in elections goes back at least as far as the Constitutional Convention. Gouverneur Morris warned that "we should remember that the people never act from reason alone. The rich will take advantage of their passions and make these the instruments of oppressing them."[389] The Founders saw that the main passions in politics were ambition and avarice or acquisitiveness. Hamilton, in a speech given to the Constitutional Convention on *A Plan of Government*, declared that both the rich and the poor had to have enough power "that each may defend itself against the other."[390] Jefferson argued that strife could only be avoided if the poor were given employment. Madison's similar warnings have already been quoted.

Another great Supreme Court Justice, Felix Frankfurter, expressed concern not only about the lack of power of the individual laborer, but also about his or her capacity for citizenship, given the dehumanizing effects of unregulated industrial work.[391] Adam Smith, of course, had made the same observations about the degrading effects of machine labor on human nature.

Few people today have heard of Herbert Croly even though he was, almost certainly, the most important proponent of active state liberalism. Through his books, and the articles he wrote for *The New Republic*, which he helped to found in 1914, Croly was a strong influence on three presidents of the United States: Theodore and Franklin Roosevelt and Woodrow Wilson. Croly also had a far-reaching influence on Justice Felix Frankfurter. Frankfurter gave Croly the epithet "the philosopher" of "progressivism."[392] Croly promoted what he called a "middle way" between the extremes of laissez-faire capitalism and socialism, what today is called a mixed economy. Croly specifically rejects the political goal of trying to equalize wealth as being "disastrous." But, he immediately adds that "a democracy can no more be indifferent to the distribution of wealth than it can to the distribution of the suffrage."[393] He argued that by its very nature a modern economy requires a more active role for government. As long as land had been readily available, Americans were able to experience an increase in prosperity by moving west. As he put it, "opportunity knocked at the door of every man, and the poor man of today was the prosperous householder of tomorrow."[394] The rugged individualism and corresponding vision of the pioneer, including suspicion of central government, became ingrained in the American psyche. But, with the closing of the American frontier and the rise of an industrial economy, the far greater concentration of wealth represented in the Gilded Age had curtailed economic opportunity for most Americans.

The phrase and term Welfare State Capitalism, for most libertarians an oxymoron, was most likely first used in Germany. Herbert Croly, in America, and later, Anthony Crosland in Britain were among its most influential architects. Although few libertarians would agree, the reforms promoted by Croly, Crosland, and other progressives were meant to rescue capitalism at a time when it was most under attack from right and left populist movements; much as it is in the West today. Instead of Sumner's Darwinian advance, progressive reformers, such as Croly, focused on the rending of the social fabric caused by unfettered capitalism. This damage has been aptly summarized as "a rising tide of misery, economic instability, narrowed paths of opportunity, shocking concentrations of wealth, the oppressive exercise of power, a debasement of moral and cultural standards, and the erosion of traditional patterns of deference and loyalty."[395] The key concept behind their reforms, *social justice*, was, as the last chapter showed, highly suspect to libertarians such as Hayek and Friedman. Croly's centrist position, however, accepts that "a democratic economic system, even more than a democratic political system, must delegate a large share of responsibility and power to the individual."[396]The use of the term *power* here is essential, as Croly's political theory has the critical virtue of emphasizing the role of "money power" in assuring justice to American citizens. He accepts the libertarian virtue of negative liberty, what he calls freedom from restraint, but includes freedom from economic exploitation, as well as the positive freedom of opportunity. The interests of the nation as a whole, and not of a select, elite, few "should be dominant."

Croly published his most important and influential book, *The Promise of American Life* in 1909. Croly's work comprises the first sustained critique of libertarian economic and political theories and policies in American political thought. He was anxious to distinguish his views from those of socialists and to establish their thoroughly American pedigree. He devoted a long section to demonstrating the lineage of his political philosophy in Abraham Lincoln's fundamental principle of equality of opportunity. What's more, as I have shown above, Lincoln was a man of the people, and he was not afraid to use the power of the presidency and government to promote equality for all citizens. Croly shared the concerns of the Founders and others that "grinding poverty" and even "partial economic privation ... constitute a grave social danger in a democratic state." Patriotic loyalty and legitimacy can only be maintained with state promotion of "a constantly higher standard of living." It is this goal of economic independence and upward mobility that is the promise of American life. Contrary to libertarian dogma this goal can be achieved "without doing any necessary injury" to the capitalist, and is actually a "positive benefit to general economic and social efficiency."[397]

A President who shared and enacted aspects of Croly's progressive vision was Theodore Roosevelt. This is not the place to give an account of his complex ideas or accomplishments. However, the year after Croly published his most popular book, Roosevelt made two important speeches in which he utilized his great conceptual and linguistic gifts to go to the heart of the problem of his day, and alas, of our current political situation. On September 6, 1910 at St. Paul, Minnesota, he summarized the progressive responsibility in these words: "The supreme political task of our day is to drive the special interests out of our public life." Eleven days later, in a speech delivered at the New York State Fair in Syracuse, he explained further that "the corporation is the creature of the people; and it must not be allowed to become the ruler of the people."[398] Michael Sandel, who quotes theses speeches, adds that Roosevelt was concerned about "the political consequences of concentrated economic power" in a democracy. A leading Roosevelt biography shows how his concern with the power of large corporations was balanced with his realization that such concentration was also the result of the modern, international, economy. Roosevelt, like so many progressives, wished to save capitalism from its worst features, rather than to get rid of it. His greatest concern was with the pain and suffering of industrial power on the workers and the poor.[399]

For a much more sophisticated and more democratically sound critique of libertarianism I must turn to the greatest political philosopher of the Progressive Era, John Dewey. Dewey had an influence on Croly's later work, and on all those who wish to preserve America democracy. I can only touch briefly here on Dewey's important criticism of the atomistic and simplistic libertarian concept of the individual. Like Croly and most of the progressive intellectuals, Dewey rejected communism and any form of autocratic government control. Instead, he wished to preserve the benefits of a capitalist economic system, while curing its ills, such as child labor and dangerous working conditions. He advocated for a "genuinely cooperative society," with as much worker control of the economy as possible, but rejected government control or "state socialism." He wanted employment for security, but also for the intellectual, moral, and personal development of the worker.[400]

Writing in 1908, Dewey refers to statistics that show a very similar level of inequality as exists in America today.[401] His concern, therefore, was for the freedom of the individual worker and consumer. Most importantly, Dewey rejected the libertarian view of the individual as something "fixed, given ready-made." Not only are individuals "achieved," but this happens in a social context, "not in isolation," but through "cultural, economic, legal, and political institutions." What's more, these institutions can "have a bearing, positive and negative, upon the growth of individuals."[402]The mere existence of democratic institutions, however, does not guarantee the nurturing or enhancement of a democratic individual. Dewey agrees with the libertarian view that rejects "society" as an abstraction that the individual responds to in a passive manner. We should substitute "law, industry, religion, medicine, politics, art, education, philosophy" for *society*, and think of all of these facets as themselves "plural".[403] Like most libertarians, he argues that "individuality is inexpugnable because it is a manner of distinctive sensitivity, selection, choice, response and utilization of conditions." But Dewey's view of individuality, though it includes this uniqueness and negative liberty, was profoundly different from the concept put forward by economists such as Hayek and Friedman in ways that are important for my critique of libertarianism. He devoted over seventy pages of his major work on ethics to ethical issues relating to "economic life."[404] He equates the views that would today come under the heading of libertarianism with a semi-mythical, classical liberal doctrine of individualism. He notes that this view of an "atomistic," rugged, independent, individual could thrive in the vast open spaces of pre-industrial America. Dewey notes correctly that this old view of the individual, like the equally mythical free market economy, never really existed in the manner described by classical liberals. All "civilized societies" have provided for certain public goods and organized markets through the state. Moreover, Dewey asserts that a number of critical public services can only be provided by government agencies if a modern nation is to "avoid discrimination." He adds that such privatization of public services only leads to more "bribery and corruption," something confirmed by countless examples since he wrote. Of course bribery and corruption have existed in government as well, since time immemorial. But, that the introduction of the profit motive creates the perfect conditions for such activity should be undeniable to anyone but the most deluded or naïve ideologues. What's more, as Dewey declares, any profits accruing from the use of public resources, such as the sale of public lands, should belong to the citizens of that land. Extraction of public resources for individual profit is inherently corrupt.

I would add that this ethical precept should apply as well to the extraction of the resources of another land without just compensation to the peoples of said country; a principle that applies to corporations working under the military force or shield of the extracting country. Naomi Klein gives many examples of the violation of this principle, with the direct involvement and guidance of libertarian economists, in her *Shock*

*Doctrine.*[405] At the time that Dewey wrote his *Ethics*, prior to the progressive reforms that he helped to inspire, he could also add that economic institutions based on libertarian lines were injurious to the health and safety of children and other workers. Today, we would add concerns about the environment and global warming to this list. Dewey's next point that "the motive of self-interest, relied upon and fostered by [this form of] individualism, is anti-social," is one I will return to in the last section of this book. Dewey accepts one argument of the socialists, namely, that "under modern capitalism a disproportionate share is sure to fall to the capitalist, and, more than this, to the great capitalist."[406]He adds that modern production has only made it all the harder for the small business to compete with large corporations; we would add, international corporations, technology, and wages.

In some ways Dewey sounds like a self-described libertarian of today, such as Narveson or Machan, when he decries the "collectivism" of modern life. But it is not the statist collectivism attacked by libertarians, but rather the concentrated power of corporate economic life that is the chief target of Dewey's concern for the survival of democratic life. In a remarkable chapter he called "United States Incorporated," Dewey decries the loss of a traditional American concept of individualism, and the rise of a new collectivism.[407] He gives this new way of thinking and organizing the name *corporateness*. The fuzzy political terms, *corporatism* and neo-corporatism have been used by both libertarians and their critics, with the former attempting to draw a sharp distinction between their views and the collective or monopolistic nature of the corporation. Dewey provides a deeper analysis of the issues in his 1927 classic work of democratic political philosophy, *The Public and Its Problems.*

Dewey basis his political philosophy on the firm foundation of actual human nature, as opposed to fanciful ideas about transforming men into angels. He begins by attacking "pseudo-scientific" views about rational choice free of human desire and emotions. I discussed the vast amount of new research that confirms his assessment in my last book.[408] Dewey is especially concerned to critique a mythical view of the individual he calls the Theory (sometimes he uses doctrine) of Individualism; a view shared by many of today's libertarians. I have already mentioned his argument that individuals are embedded in social relationships. Dewey was strongly influenced by the social theory of George Herbert Mead and Charles Horton Cooley. It is important to repeat that Dewey strongly rejects the idealist's abstraction of an organic state with an independent reality over and above the individuals who comprise any community. Dewey agrees with most libertarians that it is individuals who have thoughts, goals, desires, and who take action based on these unique interests. But, he adds an emphasis on "the consequences of their behavior upon that of others and that of others upon them."[409]He goes beyond this fact by adding an emphasis that the individual's thoughts and desires are also the result of their relationships or associations.

Even more central to this book is Dewey's trenchant critique of the dichotomy that lumps all of these various associations into the policies and actions of the state. On the one side are the anarchists, including Anarcho-capitalists, who attribute all the various evils that are the consequence of associations to the state. On the other is the equally fallacious grouping of all the good outcome of individual associations to the actions of the state. Dewey rejects this grouping of the state as "deity" or "devil." His critique reminds me of a favorite quip of Mark Twain that "the true patriotism, the only rational patriotism, is loyalty to the *nation* all the time, loyalty to the government [only] when it deserves it."[410] Dewey might not endorse Twain's quip and he would probably substitute the *public*, but he would object to the identification of the state with the government, in part because it can represent a dangerous abstraction that separates "rulers from the people."[411]

As always, Dewey is concerned to attack loose terminology and false dichotomies. He acknowledges the libertarian concern with the fallible nature and unintended consequences of laws and regulations; but, he correctly calls our attention to the central importance of understanding the motives of perpetuation of power and self-interest as the motive behind the actions of elite groups in and out of government. Whether one is speaking of the state, or the government, the focus needs to be on the employment of power in the interest of protection and advancement of public and not private interest. Dewey wished to emphasis our interdependence and our common interests. Moreover, the responsibility we have as a result of these common interests involves the preservation and utilization of *both* negative and positive freedom. Dewey spoke of our common interest in and dependence on preserving our planet, something we should be much more aware of today. I will return to Dewey's important views about community in the last subsection of this book. But before leaving this section I need to say a word about one central aspect of Dewey's concern about the dangers of inequality in a democracy, and that is what he saw as the danger of unequal education.

Dewey is rightly seen as one of the greatest progressive thinkers and activists in education. An important reform policy of the progressive agenda was to eliminate or limit labor that threatened the health, safety, and education of young children. Dewey's active involvement in the Settlement House Movement and early social services to the poor, led him to be among the early advocates for vocational training. However, Dewey was also strongly concerned about the segregation of students into separate vocational or industrial schools, especially those under the control of business. Dewey shared the concerns of other progressives, as well as America's Founders, in the dangers created by economic inequality. Specifically, he was concerned about the perpetuation of a working class that segregated institutions would encourage. Moreover, Dewey argued for the political importance of a broad, humanistic, education for democratic values and participation. He argued against any sharp dichotomy between education for labor and education for leisure.[412] He argued that an education in history, literature, as well as science, will only enhance the understanding needed for industrial work.[413] Dewey understood something very relevant to today, that vocational education needed to be about fundamentals that would equip children with skills, including a love of learning that would keep pace with future technology and automation. The importance of this for upward mobility should be obvious.[414]

The late Richard Rorty was, like his hero John Dewey, a public intellectual who gave us seminal works on the intersection of society, education, and democratic values. In a remarkably prescient series of lectures delivered in 1997 and later collected in the small book, *Achieving Our Country*, Rorty declared that America was in the midst of "a Second Gilded Age;" adding that "even Mark Twain might have been startled by the shamelessness with which our politicians now sell themselves."[415] Like Dewey, Rorty argues that citizenship should be a pragmatic effort "to forge a moral identity," to work to achieve what we stand for as a people. Rorty quotes Herbert Croly's description of American faith in democracy. But, he also draws from two powerful novels that paint a dystopian vision of a nation thoroughly in the thrall of libertarian/neoliberal values; an America, Incorporated. Rorty and Dewey argued that the kind of inequality that produces separate classes is incompatible with the level of "self-respect which is needed for free participation in democratic deliberation."The moral justification for such a classless society is simply that it is most likely one that produces "less unnecessary suffering than any other;" and, it is most likely to create "a greater diversity" of "larger, fuller, more imaginative and daring individuals."[416] Rorty's form of liberalism celebrates those who attempt to work "within the framework of constitutional democracy to protect the weak from the strong."[417]He agrees with Croly's warning that the American myth of rugged individualism, in Croly's words "has resulted in a morally and socially undesirable distribution of wealth."[418]Organized religions have often served as what Croly called a "spiritual drug," what Thomas Merton referred to as "mental tranquilizers," to subdue any rebellious spirit in the poor. Machiavelli was the master at teaching political leaders this use of "piety."[419]Rorty hoped for a "Second Progressive Era" to reform our new Gilded Age. Like Dewey and my teacher Sidney Hook, most of the first progressive reformers were staunchly anti-communist. Rorty warned that the social or cultural agenda of equal rights for minorities and others would backfire if it was not accompanied by a program of economic justice; what he called, borrowing a phrase from Richard Sennett, "the hidden injuries of class." As Rorty notes, the "dark side" of the post 1960s story is that "during the same period in which socially accepted sadism has steadily diminished, economic inequality and economic insecurity have steadily increased."[420]

The libertarian let/live cultural philosophy in America was undermined by the Reagan administration's embrace of a state sponsored morally conservative agenda, more reminiscent of John Winthrop than John Lennon. As I noted in the Introduction, this moral conservatism was wedded to a libertarian/neoliberal economic program that was anything but let/live. Libertarians profess to believe, despite all evidence to the contrary, that individual citizens will be treated fairly by a free, which is to say, unregulated or unfettered market. The fundamental irony is that a political philosophy that is essentially anti-authoritarian and anti-collectivist leads inexorably to the development of international financial and corporate institutions more powerful and intrusive than most governments.

Following Reagan, the Democratic Party felt that it needed to adopt many of the policies of economic libertarianism if it was ever to regain power. In the process, of course, Democratic administrations abandoned the interests of America's middle class and the poor. Similar accommodations were made in Europe, especially in Britain under the New Right.[421] I actually believe that Rorty was too kind to the Democratic Party, seeing them as "terrified" into adopting the libertarian economic agenda, while the Republican Establishment were the ones telling "cynical lies." Rather, government and other elites on both sides acted largely in their own economic self-interest. Rorty warned that we were likely in for an "Orwellian future," one that is a lot closer to having been realized since he made that prediction.[422] Instead of coming from a centralized planned communist economy, as Mises, Hayek, and other early libertarians feared, it has been the capitalist market system that has brought us closer to Orwell's dystopian vision.[423]Rorty draws an analogy between Orwell's Inner Party, in *Nineteen Eighty-Four* and future international financial and corporate plutocrats. It is these plutocrats, he asserts, who will make all the most important decisions; something which is already happening today. Rorty's prediction that the Inner Party will nourish an Outer Party of somewhat prosperous professionals to keep up "the pretense" of local political operations appears far less likely today. He was right about the media circuses but far less about the distribution of bread. He was also remarkably prescient about the conflict within America's Left between the desire to help the poorer, usually Southern Hemisphere countries of the world and an equal desire to raise the standard of living among America's workers. He notes that pressure from workers to close our border with Mexico will need to be addressed, since "marginally employed people can be most easily recruited into right-wing populist movements."He sees the same kind of conflict over trade deals, with workers perceiving that they only benefit the national and international plutocracy.[424]*The Politics of Unreason* by Seymour Martin Lipset and Earl Raab, arguably the most exhaustive study on political extremism and prejudice provides many examples of this link between economic decline and the destruction of democratic governments.[425] Rorty would be the first to admit that he was not alone among analysts of our social and economic situation who predicted in the 1990s that the Western democracies were facing "a Weimar-like period" of reaction to libertarian/neoliberal policies; a period that would threaten the survival of democratic institutions. We are facing that crisis of democracy today. Rorty predicts that these working class citizens will eventually wake up to the realization that their government is not even trying to meet their interests, and that they will then turn to a demagogue and trickster who will convince them "that, once he is elected" the plutocrats will be thrown out. His model is Sinclair Lewis's ironically titled novel, *It Can't Happen Here.*

As we have seen, long before Lewis or Rorty our Founders were concerned about the effects of extreme inequality and economic power on the survival of the new political system they designed. The chief designer, Madison summer-up his concern in his great *Federalist 10*; "men of factious tempers, of local prejudices, or of sinister designs, may, by intrigue, by corruption, or by other means, first obtain the suffrages [votes], and then betray the interests, of the people."[426]One analyst of the dangers to democracy from demagogues notes that the *Federalist Papers* begin and end with this concern. Michael Signer quotes Alexander Hamilton's opening warning that "of those men who have overturned the liberty of republics, the greatest number have begun their career by paying an obsequious court to the people, *commencing demagogues and ending tyrants.*"[427] Hamilton gestures at the role that rhetoric or propaganda plays in this process. Rorty notes that there is not much that governments can do about curing the human propensity to cruelty, but steps can be taken to mitigate the equally human propensity for selfishness, or what Madison called factiousness. He argues that reform must be aimed at specific abuses of economic power and not at abstractions such as what Leftists call *late capitalism.*

In an important article on this relationship between political propaganda and market propaganda, or *Marketspeak*, economist and media analyst Edward Herman notes that "a good case can be made that propaganda is a more important means of social control in open societies like the United States than in closed societies like the late Soviet Union." Herman argues that, like Orwell's Ingsoc, "Marketspeak serves to consolidate the power of the dominant elite."[428]Herman points out that the art or science of propaganda has advanced considerably since Orwell's day, with governments learning a great deal from advertising and marketing.[429]

If I had to recommend just one popular book on the dangers of inequality written since the Great Recession it would be *The Price of Inequality* by the Nobel Prize winning economist Joseph Stiglitz.[430] The book was written at a time when Stiglitz was still optimistic about the possibility of reforming an economic and political system that was no longer working in the interest of over ninety-nine percent of the American people. I do not have room here to even summarize the evidence Stiglitz provides to show that libertarian economic theory is based on mythical concepts about how markets work. I would argue that, for the most part, libertarian economic theories are the weakest link in an otherwise important political philosophy. Such concepts as trickle-down and supply-side have been repeatedly shown to be inaccurate, and they violate the realities of human nature that the kindest explanation for why they are still put forward is the self-deception caused by self-interest. I will be addressing this issue of belief in the last subsection of this book. What I wish to emphasize briefly here is what Stiglitz sees as the peril which extreme inequality presents for the survival of democratic freedom. Stiglitz is well aware that some inequality is inevitable and can even be beneficial. The great political philosopher John Rawls argued that inequalities should be permissible just so long as all citizens, especially those least advantaged, benefit from them. Stiglitz presents us with a stark choice: either we reform the economic system to make it more responsive to the majority of citizens, as was done in the Progressive and Neal Deal eras, or we risk losing our freedom. "One or the other will have to give," Stiglitz warns, "either our politics or our economics."[431]Unfortunately, in the years since he wrote the survival of those freedoms has become very tenuous indeed. What Stiglitz calls "the evisceration of our democracy" has resulted from a government that no long serves the interests of most citizens, but only the desires of large corporations and the financial sector. Stiglitz agrees with another Nobel Prize winning economist, Paul Krugman, who wrote that "extreme concentration of income is incompatible with real democracy."[432] Stiglitz is another political analyst who discerns parallels with how our current crisis of democracy came about and Orwell's insights into the role of language and the media in manipulating public opinion. He devotes a whole chapter to this subject, which I will address in the next section. In order to better understand this gradual undermining of inclusive political institutions we need to look more closely at the dynamics of power.

## Dark Arts

In the opening scene of the Swiss playwright, Friedrich Dúrrenmatt's tragicomic 1956 masterpiece, *The Visit*, the elite of the town of Gúllen (best translated as *Dungtown*) are awaiting the arrival of a former resident, Claire Zachanassian, who has since become the wealthiest woman in the world. Gúllen could stand in for any of the myriad once-thriving industrial cities and towns in Europe and America where destitution now reigns supreme. Even the town's fire bell may have been pawned, the historical museum has been "sold to America," and the elite greeters are all shabbily dressed. The town is literally bankrupt and "rotting to death."[433] As they await the arrival of this now elderly lady, the residents list examples of her major philanthropic contributions elsewhere in Europe as reasons for their confidence that she will be their financial savior. The way in which she arrives, however, tells us a great deal about the woman and the future prospects for Güllen and its residents. Claire does not deign to take any transportation as plebian as a commuter train, so she pulls the emergency brake for her stop. At first the station master threatens her with legal action for this infraction. But, when he learns who she is, he is cowed and becomes comically obsequious. Much of the sardonic humor in the play comes from this reaction to a plutocrat like Claire. At one point Claire is visited by the President of the World Bank, who flies in from California to meet with her. She is annoyed by his interruption and tells her servant to inform him that she has no time to meet with him and he should fly back to America. Famous world leaders, such as Eisenhower and Nehru, pay court to her power and influence. The Press is downright groveling in their constant coverage of her as a romantic celebrity. They totally miss any negative aspect of her power, and, at the end of the play they are completely manipulated by the residents into reporting a lie.

Another early indication of what is to come is the menagerie of odd people and objects that are part of her retinue. Among these are two gigantic, gum chewing former gangsters, bought at enormous expense by Claire, incidentally saving them from electrocution in America. Throughout the play these heavies carry Claire about in a sedan-chair like some ancient goddess. Among the menagerie are a black panther and a beautiful coffin, both of which presage what is to come. This play is rich in symbolism, and among the most important symbols are Claire's artificial hand and her artificial leg that presumably requires this mode of transportation. There is so much important material in this play that I will be returning to the moral message behind these symbols in the last subsection of this book. Meanwhile, it is the main plot and what it says about economic power that I want to focus on here.

Among the other members of her retinue are two eunuchs. We eventually learn that some forty-five years earlier, when Claire was a young adolescent, she fell in love with a young man, Alfred Ill, now a "broken-down shopkeeper," who got her pregnant. At the time, Alfred bribed two false witnesses to deny his paternity, and, it turns out that these eunuchs are those two, whom Claire has severely punished. The little girl who resulted from this sexual encounter died of meningitis at age one. Claire met her first husband, an Armenian oil tycoon in a brothel, where she had become a prostitute. We eventually learn that the explanation for the town's distress, despite the economic boom in the rest of the country, is that Claire bought all the factories and businesses and had them shut down. She tells the residents that "your hopes were lunacy, your perseverance pointless, and your self-sacrifice foolish; your lives have been a useless waste." Claire has had a long term plan to get revenge, what she and others call justice, against Alfred and the town that called her a "whore" and drove her away. She presents her proposal to the residents of Güllen. She will provide the town with a huge amount of money, half to revive the town and the other half to make each resident wealthy. Her *only* condition for this generous deal is that the town must put to death Alfred Ill, who had been the cause of Claire's pain and suffering. To make matters worse, Alfred has now become Güllen's most popular resident and he has even been slated to be their next Mayor. The initial response from Güllen's residence is shock and horror. The current Mayor recounts the humanitarian tradition of the town, noting the Goethe and Brahms produced works of classic importance while staying there. He exclaims that

Güllen has always followed "the rule of law," a claim that is repeated throughout the play. Claire's simple response is "I will wait."

Claire understands that the process of subverting institutions is a gradual one. It involves the slow, internal corruption of values and traditions internal to those institutions. We can learn a lot about this process from plays like this one; also, from Shakespeare's *Coriolanus, Othello,* and especially Shakespeare's history plays. We can even learn a lot about this use of power from organized crime families, and the dynamics of domestic manipulation, control, and violence. Demagogues with an unbridled lust for power often seem to have the kind of insight into human nature that Claire displays, giving them a leg up over liberal political efforts at governance. This same kind of subversion has been underway in the Western democracies for, at least, several decades. It begins with a transformation of ideas and public opinion. It happens in local government and at the national level. But, it also happens in various institutions within a society, including media, entertainment, and even sports. I will return to the key role that values play in the last section of this book.

Over the ensuing period, while Claire waits, taking up residence, visiting sites from her youth, Alfred becomes increasingly anxious for his life as the residents go on a commercial spending frenzy, including buying expensive items from his store, all on credit. The denouement comes after the citizens of Güllen, now hopelessly in debt and increasingly indignant at Alfred's past crimes, rationalizing their actions, ritually take Alfred's life.

Claire, of course, has had the advantage of knowing her plan in advance. Machiavelli taught us to recognize such inherent advantages to having power. It is well-known, for example, that those who play by the rule of law and justice, true believers in democratic values, can be at a distinct disadvantage compared to those who do not care about anything but power. This is particularly true if the latter can act in secrecy. Freedom is also threatened if the citizens have lost the practice and firmness of their democratic beliefs, or they are too distracted by amusements and pleasures.[434] This is also especially the case when it comes to the so-called soft forms of dominance, like intimidation and other forms of manipulation, as well as the different types of mind control. As a technique of primary prevention all young girls, for example, should be taught to recognize the early indications that a man is more likely to engage in domestic violence. These signs include certain controlling behaviors that would not necessarily be recognized as indications that the man has a thirst for power that could escalate to a far harder form of dominance. The same signals of addiction to power are usually apparent in demagogues. The Neo-Machiavellian social and political thinkers, many feminist philosophers, psychologists and social thinkers, as well as the French philosopher, Michel Foucault, have added greatly to our understanding of the depth of techniques of dominance, including authoritarian political manipulation. Even more important to this book is the growth in understanding of how to encourage the development of self-reliance, resistance, and a democratic disposition in all citizens.

In an excellent article, "The Dialectics of Domination: An Interpretation of Friedrich Dürrenmatt's *The Visit*," Alkis Kontos, Professor of Political Economy and editor of the journal *Domination*, begins with a lead quote from Jean-Jacques Rousseau: "no person should ever be wealthy enough to buy another, and none poor enough to be forced to sell himself."[435] He notes that the play presents aspects of our "contemporary industrial market society," aspects, I would add, all the more apparent since 1956. Kontos asserts that *The Visit* shows "the pernicious interdependence of wealth and poverty and the dialectics of their apogee —domination;" specifically, "the global domination of capital." Claire's "will is for others their desire." He notes that Claire's power, like that of today's multinational corporations and their executives, transcends the political power of "any office-holder or political leader." It is critical to understand how the power to manipulate and even control the poor and those of modest means has its subtle, psychological aspects. Absent any rational understanding of why Güllen and its residents have fallen into extreme poverty while the rest of the country thrives, they adopt a posture of "victimization" and turn to conspiracy theories, blaming the Jews, the Communists, and even the Free Masons for their fate. It is this, all too common, reaction that has historically proven to be most dangerous, leading to a turn toward rightwing political populist demagogues. Kontos notes that "the psychological death of the poor occurs when their condition is perceived as an inescapable fate." He brilliantly sums up this central aspect of the play in a sentence. "Dürrenmatt," he states, "concerns himself with a poverty that dehumanizes, exposes human fragility and weakness, denies heroic action, undermines consciousness, and forces the surrender of freedom."[436]

The German poet and playwright Bertolt Brecht wrote his play, *The Resistible Rise of Arturo Ui* in 1941 while he was an exile from the Nazis. The rise to power of the Chicago mobster Ui, a character modeled on Al Capone, was clearly meant to represent the rise of Hitler, and especially the role played by German industrialists. Ui comes out of the corrupt business which is referred to as the Vegetable Trust. Historians have mostly discredited the crude Marxist equation of capitalist corruption and the rise to power of Hitler. Robert Paxton's great book on fascism notes that the business leaders, even those who have rejected democracy have also "mostly preferred authoritarians to fascists."[437] Another authority on fascism notes that the business community was initially wary about Hitler and the Nazis, though many became enthusiastic supporters, partly from self-interest, but largely out of a greater concern about communism. However, Hindenburg's involvement in one financial scandal, about an estate, did play some role in Hitler's rise.[438] Brecht's play though is not important for its historical allusions or reporting. Rather, it is what the play says about power that makes it worth mentioning here, especially if one substitutes more subtle and gradual forms of corruption of the body politic, threats, and economic manipulation for direct physical force or violence. If a citizen does not have the resources, including the required information or the capacity to resist, physical force may not be necessary to control or coerce.

Libertarians are correct to remind us of the inherently coercive nature of political power; but, they tend to minimize, ignore, or deny the intrinsic coercive, manipulative, controlling, and exploitive nature of economic power wielded by a plutocrat like Claire. As Kontos puts it, "Dürrenmatt forces us to see that poverty is a condition of powerlessness, of denied freedom."[439] The flip side was summarized by Joseph Stiglitz in a famous article in *Vanity Fair*: "wealth begets power, which begets more wealth."[440] James Madison understood, both from his extensive reading, as well as his personal experience in the Virginia legislature, that government officials could easily be corrupted by economic interests. In his great *Federalist No. 48*, he noted the "encroaching" nature of power; that it was hard to restrain, requiring constant vigilance; that written laws alone were not sufficient to ensure this restraint; and, that legislators, given their financial powers, were even more subject to this insidious economic corruption.[441]

One of the greatest political theorists in American history, one who also understood a great deal about the nature of power, including economic power, was Reinhold Niebuhr. He was careful to draw a sharp distinction between the kind of absolute power seen in communism or fascism and a softer form exercised by titans of industry, while asserting that, whatever the cause, "disproportions of power in the human community are fruitful of injustice."[442] Niebuhr believed that the opposite extreme economic views of communism and libertarianism "were almost equally erroneous." Writing directly after the Second World War, he foresaw that communism would only lead to a far greater concentration of both economic and political power in the hands of a few oligarchs. However, more germane to my argument here are Niebuhr's insights concerning the central problems with the beliefs known today as libertarianism. Having come to the same conclusion a long time ago, I was excited to encounter his assertion that the key fallacy of libertarianism, or what he calls classical liberalism, was "its strange blindness to the factor of power in man's social life and more particularly to the possibility that great disproportions of [such economic] power would result in injustice." What was missing from libertarian economic theory was a realization of the fact "that every economic process begins with a disproportion of economic power."[443] The blindness here is all the more remarkable in that every business school spends a lot of time teaching students how to gain and take advantage of such power The real question is whether or not this is willful blindness. However, since all motives are mixed, and since confirmation and other forms of bias are clearly influenced by issues of personal gain, economic and political blindness is endemic on all sides. Moreover, in his great work on the nature of power, *The Children of Light and the Children of Darkness,* Niebuhr adds another important insight about capital, namely, that it is both a "defensive and offensive" source of power. He points out that "it is defensive only so long as the individual possesses so little of it that he will not be tempted to use it for domination over others."[444]Niebuhr correctly connects the blindness of libertarian ideas to the reality of power to the mythical view of individualism, which he notes runs up against the complexities of modern societies and economies. Libertarians long for an equally mythical rural simplicity of life prior to the twentieth century. They blame the huge increase in the size of government on the desire of agencies to expand their power and influence. No doubt, they are correct to identify this as a major factor. However, just as they are blind to the enormous growth in the power of private corporations and their coercive influence in all aspects of daily life; they tend to ignore the tremendous growth in private bureaucracies in response to modern realities. This aspect of modernity shows no sign of abating given the exponential growth of technological innovation. Niebuhr correctly notes that the individual worker is at an enormous disadvantage given the power of corporations.

Niebuhr's second major error of libertarian ideology is what he calls its "economic rationalism," which assumes that the individual player in economic transactions acts out of rational self-interest. I have already noted that the new field of behavioral economics has added a good deal of evidence to verify Niebuhr's penetrating analysis about passions and motives that sometimes conflict with personal interest. Niebuhr was alert to the limitations of rationality and the reality of irrational forces in human nature that call into question the libertarian optimism about economic interactions. Niebuhr opposed ideological fixes for questions of economic power. He argued that questions about how much freedom and how much social control will bring the right balance of power had to be answered pragmatically in each situation. He understood that the power of unions had already brought large improvements in the well-being of workers. Modern technological economies require a balance of the power of labor against the power of the corporations to ensure justice.

Economists have labeled these balancing forces *countervailing powers*, the same term and concept of balance used by Justice Brandeis.[445] John Kenneth Galbraith's 1952 book, *American Capitalism: the Concept of Countervailing Power,* was a critique of libertarian ideas about markets. The major balancing power source at the time was the labor movement and unions. Galbraith expanded his insights about corporate power over thirty years later in his book on *The Anatomy of Power*.[446] In this latter book, Galbraith asserts that "economics divorced from consideration of the exercise of power is without meaning and certainly without relevance." He goes on to note that, in addition to influencing consumer behavior, corporations also exert their power to defeat any regulations that would reduce their power. He coins another term, *conditioned power*, for efforts by corporations to exert pressure on government by changing public opinion.[447] Niebuhr, however, saw that both big unions and big business take on "semi-governmental functions" and authority that required the same kind of rules of justice as political institutions. As I noted in chapter one above, labor and trade organizations can work against the general interest of segments of society, such as children, or the greater good of the whole nation. Niebuhr was correct that each and every powerful faction, he uses Hobbes's phrase "chips of the block of sovereignty," need "constitutional restraints."[448]

Niebuhr's insights came in part from another great political economist, who wrote a generation after Adam Smith, namely, David Ricardo. Ricardo is usually thought of as a technical economist, who had little of importance to contribute to political thought. Niebuhr knew that this was far from a true characterization of Ricardo's contribution. Ricardo was concerned that governments should promote the interests or material well-being of workers, and curtail the self-serving legislation of powerful interest groups. He asserted that "the laboring class have no small interest in the manner in which the net income of the country is expended."[449]He understood that the way that wealth is determined, and the way that laws and regulations are written, plays an enormous role in how economic power is distributed.

Joseph Stiglitz and others have shown why this is even more relevant in today's economy. Stiglitz shows how, just like governments, markets fail to be efficient, and, therefore, "there needs to be a balanced role between markets, government, and civil society."[450] As Stiglitz shows, government laws and policies often have "distributive consequences," and in recent decades these outcomes have all-too-often worked to the advantage of our plutocrats at the expense of everyone else.[451]The power of the wealthiest has even extended to writing the very regulations specific to their industry or even company. In a repetition of what happened in the first Gilded Age, President Trump has taken this one step further by appointing a cabinet of corporate leaders and champions. Libertarians show less concern with the massive increase in the lobbying industry than they do in the government agencies being lobbied. The power of special interest groups, such as the energy sector to influence government should be as great a concern to those who support liberty. This was seen in its most blatant form with the financial industry leading up to the Great Recession of 2008.[452] Stiglitz summarizes a great deal of evidence that shows how libertarians shaped public opinion in a way that allowed America's wealthiest citizens to control the political agenda to benefit their own self-interest to the detriment of everyone else, and to the detriment of a more robust economy.

Wealthy individuals and corporations also utilize their asymmetric power by filing lawsuits to intimidate low income individuals or institutions with high legal costs they cannot afford. This process has become so ubiquitous that it has a title, *strategic lawsuit against public participation* (SLAPP). An especially egregious example involves efforts to silence news organizations with the fear of a massive court case; something that can undermine the viability of free speech and a free press.

In their excellent book about *Ricardian Politics*, Murray Milgate and Shannon Stimson contrast Milton Friedman's subordination of political concerns to those of economics with Ricardo's concern that the political system represents the interests of every economic group equitably.[453] Even Adam Smith showed some understanding of this aspect of capitalism. He called attention to this inefficiency of markets when he wrote that "people of the same trade seldom meet together, even for merriment and diversion, but the conversation ends in a conspiracy against the public, or in some contrivance to raise prices."[454] Libertarians like to point out that Smith follows this famous quote up with negative comments about regulation. But, the full context, as I noted earlier in this chapter, is that Smith knew that the love of power was as strong, if not a stronger motive, and that trades would work on government to obtain such legal advantage, including doing away with regulations. Moreover, he correctly foresaw that these errors in and problems created by the extreme economic doctrines would only magnify as a result of modern technology. Niebuhr was well aware of the less apparent features of economic power that involve subtle manipulation, corruption, and which are often hidden until it is too late to counter them.

James Fenimore Cooper devoted a few illuminating pages to the subject of demagogues in his 1838 political treatise, *The American Democrat*.[455] He notes that democracy is particularly susceptible to the wiles of demagogues. "The peculiar office of a demagogue," he states, "is to advance his own interests, by affecting a deep devotion to the interests of the people."[456] Cooper describes the "cunning" and "sly" methods that the demagogue uses to manipulate the people, playing upon their "passions" and "prejudices" through flattery, which he describes as "a corrupting and dangerous poison." He notes that some of these methods of intrigue and deception are utilized by other politicians who do not rise to the level of true demagogues. He spends most of this section on the antidote to demagoguery, namely, education and knowledge of the truth to protect against "sophisms" and "the audacity of falsehoods." For the same reason, he argues for the necessity of a free press. There is much that moderate libertarians will find agreeable in Cooper's treatise; some may even agree with his stern warnings against economic inequality and the dangers of economic power. He observes, for example, that "when property rules, it rules alone; but when the poor are admitted to have a voice in government, the rich are never excluded." For good measure, he adds that "such is the nature of man, that all exclusive power is uniformly directed to exclusive purposes." The end result of failing to protect the poor is "to make the strong stronger, and the weak, weaker."[457]

The frequent invocation by libertarians of concepts like "free" market and individual "freedom," as a matter of wanting, as well as a focus on mathematical formulas and data, blinds them, I believe, to the essential role that power plays in a capitalist system. Milton Friedman often gave the counterfactual argument that, if only the system were allowed to function without governmental interference, individuals would be free to attain what they wish. Speculations that, by their very nature, cannot be falsified do not advance the libertarian cause. Moreover, the predominance of historical evidence shows that inclusive economic systems which share power broadly are the ones which have enhanced freedom, whereas in extractive systems the powerful few "set up economic institutions to enrich themselves and augment their power at the expense of society."[458] Also, the mythical individualism of most libertarian theories contributes to a mis-understanding of the intrinsically social nature of power. Libertarians have usually demonstrated a lack of any full understanding of the individual psychological aspects of power. It is interesting to note that there is a relationship between the negative concept of freedom promoted by libertarians and the conception of power as power-over another person. It is this latter way of defining power that is associated with Thomas Hobbes and Max Weber. Weber admitted that his own economic ideas were strongly influenced by Ludwig von Mises. This idea of power is based on German ideas about the will. It is a view of human nature that contrasts with ideas about positive freedom and power-to or empowerment. In the next section I will examine this latter way of looking at freedom and power, one which has been promoted by certain active state liberals, as well as by prominent feminist social theorists.

The use of a technically sounding term, *externalities*, by economists for the social and other unintended consequences of economic actions, also contributes to a failure to fully appreciate the coercive nature of capital and the capitalist economic system. In a similar manner libertarian economists coined the positive sounding term, *liberalization*, for the process of loosening of controls by doing away with regulations. Economic liberalization is most often used as a term for developing countries that are breaking free from state controls and are said to be "opening up" their economies to outside investment. In many cases a more accurate and descriptive term is corporate welfare, but this tends to call undesired attention to the fact that payouts to corporations far exceed any amount spent on welfare for the poor. Stiglitz notes that one financial corporation alone, AIG, received a taxpayer bailout in 2008 that was more than the amount given to poor welfare recipients from 1990 to 2006.[459]

There is no room here to go into the myriad ways in which such activities distort markets, contribute to extreme inequality, and lead to corruption, all of which is fully covered by Joseph Stiglitz with admirable thoroughness and clarity. Libertarians tend to emphasize benefits in the form of welfare assistance to the poor. However, as Stiglitz and many others have shown, the enormous power at the very top of the wealth pyramid translates into a government for the wealthiest, and, increasingly, by the wealthiest, with fewer and fewer resources going to the ninety-nine percent of Americans. This process is a direct consequence of governmental actions, some direct, but others such as deregulation and privatization that are hidden from all but the most discerning citizens.

Libertarians have played an important watchdog role for governmental coercion, but they have mostly turned a blind eye toward coercion of government from the power of the wealthiest individuals and corporations. Democratic institutions need to protect citizens against the monopoly of economic power as well as political power. As I stated early in this book, power abhors a vacuum, and restraining the role of government to protect citizens and to enhance well-being only leaves the door open for the rent seeking or extraction of financiers and corporations. Moreover, the propaganda that libertarian policies are defensive is a total ruse meant to hide the manipulation of government to benefit a few of the wealthiest citizens at the expense of everyone else.

Traditional democratic norms of fair play are just that, norms, and do not protect a free society against powerful extractive forces. As Madison noted, even written laws will fail to protect citizens who are not vigilant. Power is such that if one side follows these norms, a political faction that is willing to violate them with impunity is at an advantage. Moreover, like Claire in *The Visit*, the authoritarians often have a long perspective and plan, one that is satisfied with small incremental steps which eventually subvert freedom. Americans were faced with the first of a series of bold violations of such norms when a Republican controlled Senate refused to discharge its responsibility to hold hearings to most likely confirm President Barack Obama's Supreme Court nominee. As I have noted above, the libertarian agenda has been advanced as much, if not more, by legislative inaction and deregulation. The same inaction technique has resulted in vacancy of a hundred Federal judges that will be replaced by judges pledging to advance a libertarian economic agenda. The end result of this power grab will be the further enhancement of the economic power of a plutocracy for many years to come. Adam Smith's warned that a "standing army" of economic "masters" will control government regulation for their own gain, instead of doing what he argued was desirable, passing legislation that would benefit and protect workers. The United States Supreme Court has recently been fully complicit in this takeover by this economic elite.

This activist intervention on behalf of the wealthiest has been chronicled in great detail by many of our best political scientists and economic journalists. Milton Friedman and a group of his students at the Chicago School of Economics are the chief activist villains of Naomi Klein's *The Shock Doctrine: The Rise of Disaster Capitalism.* Klein acknowledges that Friedman had an enormous influence with the leaders of a wide range of different countries around the world over his long life. Klein also notes that the ideas behind the shock doctrine were outlined by Friedman in his most influential book, *Capitalism and Freedom.*[460] The basic idea is a simple one, namely that libertarians should take advantage of crises, whether "actual or perceived" in order to promote their agenda of unfettered capitalist markets. What should be shocking to professed lovers of liberty is the story of how Friedman and his followers carried out this simple strategy and the devastating outcomes that Klein spells out in all its sordid details in her important book. Klein details the disastrous results from the so-called "Chicago School Revolution," when Friedman and a number of his students took advantage of the power of the ruthless dictator, Augusto Pinochet in the 1970s to completely transform the Chilean economy into a libertarian Arcadia. Friedman described his prescription for ailing economies as a form of shock therapy, and like electroconvulsive therapy it often carries negative effects on those unfortunates who undergo it. In fact, one Uruguayan commented rhetorically "how can this inequality be maintained if not through jolts of electric shock?"[461]

Klein gives many examples of the use of Friedman's therapy and its devastating effects on economies and citizens around the world. But, nothing is more shameful than the involvement of the Chicago Boys, as they came to be called, in helping Pinochet's transformation of a relatively free country and thriving economy into a brutal dictatorship and economic basket-case, with the backing of the United States and with corporate assistance. Klein does acknowledge that the Chicago economists had unsuccessfully attempted to introduce their libertarian agenda when Chile was still relatively free and peaceful under President Salvador Allende. The authors of *Why Nations Fail* report that some 2,279 Chilean citizens were put to death for political opposition to Pinochet. Many more Chileans opposed to Pinochet's agenda were tortured in the chambers that are now a tourist attraction.[462]Milton Friedman had argued that capitalism was a necessary prerequisite for freedom, but here he was supporting a ruthless dictatorship. The Chicago Boys went along with these brutal tactics because their own agenda of completely overhauling the economy could only be accomplished over a number of years of tight control and they were convinced that they were following necessary laws of nature. Hayek even brought the Mont Pèlerin Society's annual meeting to Chile to witness directly the fulfillment of a libertarian led economy.[463] Klein summarizes the debacle that resulted from the shock application of Friedman's economic program. The main problem came from deregulation of the financial markets which led to the kind of speculation we are all-too-familiar with from our recent history. The end result was similar to our Great Recession, "where a small elite leapt from wealthy to super-rich in extremely short order."[464] Among the beneficiaries of Friedman's shock therapy, in Chile and elsewhere, were large, often American, corporations who gained wealth and power through privatization of Chile's economy.

Far less dramatic is the clever strategy, that I mentioned earlier, of cutting public services to the point that they are not able to function in the manner they were intended, and then to use their dysfunction as an excuse for their elimination or privatization. This has been a pattern with the move to replace public schools with charter schools and other privatizing schemes. Diane Ravitch shows how the "far-right wing of the Republican Party" has succeeded in "branding" their privatization moves as providing families with "choice," while race and pecuniary self-interest have been the thinly disguised actual motivation.[465] These moves are often sold as a means to save on taxes, even though it sometimes involves the use of public funds given to private for-profit or not-for-profit agencies. The end result is to undermine the public system that has benefitted so many with upward mobility while also helping to safeguard our democracy. I believe that many libertarians and others are not conscious of this dynamic behind destroying public institutions and its ultimate consequences. Most parents just want the best education for their children. Nor were individual citizens always conscious of the racial aspects of urban flight; convincing themselves that they just wanted a better environment to raise their children.

The extreme example of this great separation of classes has been the growth of gated communities, most with their own private security, garbage, and other services. Whole new industries have developed to accommodate this lucrative market. This great separation has allowed the wealthy to be shielded and protected from the effects of our growing inequality and the suffering of the poor. The psychological effects of such separation on the lack of compassion have been well demonstrated by psychologists and such dystopian novelists as Margaret Attwood and others. Libertarians who choose to live in such close-knit communities, and even those who are active members of the Libertarian and Tea Parties ought to ask themselves whether they have chosen this kind of tribal lifestyle because they really believe their extreme individualist and anti-communitarian precepts, or is their primary motivation that they are opposed to associating with certain types of people.

Klein notes that Friedman's last act was to champion what amounted to the privatization of many governmental services in Louisiana after the shock caused by hurricane Katrina in August of 2005. Friedman argued that the tragedy of the New Orleans flood was a once in a lifetime opportunity to privatize a whole school system. With the full support of the George W. Bush administration, a substantial portion of the funds meant to rebuild the city's broken levies was quickly diverted to this goal, with, as Klein notes, a speed that did not characterize efforts to help shelter and feed Louisiana's displaced citizens. What followed has been described as "an educational land grab." The number of New Orleans's private schools went from 123 to just 4.[466] Former teachers were fired, with mostly younger teachers hired back at a reduced salary by the largely for-profit system that had replaced public education. Klein recounts what happened to the quality of the New Orleans educational system. As has been the case with so much of libertarian inspired privatization the beneficiaries have been large corporations, some with direct financial and other ties to the very government awarding them contracts. The case of Dick Cheney and Iraq is too well-known to need recounting here.[467]

At least since the time of Polybius historians and social theorists have noted that demagogues and other authoritarian leaders have engaged in foreign conquests and other violent adventures for personal economic gain.[468] The great German philosopher Immanuel Kant made an important contribution to questions about the relationship between freedom, economics, and international aggression in his 1795 classic essay, *To Perpetual Peace*.[469] Kant recognized that "the inclination of those in power [to wage war was] an inclination that seems innate in human nature." He also recognized the role which the new capitalist economy could play in exacerbating this tendency. But, on the positive side, he believed that the equally new adoption of republican or democratic constitutions by more and more governments would work to enhance a tendency toward perpetual peace. Despotic rulers who waged war were in effect using their citizens as their personal property. In Kant's conception of democratic rule, "the consent of the citizenry is required in order to determine whether or not there will be war." The citizens are the ones who have always born the personal costs of war, in the form of taxes and other financial costs, as well as with their very lives. As the main victims of the evils of warfare, he reasoned, the people will be far less likely to initiate aggressive action against other states, and more willing to enter into negotiations for peace. Kant had other suggestions for how to institute perpetual peace between nations, but this argument was clearly central to his recommendations.

Some libertarians have argued similarly that the expansion of unfettered capitalism will have the same effect of lessening the amount of warfare. Montesquieu had put forth the same hope in his highly influential *The Spirit of the Laws*.[470] The Libertarian Party in America has generally upheld a consistent policy of non-interference in the affairs of other nations, something Kant also advocated. However, what Kant could not have anticipated and libertarians tend to ignore is the rise of corporate power to influence governments to engage in extractive acts against other countries, to advance their self-interest, as well as the power to engage in such acts directly despite international laws and agreements. Kant opposed standing armies; but, he also could not have anticipated a democracy where inequality made it inevitable that only the poorest citizens are required to sacrifice their children to fight wars started by plutocrats.

Franklin Delano Roosevelt warned us that "the liberty of a democracy is not safe if the people tolerate the growth of private power to a point where it becomes stronger than their democratic state itself."[471] Arguably the most pervasive experiment in privatization came after the fall of the Soviet Union in 1989. Few would disagree with the argument that this great and rapid transformation has brought with it mixed results, with many of the new private owners resembling "criminal mafias."[472] Instead of real democracy, which as we have seen requires a thriving middle class, many of the former communist states have developed new, authoritarian, oligarchies along with crony capitalism. But, a number of economists have pointed to countless examples of similar "extreme racketeering" that has resulted from deregulation and privatization in the developing countries around the world.[473]

The deregulation championed by libertarians in recent decades has had the exact opposite effect predicted by their ideology. Rather than promote increased competition, with lower prices for consumers, the world has seen the rapid growth of oligopolies in all sectors of the economy. An *oligopoly* results when a few giant corporations or producers dominate a given sector of the economy, such as health care. Cartels, mergers, and other forms of monopoly, resulting from the demise of antitrust regulations, have all led to the growth of oligopolies in every sector of the world economy. Libertarian theory held that deregulation would encourage an opening of new competitors to enter a given sector, but instead many new barriers were used to keep competitors out.[474] In turn, this has brought the development of a great deal of mutual collusion within sectors, among other things, greatly reducing the costs of production, for example by outsourcing and through various forms of corporate welfare. For the most part, the resulting cost savings have not been passed along to consumers in the form of lower prices. Rather, corporations have become wealthier and more powerful than many countries in the world. This has allowed them to further increase their economic and political power through such activities as lobbying and more direct forms of manipulation. The corruption of democratic institutions has reached a crisis point.

Two recent works have very thoroughly documented the methods used to corrupt democratic traditions and institutions in America: *Dark Money* by Jane Mayer and *Corporate Power, Oligopolies, and the Crisis of the State* by Luis Suarez-Villa. Both books emphasis the key role played by libertarian/neoliberal propaganda in setting the stage for this corporate subversion of political power. Mayer documents in great detail how the Koch brothers used the enormous wealth from their vast empire of fossil fuel companies to fund Hayek's idea of think tanks, other institutes, economics departments, endowed academic chairs, and media outlets to promote libertarian ideas and influence politicians in both parties. Mayer notes the shocking suggestion of a libertarian historian that the successful Nazi youth movement made their tactics a good model for organizing libertarian-minded university student groups.[475] One especially telling anecdote involves Charles Koch's demand that computers scan the applications of prospective teaching positions for how often they referred to Ayn Rand and Milton Friedman.[476]Far more sinister is her documentation of the many ways that the Koch brothers and other plutocrats used dark money and tactics to directly manipulate campaigns and legislation to get a legal system that undermined environmental safeguards and led to a tax structure that "directly increased their own wealth at the expense of everyone else."[477]Luis Suarez-Villa further documents how corporate economic power has been used to undermine democracy through "political contributions, lobbying, and a *revolving door*" of employment between lobbying agencies, regulators, and members of Congress, their family and friends, as well as former members of their staff.

This kind of corruption was on full display when the Bush and Obama administrations brought in leaders of top Wall Street financial corporations who proceeded to pump hundreds of billions in taxpayer dollars into the very institutions that had brought the world economy to disaster. Moreover, the money was simply given to banks without any strings attached as to how this unprecedented bailout would be spent. Similar kinds of corruption of power exist within corporations between boards of directors and executives, which meant that much of this taxpayer money went into the pockets of some of the very individuals who had brought their corporations and the world economy to crisis. Even some financiers who had engaged in major white-collar crimes not only escaped prosecution, but some received these economic rewards, setting a "moral hazard" precedent which can only encourage future corruption. Traditions that were set up to avoid conflicts of interest are now flouted with abandon.

Already watered-down legislation passed in the hope of avoiding another Great Recession is under threat from the Trump administration. The libertarian mantra of efficiency of unregulated markets was shown to be largely a chimera. Suarez-Villa shows how libertarian backed deregulation also shifted market risk from the corporations onto the average taxpayers. The taxpayer gets all the risk, the corporations get the rewards. Heads I win, tails you lose.[478]

Arguably the most dangerous threat to the survival of liberty comes from the extreme level of control of the news resulting from three decades of media consolidation and corporate and hedge fund purchases. Rupert Murdoch's media empire is only the most visible example of this oligopoly; others include News Corp., Comcast, and AOL-Time Warner.[479] Al Gore, in his book *The Assault on Reason* gave a detailed accounting of how this concentration and corporate control violates our Founder's precepts and warnings.[480]

The final example of the corrupting influence of corporate power and libertarian ideology I will mention is perhaps the most egregious. Right after the George W. Bush administration destroyed the government and much of the infrastructure of Iraq with Shock and Awe they implemented Friedman-style shock therapy to its economy under the command of Paul Bremer. Bremer announced triumphantly that Iraq "was open for business." What he meant by this was soon apparent when he instituted one hundred economic rules that came to be called the Bremer Orders. In case anyone had doubt about the real motivation behind that illegal invasion this blatant imposition of economic power should make it crystal clear. Naomi Klein shows how the Bush administration was itself ruled by the "triple obsession" of libertarian political economics —"privatization, deregulation, and union-busting."[481]She notes the alarming fact that the Bush cabinet officials had no compunction about simultaneously keeping their hand in both government and the corporate world, in a manner reminiscent of politicians during the first Gilded Age. The new Trump administration seems poised to take this conflict of interest form of corruption to a level that has never been seen before in American politics.

In her excellent book, *Undoing the Demos*, Wendy Brown shows how the imposition of these Bremer Orders on an occupied country was a clear violation of international law.[482]Liberalization of a sovereign nation's economy becomes a cloak for exploitation by corporate oligopolies, most, not surprisingly, with headquarters in the United States. A clearer example of an extractive foreign policy would be hard to find. These were laws that were clearly enforced on Iraqi citizens by American military power. Power and self-interest are always easier to impose when ones moves can be cloaked in the guise of benevolence. The authors of *Why Nations Fail* show how certain abstract theories about modernization and liberalization of national economies were believed to especially apply to Iraq, with its many resources including a relatively well-educated population.[483]

Arguably the most egregious example of this blatantly extractive corporate power was Bremer Order No.81. One provision of this law required that Iraqi farmers only use "crop seeds of protected varieties."[484]It just so happened that these required seeds were those produced by American petrochemical corporations, such as Monsanto, Dow and DuPont. Furthermore, the use of these varieties of seed would require farmers to also use the modern chemicals developed by these same corporations in order to produce their crops. Brown points out that Iraq has been the center of food production for thousands of years using methods that not only worked for their people but were far healthier and safer for our environment. She also notes that the agrichemical oligopoly has been pushing this same package of seeds and chemicals on other small countries around the world, thus hooking them for life. Given its nature and strength, it should not be at all surprising that the agricultural, chemical, and food corporations would have their greatest interest and influence on foreign policy.

Wendy Brown has a lot of interesting things to say about the interplay between values and economic power. It is to this centrally important topic of values that I need to turn in the closing pages of this book

## Values

Aristotle had a realistic conception of political life which came from his profound understanding of the limitations of human nature, the central role of our appetites and passions, and the resulting reality of human conflict in public and private relationships. These conflicts tended to arise around issues of economic power and the distribution of goods.[485]Libertarian political theory shows a keen awareness of the dangerous nature of state power, but a strange lack of concern about the same human tendencies when they are manifest in economic transactions, asymmetries of economic power, and the consequences of economic injustice. After all, as Aristotle points out, even the smallest economic transaction is a form of communal relationship. These economic transactions, therefore, must involve interests, desires, and values. For that reason, it is not really possible or desirable to draw a sharp distinction between ethical, economic, and political concepts.

One place where this can be seen is in Aristotle's famous enumeration of three different types of friendship in his great work on ethical theory.[486] Modern science agrees with Aristotle that human beings are by nature both social and political. In opposition to Plato, Aristotle's conception of community respects difference and rejects a need for a common identity. For my purposes here, what is important is Aristotle's famous distinction between three different types of friendship, especially the kind of relationships based on a mutual concern of utility, usefulness, or self-interest. This is sometimes referred to as *instrumental* friendship. We all know relationships of this nature; a person who is your friend just so long as you can do something for her. He or she is always looking out for their personal advantage in relationships. We call them self-serving, opportunists, or fair-weather friends. A fictional example might be the character of Max Detweiler in *The Sound of Music.* This type of person is always asking themselves whether or not they should invest their time and energy in a particular relationship. Aristotle notes that such relationships will continue so long as there is some reciprocity and each party feels that they gain some mutual advantages. He states that "those who are friends on account of advantage cease to be such at the same time as the advantage ceases; for they were not friends of one another but of the benefit to themselves."[487] In my book, *Love of Having*, I explain why it is better, following Aristotle and certain modern psychologists, to speak in terms of forming a disposition to act in certain ways, rather than in designating special types of persons. To the extent that we habitually seek some greater advantage in an economic or business relationship, we are engaging in this kind of instrumental friendship.

In a highly influential essay, the Canadian philosopher Charles Taylor noted that the libertarian conception of the individual and of society is instrumental in this sense of instrumental friendship.[488]This should not be surprising since Taylor correctly traces these individual rights based concepts back to the origins of classical liberalism in the seventeenth century. Taylor's contemporary target is libertarianism, especially, the views of Robert Nozick. Taylor contrasts this instrumental view with Aristotle's argument that human beings are not self-sufficient, but are social in nature. The libertarian view of the individual is week to the point of being vacuous. Human beings are socially and historically embedded creatures, with certain socially developed capacities for self-fulfillment. Libertarians tend to put forth an instrumental view of individuals as passive consumers of services rather than as active citizens, while meanwhile holding that market forces and values preempt long established traditions, principles, and customs. The very concepts which libertarians wish to promote are themselves embedded in this rich liberal history and cultural tradition. To speak of individual choice and rights without taking these realities into account is just as specious as to speak of the state as having a will and a mind of its own. Moreover, the independence, autonomy, and self-determination of citizens can only be fully fostered in a socially nurturing and empowering context of freedom and encouragement of these individual capacities for fulfillment.

In an equally important essay in the same volume, Taylor takes on, what he calls the "caricatures" of both negative and positive freedom confusing both libertarians and their critics.[489] Libertarians have too crude a notion of human flourishing and self-realization, what I called above a moral psychology, which mirrors their crude view of individuality. The external constraints imposed by government regulation, for example, are far from being the only cause of the lack of freedom to choose and exercise control over your life and your personal goals. A more realistic view of freedom needs to include other forms of external constraint, other sources of power, as well as such internal capacities as "self-awareness, self-understanding, moral discrimination, and self-control."[490]

There is some danger in using the English term friendship for the Greek *philia*, and certainly we do not think of business transactions as acts of friendship. But, Aristotle calls attention to the communal aspect, as well as the ethical component of such relationships, which is what is important for my purposes here.[491] Of course, there can be differences of degree of fellow-feeling in various types of economic transactions, for example face-to-face as opposed to electronic. Individuals are clearly more willing to engage in fraud and deception with individuals they never meet.[492] What is important here is that Aristotle contrasts this disposition of advantage-based friendship with what he calls complete friendship. This higher type of friendship, sometimes translated as perfect friendship, is directed at the virtuous character of the friend.[493] An important aspect of the goodness of the friend is her trustworthiness. People who have a virtuous character treat others as valuable in their own right, and not as means to their own pleasure or economic benefit. For example, they are generous and magnanimous, rather than miserly. This type of relationship is complete to the extent that it expresses the major dispositions of a virtuous character. In contrast, a person who focuses on her own self-interest is not likely to fully understand what her friend needs for his own personal well-being. Aristotle makes this clearer with his definition of friendly feeling in another work, his *Rhetoric*. "We may describe friendly feeling toward anyone," he asserts, "as wishing for him what you believe to be good things, not for your sake but for his, and being inclined, so far as you can, to bring these things about."[494]

Moreover, Aristotle presents a strong contrast between the value of friendship as such and the value of material goods. In fact, he notes that the rich and powerful are actually in greater need of friends that value them beyond their own riches and power. The more of these external goods a person has "the more precarious" is their situation without friends to help them. Moreover, friendship is intrinsically a greater good than riches or political power.[495]

There has been a growing tendency in the western democracies to accuse those who do not agree with us of being children of darkness or evil. The very best political thinkers, Aristotle, Madison, Niebuhr, Dewey, realized that we all harbor the seeds or traits of the destruction of democracy in ourselves. Pericles's famous funeral oration, a model for Abraham Lincoln and many others, extolled the supposed virtue of Athenian democracy for choosing its leaders based on their character and merits. Of course Athenian and all prior democratic systems were far from the equality of our modern systems. Pericles also praised the civic virtue of the Athenian citizens, their respect for customs, traditions and laws, their patriotism, and the virtue of their relationships. These virtues were a prominent component of early civic education in America in the 1940s and 1950s. For Aristotle, the virtue of its citizens, and especially its leaders, was an essential preservative of democratic rule. Aristotle warned against the corruption of even the best constitution that can come from unchecked self-interest. As is the case with personal friendships, the most corrosive type of self-interest in government is economic, especially in societies with extreme economic inequality.

In a fascinating discussion of Aristotle's views about self-interest, Richard Kraut contrasts Aristotle's belief that individual citizens should be willing to forego some of what they most value for the good of others with three different forms of egoism: pure, combative, and benign. These latter views all hold that goods that benefit oneself should have priority over any similar goods that benefit others, but what Kraut calls *combative* egoists admit that their interests may conflict with those of other citizens, whereas *benign* egoists argue that pursuing one's own interest is not only the best plan of action, but it will also benefit others. It should be clear that this last approach is similar to libertarian views about the natural functioning of markets.[496] Aristotle's great insight, confirmed by modern social science, is that we are a social animal, and, at least partially, other-directed; also, that the kind of friendship that is concerned for the well-being of the other person is the bedrock of community. Moreover, he taught that the justice and the very survival of the state depends on the moral character and practical wisdom of its citizens, and, especially, of its leaders. The health and survival of democratic institutions can be assessed by examining the character of its citizens and its leaders. Aristotle puts forth a very sophisticated moral psychology, one that has been largely confirmed by modern research. Arguments, fear of punishment, or threats do not make someone good. Rather, it is the gradual process of habituation to moral acts that lays down settled dispositions to act in accordance with virtue. Contemporary multidisciplinary studies of individuals who act altruistically, for example those who helped save Jews in Nazi occupied

Europe, shows that these individuals typically did not have time to deliberate about their actions. Instead, those who put their life on the line to save the life of another human being do so because of a settled disposition of care and compassion.[497] As Aristotle knew, it is only by habitual acts of kindness and courage, beginning with parenting, that individuals develop a settled disposition to act in a virtuous manner. The opposite is also true, namely, that the process of corruption of character is a slow habituation to behaviors that reinforce corrupt practices.

This last point is one of the moral lessons of Dürrenmatt's brilliant play, *The Visit.* The gradual deterioration or subversion of the moral character of the citizens of Güllen involves internal processes of rationalization and other forms of self-deception that take their time to work their transformation. The power of wealth would not be capable of countering justice if it were not for the power of self-interest and greed to undermine virtue. This is not something as simple or as crass as direct bribery. It is reinforced by the character of those we choose to associate with, as well as the propaganda we ingest. But also by the fact that it appears harder to convince the egoist that her happiness is dependent on the well-being of others rather than on the cunning and manipulative behaviors which seem to have benefited a wealthy person, such as Claire. Also, it would be hard to argue that the market transaction in this case was free. Michael Sandel points out that this claim of free market exchange is often more complicated than libertarians would wish us to believe.[498] We can question to what extent any of the choices that the citizen's of Güllen make are really free, including their choice of lifestyle.

Aristotle's focus on treating friends as ends in themselves rather than merely as means to our own ends became a central tenet of the moral philosophy of Immanuel Kant. Kant's famous formulation of this practical rule is "so act as to treat humanity, whether in your own person or in that of any other, always at the same time as an end, and never merely as a means."[499] The Austrian libertarians Mises and Hayek, though fully versed in Kant and accepting of some of his nonpolitical and moral ideas, rejected this formula because of its emphasis on positive freedom. Just as a reminder, negative freedom is freedom *from* interference, restraint, or coercion, whereas positive freedom is the ability *to* be able to achieve one's goals, which includes the component of having the necessary resources and capabilities. Positive freedom involves having the capacity to choose from a range of different options. Mises and Hayek saw this latter type of freedom as encouraging paternalism. There are some differences between Hayek's views on negative liberty and those of others. As I showed Hayek accepts the necessity of a rule of law in any society. But, like other libertarians, Hayek argued that individuals should be free to engage in private activities that do not infringe on the rights of others. Even those liberals who reject libertarian economic policies usually embrace the view that citizens should be allowed to engage in whatever activities they wish in their own home and with their own body, so long as these activities do not harm or restrict other individuals. Although Hayek recognizes the harm that unregulated economic competition can bring to certain individuals, his moral philosophy, and that of many libertarians, is too strongly influenced by the scientism of Social Darwinism.

The greatest defender of libertarianism Robert Nozick, however, embraced this Kantian imperative. As I noted in my discussion of him above, a central principle of Nozick's argument is the doctrine "that individuals are ends and not merely means." He goes on to add "[individuals] may not be sacrificed or used for achieving other ends without their consent. Individuals are inviolable."[500] Nozick's formulation is clearly rights based in a way that Hayek would appear to reject. However, the differences between Kant and Nozick could not be more critical and central to my own position in *Love of Having* and in this book. The first thing to note is that Kant was very concerned that extreme inequality in relationships and in a nation precluded the possibility of true political freedom.[501] As I also noted above, John Locke was concerned about our natural "covetousness" and narcissistic "bias" and that we would tend to injure those unfortunate individuals who did not own property by taking all for ourselves.[502] Nozick wrestles with these concerns about "leaving enough and as good for others," and not "spoiling" the environment, which he calls the "Lockean proviso," but he comes up short. After all, Locke was very clear about our obligation to provide for the poor, and there is a very real problem with relying entirely on voluntary charity in order to meet this obligation.

The second major difference, one that is central to the question of values, is that Kant's conception of liberty is far more nuanced, and I would argue closer to reality than the libertarian view of negative freedom and self-ownership. His conception does not even rest on the results of mutual consent. Rather, as Michael Sandel notes, Kant's moral view of liberty "depends on the idea that [humans] are [all] rational beings worthy of dignity and respect."[503] For Nozick, the reason that humans should be treated as ends rather than as instruments or tools for another's satisfaction is that we are capable of formulating our own plans or goals in life. However, as I have shown, Nozick's libertarian individualism is a far more restricted view of life's meaning and human rationality than the social or relational view of Aristotle and communitarians. In addition, the guiding value of the capitalist profit motive is essentially instrumental, and involves using others to gain winner-take-all advantage. In explanation to a reference Kant makes to teeth, Sandel describes a cartoon drawn by the British artist Thomas Rawlandson entitled *Transplantation of Teeth.* It depicts "a scene in a dentist's office," Sandel tells us,"in which a surgeon extracts teeth from a chimney sweep while wealthy women wait for their implants."[504]Sandel gives a number of modern examples of the sale of body parts that demonstrate major problems with the whole idea that we own our body and can treat it like a mere object.

It is important to note that one can have positive freedom without a paternalistic government, just as one can have paternalism without government. This latter existed in Britain, especially during the Victorian years in what is called *industrial paternalism* or, sometimes, welfare corporatism. Similar practices thrived in America during the Progressive Era, with somewhat different motivation. The interest was not just control of employees, but to show that capitalism could be benevolent. The effort to hold off unionization was certainly no small additional motivation.[505]

It is interesting to note that this industrial paternalism has mostly disappeared, due in part to the decline of unions, as well as the rise of large international corporations and financial institutions with employees who are now largely faceless to their executives. Brian Alexander gives a detailed analysis of how these economic changes and the power of finance and the enormously wealthy transformed his home town of Lancaster, Ohio.[506] Lancaster can stand in for a real world Güllen. Alexander is careful to note that other economic factors beside the maneuvers of Wall Street led to the precipitous decline of Lancaster's main employer. But, his account of how that giant company was transformed from the bedrock of a very typical town's economy and the devastating inequality which resulted goes a long way toward explaining the success of the populist rhetoric of Donald Trump in Lancaster and many similar towns. Though there had always been periods of some labor unrest, the efforts at paternalism, some of it informal, had been largely beneficial to the company, its employers, and the whole town.

There are still many wealthy capitalists, of course, who are willing to invest in new industries and businesses that create prosperity for all our citizens, not just for themselves and their immediate family. Not all our wealthy capitalists have squirreled away their capital in hidden accounts, and many smaller banking institutions and businesses are still willing to invest in their local communities. The city that I grew up in and love, Worcester, Massachusetts, has been buffeted by the same economic forces as Lancaster, Ohio. However, Worcester has had resources, a politics, and a different history which have made for a contrasting outcome and the possibility of a much more promising future; assuming, that is, that America does not turn into a failed nation, a prospect very much in play. Since these differences are highly relevant, I need to touch on them briefly here.

Worcester was one of the early sites of the Industrial Revolution in America, and it prospered enormously during the nineteenth and early twentieth centuries. Like all such cities, its major industrial employers have either left, been absorbed by international firms, or have been sharply reduced in size. However, Worcester has long had several major advantages going for it, two of which I want to mention here. Chief among these advantages is education. Worcester has a rich abundance of public and private educational institutions, colleges, universities, but also other research centers or institutes. Its other major advantage is also highly relevant to these times and the thesis of this book. Worcester has always welcomed new immigrants and refugees from all areas of the world. I'm told that today, some 40,000 residents of the city are foreign born; but, though the numbers and ethnic mix has varied, the spirit of a highly pluralistic community has long defined the city. A wonderful smorgasbord of ethnicities and religions with different foods, music, customs and beliefs has enriched the city and my own life. Although there are many reasons why people may need to stay in the country of their birth, despite wars, persecution, and financial ruin, it has always been true that those who risk leaving tend to be the most adventurous and creative, and the individuals most willing to give their all to improve their well-being and that of their children. I wrote about this subject of immigration in my biography of Dr. William James Macneven, himself a refugee, an innovator of social welfare for immigrants, and an enlightened promoter of immigrant rights and their contributions to a flourishing society. Encouraging education, vocational training, research and development, new ideas and a spirit of openness and creativity, public/private cooperation, a mixed economy, and development of individual capabilities are all features of inclusive and flourishing economies and societies.

Libertarians are right to warn us against the dangers to our negative freedom from governmental paternalism. We can also agree with the Austrian libertarians and their disciples that heavily planned economies will inevitably intrude into more and more areas of personal life, fostering a dependence that impedes the development of democratic autonomy. However, not every form of governmental paternalism has resulted in negative consequences. I have in mind 1960s civil rights legislation which eventually brought about some acceptance of African American rights, however begrudging this might still be in some quarters. John Dewey was mostly correct when he asserted that "only by public agency can discrimination be avoided."[507] But of greatest importance here is the fact that industrial or corporate paternalism has been allowed to infiltrate, transform, and corrupt every segment and institution in our society, including medicine, journalism, even religion, sports and entertainment. The slow process of this transformation of values involves internal mechanisms similar to the process by which the citizens of Güllen became the willing tools of Claire Zachanassian's evil plan of revenge. I presented some of the complex psychological dynamics of this slow corruption of character in my last book.

Libertarians are also correct to point to the phenomenal positive rewards that capitalism has brought in so many areas of our life, not least of all in the areas of medicine and technology. However, the values associated with the marketplace have been allowed to slowly undermine the intrinsic set of values that have traditionally defined social institutions, including medicine and my field of social work. The profit motive, the importance of the bottom line, competitive advantage, price, consumer manipulation, the value of material goods, creative destruction, in short, instrumental and external relations and values have slowly replaced the intrinsic goods associated with specific sectors of society. There are countless tragic examples of what happens when an obsession with profits, balance sheets, greater efficiency, and reducing the bottom line replaces concern with community and the safety of men, women, and children. I will mention just two additional examples besides Lancaster, Ohio: the

Flint, Michigan water crisis, where thousands were exposed to extremely high levels of lead in their drinking water; and, the alarming rise of serious earthquakes in Oklahoma directly resulting from the practice of hydraulic fracturing or fracking for oil and gas. The general decline of the social fabric, leading to multiple addictions, dependencies, suicides, and a breakdown of community and personal relationships has spilled into small towns nationwide; areas far less equipped to deal with such devastation. The highly predictable political result was an extreme populist backlash.

This line of argument owes a lot to the moral philosophy of Alasdair MacIntyre, who I had the honor of studying with for several years. I have room here only for a brief look at one aspect of MacIntyre's influential concept of social practices. MacIntyre provides a lengthy and complex definition of what he means by a social practice in his major work, *After Virtue*.[508] He distinguishes practices from what I referred to above as institutions and sectors; in other words, the practice of architecture should be distinguished from any architectural firm or society. For my purposes here, what is important is that a "socially established cooperative activity," such as architecture or medicine, has what MacIntyre first called *internal goods* and later *excellences*, and which I will call intrinsic rewards and virtues. Each specific social practice has its own unique set of such standards or virtues. MacIntyre distinguishes these internal goods from those that are *external*, such as money, power, and fame. These latter, of course, are contingent, in that they are based on what a given society at any one time happens to value. There is, therefore, a certain amount of luck involved with external goods, which is a counter argument, as I mentioned above, against Nozick's reasoning about property rights based on self-ownership. It is important to note that these external rewards are not specific to any given social practice. MacIntyre and others have also noted that internal goods tend to benefit society as a whole. It is also interesting to note that at least one of these external goods, namely money, is a prime intrinsic good for the social practice of business.

What is most important for my argument here is that a primary consequence of libertarian theory and practice has been the gradual domination of all social practices by a value system based entirely on external rewards. The profit motive, the bottom line, the importance of financial rewards have overwhelmed or engulfed the specific intrinsic virtues of each and every social practice in modern western societies. What is problematic here is the exclusive or at least predominant dependence on instrumental values in all social practices. Practical considerations can arise in all interpersonal relations but they are external to other concerns and interests that define the nature of a social practice such as medicine. Market transactions, on the other hand, are situations where we primarily treat others as means. As Michael Sandel shows the most important transformation is "the growing reach of money and markets into spheres of life once governed by nonmarket norms."[509]

It is also important to point out that politics is itself a social practice, one that it has long been argued has its own specific virtues. MacIntyre and others, such as Jeffrey Stout, look to Aristotle for a list of specific virtues that should be standard in any political leader of a democracy or republic.[510] Stout, MacIntyre, and others warned about the corrupting dominance of instrumental values in all areas of society. Tocqueville and other acute commentators on democracy warned that if we do not value freedom for itself, we will soon lose it. It is instructive to point out that one of the key virtues that Aristotle saw in a good leader was that of temperance. I showed in my book, *Love of Having*, just how far our society has come from valuing temperance in our leaders and citizens. It is also instructive to see just how important this disposition of "self-command" was to Adam Smith, as well as how much he worried about the negative effects of "a commercial spirit" on moral education and society in general.[511] It is also instructive to call attention to how many American citizens seem to have ignored, in the last presidential election, the importance of virtuous character as an essential aspect of leadership.

It would take me too far afield to give an analysis of MacIntyre argument about the type of moral theory that has come to dominate our society. But, it is highly relevant to include his conclusion that it has led to "the obliteration of any genuine distinction between manipulative and non-manipulative social relations."[512]Despite Robert Nozick's desire to appropriate Kant's view about treating individuals as ends rather than as means to our own ends, the real consequence of libertarian political philosophy and policies has had the opposite effect. Kant explicitly highlighted the difference here and countered Nozick's usage when he wrote that "what is related to general human inclinations and needs has a *market price* … but that which constitutes the condition under which alone something can be an end in itself has not merely a relative worth, that is, a price, but an inner worth, that is, *dignity*."[513] Kant's contrast in this passage is with the dignity, benevolence, faithfulness, and respect which are the intrinsic values of a human being and the external goods intrinsic to the marketplace.

Even some theories that oppose libertarianism accept the market as the principle model to compare or measure against the state. The intrinsic values of a market economy have become the standard of rationality in all spheres of social practice. Individuals are measured by their degree of *human capital*. Social spheres that once functioned under very different intrinsic values are threatened with extinction if they fail to adopt these economic performance standards.[514]This is far from the kind of creative destruction that finds new, more efficient replacements for old traditions and values. Leaders of large corporations mainly pursue the intrinsic values of their own social practice when they pursue all avenues available to maximize market share, stock value, and other corporation revenues. It is by this standard of external rewards that they will be judged. The problem for a healthy society is that all other disciplines have been manipulated into adopting these same standards and values.

One discipline essential to the health of any democracy is that of public education. The Founders of American democracy, not least of all Thomas Jefferson understood that a certain kind of education, one that has intrinsic standards of value very different from commercial interests, would be essential to maintain freedom.[515] Madison said it most starkly and clearly when he wrote that the "blessings of liberty cannot be fully enjoyed or long preserved" without the advancement of knowledge and educational instructions "as a nursery of enlightened preceptors" inculcating "those national feelings, those liberal sentiments, and those congenial manners which contribute cement to our Union and strength to the great political fabric of which that is the foundation."[516] Many similar expressions from all the major Founders of American democracy could be quoted about this necessity for the education of all citizens in critical thinking and democratic values if the government they created was to survive. Writing only a few decades after Madison the great abolitionist and educational reformer Horace Mann agreed that an educated citizenry was necessary to maintain freedom, as was the enhancement of their capabilities to ensure their "physical well-being." Mann argued that "poverty is a public as well as a private evil," one that destroys political liberty.[517] This warning was central to John Dewey's concern about preserving American democracy. One of his clearest statements against the libertarian belief that democracy can be based solely on a negative conception of freedom came in a little book he wrote on *Experience and Education.* "The only freedom that is of enduring importance," Dewey asserted, "is freedom of intelligence." He went on to define this essential capacity as "freedom of observation and of judgment exercised in behalf of purposes that are intrinsically [of value]." Dewey made his strong concern about basing democracy on a purely negative definition of liberty by adding that "the commonest mistake made about freedom is, I think, to identify it with freedom of movement, or with the external or physical side of activity."[518]

As is the case with extreme economic inequality, libertarians who share a concern about the stability and very survival of democracy need to question some of their basic ideas about freedom and education. Moreover, the origins of this anxiety about the need for a certain type of education for the preservation of freedom, as was the case with inequality, goes back to the very beginnings of democracy in Athens. Dewey, Tocqueville, and almost all of the great thinkers about democratic governance drew upon the Greek experience that citizens learn the social practice of freedom from habits of acting democratically, something that goes well beyond voting.[519]Development of democratic dispositions, as I noted in my discussion of Aristotle, is a very long educational process that involves repeated or habitual practice. It would require a separate book to spell out all that needs to be part of developing democratic dispositions. However, one thing is clear, namely, in a representative democracy citizens need to develop a level of critical thinking that allows them to understand the character traits that make for good leadership, as well as how to distinguish between reasonable persuasion and pure manipulation. Historical and psychological knowledge is as important for developing this skill as is the kind of reasoning needed in science, technology, and business.[520] Martha Nussbaum, Wendy Brown, following Adam Smith and so many others concerned with freedom, have sounded an alarm about the supplanting of humanistic with purely commercial values and the attack on the humanities and critical thinking in all levels of our education.[521]

In order to move beyond the sharp partisan rhetoric that divides and threatens our freedoms and the stability of our democratic institutions we must first acknowledge the appropriateness of libertarian concerns about the dangers of certain uses of positive freedom and paternalism by government leaders to advance their own power and self-interest. We all need to broaden our concern about paternalistic domination beyond just government to any source of concerted power, including uses of soft power. This awareness should take advantage of our new deeper understanding of the moral psychology of propaganda and persuasion. Libertarians must also acknowledge the appropriate concerns of active state liberals about the dominance of corporate self-interest which results from a reliance solely on negative freedom. Deregulation of financial institutions, cutting government programs till they can no longer function and then using their inefficiency as an argument for their elimination, privatization and commercialization of services that benefit all citizens, have all resulted in extreme inequality, plutocracy, and the almost complete erosion of civic virtue.

Although not as well-known a political philosopher as those I've discussed so far, Samuel Fleischacker is one who has attempted to move beyond these divisions while acknowledging the positive contributions of both sides. His contribution goes back to the original foundations of modern democracy in the period known as the enlightenment; specifically to the ideas of Adam Smith and Immanuel Kant. Fleischacker finds in Smith and Kant the outlines of a third concept of liberty beyond Isaiah Berlin's division into negative and positive.[522] I will conclude this book with an all-too-brief outline of this third concept of freedom, one that can move us beyond our current partisan rancor.

I have already noted that Adam Smith has been misappropriated by libertarians, but it is still instructive to note Carl Menger's summary statement, which was obviously passed over by the Austrian libertarian economists who saw Menger as their mentor. Any careful reader of Smith's entire works will see very early on that far from being an economic libertarian he had an abiding and deep concern for economic equality, for adequate wages, and for governmental action to minimize the suffering of the poor.[523] Rather than these active measures taking away from a nation's economic advancement, Smith sees them as ensuring the wealth of nations. Fleischacker quotes Menger as stating that "there is not a single instance in A. Smith's work in which he represents the interest of the rich and powerful as opposed to the poor and weak."[524] Fleischacker states flatly that Smith's prescription for a nation's wealth is "linked inextricably to the well-being of the poor."[525]

Fleischacker begins however with Kant's famous contribution to the late eighteenth century contest to define *enlightenment*.[526] Kant defined enlightenment as involving "man's emergence from his self-incurred immaturity," and he went on to define immaturity as "the inability to use one's understanding without the guidance of another." Kant's examples of daring to think for oneself show that he had in mind the kind of ideological rigidity that Enlightenment thinkers reacted against, including the fundamentalist religious movements that have reappeared in the twenty-first century. I agree with those interpreters of Kant who see in him a broader social, political, and even moral/psychological conception of autonomous and critical thinking than has been traditionally attributed to the great philosopher of Königsberg. This reading of Kant sees in him a more empirical, less rigidly metaphysical social and political philosophy. Freedom is seen as something that individuals and society needs to work to produce and to preserve. One of these interpreters notes that Kant could not have anticipated the modern advance in techniques of persuasion, what he calls the "brave new world syndrome."[527] This technology, of course, has only made the need to develop a disposition for autonomous thinking all the more crucial. The latest of these modern methods include the doctoring of video recording so that it seems to show a person saying something which they didn't actually say, making photo-shopping still images seem primitive in comparison. Moreover, creeping authoritarianism, each loss of freedom alone appearing inconsequential, requires almost constant vigilance and a level of political awareness and engagement unusual for most citizens.

Fleischacker, building on the important work of Barbara Herman, makes good use of Kant's highly influential views on judgment. Kant was opposed to any form of paternalism, not least of all that of the state toward its citizens.[528] He shared this antipathy with Smith, Benjamin Constant, Wilhelm von Humboldt, and many other Enlightenment political thinkers.

Fleischacker notes that Kant's views on the economy and markets seem very similar to modern libertarianism; for example, his suspicions about government regulation as paternalistic. However, Kant's is a libertarian philosophy with a difference and it is that difference that can be used to break through the partisan divide. Kant sees the public and the private sectors of society working together to promote the good of all. Also, Kant shared the view that in order to develop a disposition to act freely an individual needs to practice such actions over years of moral development.

Kant briefly returned to the topic of his essay on enlightenment and mature thought in his last great work of critique, his *Critique of Judgment*.[529] He notes that individuals progress beyond the "illusion" of their personal prejudices by "comparing our judgment with the possible rather than the actual judgment of others, and by putting ourselves in the place of any other man, by abstracting from the limitations which contingently attach to our own judgment." He follows this counsel with three guiding maxims: "(1) to think for oneself; (2) to put ourselves in the place of everyone else; (3) always to think consistently." He calls the first "the maxim of *unprejudiced* thought; the second of *enlarged* thought; the third of *consecutive* thought."[530]In this passage Kant defines enlightenment as an active reasoning mind that is free from the control or blindness of superstitious beliefs. As with other dispositions, the realization of these judgment skills can only come after long repeated applications. These maxims are rules for the process of the give and take of views and policies that is an essential standard of the specific social practice of politics. In fact, Kant draws a very similar distinction between intrinsic and external goods of social practices when he discusses the differences between art and commerce in a later section of this work.[531]

Fleischacker points out that in an essay published three years after his *Critique of Judgment* Kant spelled out how these standards of good judgment are essential to the healthy functioning of a free and peaceful state.[532] Freedom of thought, being able to think for ourselves, and doing so by attending to the ideas of others, are all key virtues of any democratic government. Kant asserts that for this essential freedom to work certain other freedoms and capabilities need to be protected, including freedom of speech and the press, but also public education and certain human faculties, especially judgment. A healthy democracy encourages constructive dialogue between opposing views, the working out of differences rather than ideological solidarity. As I noted in the introduction, for John Dewey this involved the internalization of "the scientific method" so that it becomes a citizen's disposition.[533] In other words, citizens need to be able to use the same critical thinking capability or assessment techniques which will allow them to distinguish between truth and propaganda, self-interest or manipulation. Fleischacker would no doubt argue that Dewey's generalization of science to politics is both too demanding and dangerous, too much like Plato's philosopher kings. I agree that Fleischacker's concept of judgment is preferable to Dewey's in that it allows for a capacity that all could aspire to, just so long as it includes, like Dewey's an ability to see through propaganda and political manipulation. Fleischacker's views need to be supplemented by a more realistic awareness of the dark arts of politics which I discussed in my last segment above.

As an example of this sort of open dialogue, Fleischacker sides with moderate libertarians against what he argues are extreme egalitarian views about a person's moral right to benefit from the rewards coming from her natural endowments or talents, birth advantages, and luck. He points out, correctly I believe, that some inequality in a society has benefits for all, and that rewarding people for the cultivation of their talent and their industry is also beneficial. He also shares with libertarians a skeptical attitude toward arguments and policies based on the supposed will of the people, and whether there really is any such thing; concerns about who is qualified to announce it even if it exits; and, the violent history of revolutions based on this delusion. This makes him understandably nervous about a politics based on concepts of positive freedom.

Although Fleischacker is sympathetic with some moderate libertarian arguments, he points out that libertarians have made three specific errors in their reasoning. He believes that they have misinterpreted the position of Locke and Kant that one way that government ensures the freedom of its citizens is by "restricting the power of some individuals." The first error in interpreting this liberal principle comes from the extreme individualism of libertarians that I analyzed earlier. Fleischacker criticizes the atomistic conception that sees each individual's freedom as "absolute" and apart from others. I would add that one can agree with libertarians that the state is not some separate entity with a will and a set of goods of its own, while also arguing that individuals are innately social and political, with interdependent needs and values. Fleischacker's second criticism is also one that I have made earlier, namely, the narrow view of the government as the source of dangerous power rather than "groups of individuals." Active state liberals can and do share a deep concern with state power and with positive freedom as moral prescription, while holding, at the same time, that genuine freedom must include the opportunity and ability to act on ones rights.[534] His last criticism goes to the heart of the narrowness of the views of libertarians. They assume that the values related to ownership, "rather than any mental or physical ability" should be the central element that defines what needs to be protected from power. Fleischacker holds that these three "mistakes" are interrelated. Concentrating only on the coercive power of the state allows libertarians to ignore the enormous power of concentrated wealth in the private sector.

Fleischacker draws on Kant and Martha Nussbaum's masterful *The Fragility of Goodness*, itself a synthesis of ancient wisdom about moral luck, to outline a political economy that differs in essential ways from libertarian views. He argues that economic policies that promote the human abilities related to good judgment and "judicious choice" must require providing "a guaranteed minimum" of resources. This is especially the case when it comes to children. Fleischacker accepts the desirability of providing the required resources through market mechanisms "*as much as morally justifiable.*"[535] He would also prefer a market system that develops and favors small businesses, even at the risk of increased prices for commercial goods. His fear here is clearly the monopolistic power of corporatism. Adam Smith's warning about the lack of compassion which comes from the abstraction and distance of corporations has certainly been magnified many times with the global financial markets of today. Fleischacker is correct to favor earning this minimum over government distribution. I would add however that the very survival of democratic institutions, as well as free markets, depends on the development and maintenance of the dispositions of good judgment, critical thinking, and self-esteem necessary for healthy relationships at any level. Moreover, a too exclusive focus on material capabilities both ignores the importance of capacities for judgment, mental resilience, and education, while encouraging political conflict over material resources, as well as the unhelpful labeling of socialism.

It is important to emphasize that the justification for this minimum of income is not simply benevolence, but can rest on the practical self-interest of all citizens, even our plutocrats. Not only is there the virtue of political stability and the survival of democracy, but the evidence is overwhelming that societies and economies flourish much better when their citizens have the educational and other capacities that allow for their own flourishing. Before ending I must spell out a little further why this is the case. That involves looking very briefly at Fleischacker's conception of a *liberty of judgment* and the related concept of *agency liberty* of the Nobel Laureate economist and philosopher, Amartya Sen, but in the context of ideas from feminist theory about self-esteem and soft power.

Fleischacker argues that his third concept of freedom, one based on each individual's independent cultivation of skills of interpretive judgment can bridge the current divide between libertarians and welfare state liberals, synthesizing the best of negative and positive freedom. Governments must leave their citizens free to pursue their own goals and desires, but citizens also need at least a minimum of resources, including job retraining and an "excellent education" in order to be able to develop the judgment that supports the free realization of such goals. An education for judgment must include a firm grounding in the humanities and cannot be limited to the instrumental skills necessary for the external values of market competition. He favors indirect methods of providing such assistance, including Milton Friedman's negative income tax. He is justifiably concerned about the promotion of paternalistic social values associated with communitarian views of civic virtue. He does also warn in passing that other groups in society, including large corporations, unions or professional associations, and religious groups can work to reduce individual freedom of judgment and will possibly need to be restrained. It is consistent with libertarian values to favor local government over the large, centralized, federal bureaucracy, but also to support small business over large international corporations and monopolies with antitrust regulations. He also points to the essential need for complete access to information in order to correctly judge the activities required for good judgment in markets and in government. Fleischacker is fully aware of the dangers of undue power and influence over government. I agree with him that a consistent libertarian philosophy would see the need to balance such forces in the interest of both the individual and the market.

On the face of it positive freedom, the freedom to do things, should not be problematic. But, Fleischacker like Isaiah Berlin and other realists of power, correctly points to the many historical examples of where this benevolence has led to government coercing citizens in the interest of their supposed good. I warned about this danger in my critique of consumerism in *Love of Having*. Amartya Sen's highly influential *Capability Approach* avoids this danger by its focus on enhancing individual *agency* and by its pluralist or open view of well-being.[536] The focus is not on some pre-ordained or externally imposed prescription for a full life, but rather on helping the individual achieve her own defined and chosen goals and achievements. Agency is defined as "what a person does or can do to realize any of his or her goals and not only ones that advance or protect his or her well-being."[537] Of necessity, this has to involve the identification and possible elimination of constraints on personal freedom, from whatever sources such negative forces come, including prejudices such as those relating to class, race or gender. This approach is practical in that it focuses on the actual possibilities open to individuals rather some abstract concept of well-being. It also focuses on intrinsic values as defined by each individual rather than only on instrumental or market capacities.

However, I would argue that Fleischacker does not go far enough in his skepticism about the actions of individuals and groups, public or private, to control the individual for their own personal power and selfish ends. He also underestimates the need for each individual to develop a healthy self-esteem in order to be able to, not only interpret but resist such efforts at control. In order to be able to access or interpret the motives behind ideas and actions, you not only need to recognize when you are being used, lied to, being taken advantage of, you need the confidence and support in order to effectively resist. I already wrote about the role of consciousness-raising support groups in helping to develop healthy self-esteem in my book *Love of Having*; so I will turn here to some final words about the role of government in building citizen capabilities. As John Dewey taught, genuine equality of opportunity should enrich and strengthen the individual and her capacities to withstand coercion.[538]

I pointed out at the beginning of this book that, like all such political viewpoints, libertarianism is hardly monolithic. There has been a growing dialogue between those who embrace the libertarian label around questions of value, and, specifically, the degree to which compassion for those who live in extreme poverty, in many cases through no fault of their own, should be a motivating factor in society. A spectrum of compassion has emerged, with the followers of Ayn Rand's so-called objectivism and a morality of quid pro quo at one end and individuals who call themselves left libertarians at the other. Many have noted the danger that extreme inequality and callous disregard for those in pain poses for the stability of any democratic government. Given my desire to engage with the best arguments for and against libertarianism, I have all but ignored the extreme views of anarchists as too utopian, or the Randians as too dystopian for any reasonable debate. Many libertarians bemoan the fact that so-called leftists dismiss their views as lacking in compassion. However, it does not help their cause when some blithely dismiss left libertarians as "do-gooders." What does it mean not to want to engage in actions that result in doing good for other human beings? Those libertarians who wish to include the value of compassion, even if only for reasons of their own interest in political stability and possible violence, should skeptically and openly question the evidence for their beliefs. I will end with part of a prayer written by Martin Luther King, Jr.:

> To build together a city of justice where none shall prey upon the weaknesses of others, a city of plenty where greed and poverty shall be eliminated, a city of brotherhood where success is founded upon service, and honor given for nobleness alone.[539]

---

# Notes

Introduction:
[1] Keats, 1958, 1, pp.193–194
[2] Herbert Croly, quoted in Frankfurter, 1939/1962, p.311
[3] Dewey, 1930, p.163
[4] Lincoln, 1848/1989, Fehrenbacher, ed., p.192
[5] Nozick, 1974, p.x–xi
[6] Appiah, 2008, p.198
[7] Mencken, 1956, p.369
[8] Gadamar, 1982, pp.245–274
[9] Piketty, 2014, p.4

[10] Lasswell, 1971
[11] Finn, 2006, p.11
[12] Orwell, 1943
[13] Dewey, 1938/1971, p.6
[14] Dewey, 1939, pp.95–96
[15] Banaji & Greenwald, 2013
[16] Dewey, 1927, p.110
[17] Engelhardt, 1986; Pellegrino & Thomasma, 1988; Veatch, 1981
[18] Mulhall & Swift, 1992, p.151
[19] Sandel, 2009, p.62
[20] M. Friedman, 1962, p.158, pp.137–160
[21] Starr, 1982
[22] M. Friedman, 1962/2002, p.2
[23] Bird, 2004, p.139
[24] D. Boas, 1997, p.2; cf. also, Boas, 2015; Brennan, 2012; Miron, 2010
[25] Kant, in Schmidt, ed.,1784/1996, pp.58–64; cf., also, Kant, 1798/2012
[26] Frankfurter, 1939, p.312
[27] L. White, 2012, p.5
[28] Vallentyne & Steiner, 2000
[29] Hamowy, 2008, ed. In chief
[30] Skocpol & Williamson, 2012
[31] T. Boas & J. Gans-Morse, 2009; Steger & Roy, 2010
[32] Hayek, 1994, p.xxxv
[33] Nash, 2008
[34] Kirk, 1953, especially, pp.1–79
[35] Brittan, 1988, pp.37–44
[36] Skocpol & Williamson, 2012
[37] Rawls, 1993, p.5
[38] Sumner, 1883, p.19, emphasis in original
[39] Hayek, 1960, pp.397–411
[40] Scruton, 1980, p.36
[41] Op. cit. pp.133–252; Hayek, 1973
[42] D. Mayer, 1997, p.79
[43] Ingham, 2015
[44] H. Adams, 1905/1931, Ch.12, p.180
[45] Locke, 1690/1965, p.148
[46] Op.cit. p.167
[47] Sally, 1998; Lal, 2006, pp.48–50; Petsoulas, 2001
[48] Singer, 2015, pp. 51–4
[49] Epstein, 1985
[50] Locke, 1690/1965, p.134
[51] Madison, 1792/1999, pp.515–517
[52] Rousseau, 1988, pp.1–83; Rousseau, 1979, pp.453–480
[53] Douglas, 1996, pp.xviii–xxvii
[54] R. Ellis, 1993
[55] Ingham, 2015
[56] Caldwell, 2005, p.291

[57] See Chapter 2 for what went wrong
[58] Risen, 2014, pp.5–30
[59] See Hayek, 1948, p.14 for an example
[60] See Winters, 2011 for different types of oligarchies
[61] Quoted in Morton White, 1987, pp.78–81, p.224
[62] Tax Foundation, "Federal Taxes Paid vs. Benefits by State"
[63] Dewey, 1935/1963, p.6
[64] Ibid., pp.15–16
[65] Quoted in Fink, 1997, p.21
[66] Westbrook, 1991, p.166
[67] Hofstadter, 1955, p.46
[68] Tocqueville, 1840/1969, vol. II, pp.690–695, p.692
[69] Zakaras, 2009, pp.14–18
[70] Nussbaum, 2016, p.27
[71] Dionne, Jr., 2016, pp.41–63, 250–254
[72] Gordon, 2016, pp.541–543, 613–614
[73] See, Fleischacher, 1999 for this terminology
[74] Piketty, 2014, pp.16–22, 571–577

## Chapter 1, Pro:

[75] Gruber, 1991; Gulick, 1948, vol.1, pp.407–504
[76] A. Ebenstein, 2001; Caldwell, 2004
[77] Hayek, 1977/1992
[78] He did do some important work on perception (Hayek, 1952)
[79] L. Hunt & P. McNamara, eds., 2007, p.viii
[80] Keynes, 1936, p.32
[81] Hayek et al., 1929/1972; Hayek, 1960, pp.340–357
[82] Ranelagh, 1992, pp.190–195
[83] Gruber, 1991, p.47
[84] Quoted in Hayek, et al., p.76
[85] Gulick, 1948, pp.446–449
[86] Gruber, 1991, p.46
[87] For examples, see Friedman & Friedman, 1990, pp.110–112
[88] Hayek, 1960, p.341
[89] Gruber, 1991, pp.146–179
[90] Hayek, 1944/1975, p.125
[91] M. Friedman & R. Friedman, 1990, p.97
[92] See Stern, 1977, pp.208–225 for confirmation
[93] M. Friedman & R. Friedman, 1990, pp.110–112
[94] Hayek, 1944/1976, p.201
[95] Wapshott, 2011, pp.198–199
[96] Hayek, 1944/1976, pp.64–67
[97] A. Ebenstein, 2003, pp.203–204
[98] Caldwell, 2005, p.105
[99] Cassels, 1975, pp.152–177; Paxton, 2005; Sternhel et al., 1994
[100] Quoted in Caldwell, 2005, p.239
[101] Ibid., p.156

[102] Polanyi, 1967; Mitchell, 2006, pp.21–103; Caldwell, 2004, pp.294–307
[103] Quoted in, Mitchell, 2006, p.22
[104] Polanyi, 1967, p.4 (emphasis in original)
[105] For differences, see, Petsoulas, 2001; Bianchi, 1994
[106] Smith, 1776/1990, Bk.1, ch.2, para.2
[107] Crèvecoeur, 1782/2013, Letter 3
[108] Mises, 1920, p.49
[109] Ibid., pp.31, 50–51
[110] Hayek, 1944/1994, p.41
[111] Hayek, 1960, pp.145, 451n18
[112] Ibid., p.141
[113] Caldwell, 2005, p.289
[114] Simons, 1948, p.43
[115] Madison, pp.160–168, 92–93, 423
[116] Hayek, 1973, p.9
[117] Keynes, 1964, p.379
[118] Mises, 1944, p.21
[119] Ibid., pp.41–50
[120] Mises, 1949, pp.692–723
[121] Ibid., p.47
[122] R. Miller, 2002, pp.73–74
[123] Hayek, 1960, p.29
[124] Ibid., p.21
[125] Bentham, 1800, Ch.1, p.35
[126] Berlin, 2002, p.169
[127] Quoted in Binswanger, 1986, p.228
[128] Hayek, 1960, pp.15–20
[129] O'Hear, 2006, p.135
[130] Berlin, 2002, p.170
[131] Schaar, 1991
[132] Hayek, 1960, pp.62–64
[133] Ignatieff, 1984, p.11
[134] See Ingham, 2015 for more on this error
[135] M. Friedman & R. Friedman, 1990, pp.226–227
[136] Hayek, ed., 1954
[137] Hayek, 1948, pp.1–32; Hayek, 1960; Hayek, 1967/1978
[138] Ibid., pp.11, 17
[139] Ibid. , p.19
[140] Hindess, 1987, ch.9; O'Neill, 1998
[141] Hayek, 1948, p.6
[142] Ibid., pp. 30–31; see, also, Hayek 1960, pp.85–102
[143] See, Ingham, 2015
[144] Hayek, 1960, p.87
[145] Hayek, 1948, p.31
[146] Hayek, 1960, p.94
[147] Ibid., p.101
[148] Ibid., pp.306–324

[149] Hollander, 2008, p.448

[150] Ibid., p.308

[151] Reeves, 2007, p.211; Mill had quite different views on equality

[152] See Ingham, 2015, for more on satiation

[153] Hayek, 1960, p.321

[154] Brandeis, 1914/1967, p.12

[155] Parfit, 2002, pp.81–125

[156] Jacobson & Hamowy, eds., 1965

[157] Haidt, 2013, p.350

[158] Stenner, 2005

[159] Madison, beginning of Federalist No. 10; of course, there are major differences

[160] Hayek, 1976, II, pp.62–100

[161] Hayek, 1988, pp.114–116

[162] Hayek, 1979, pp.3–4

[163] Ibid., p.7

[164] Ibid. p.11

[165] Madison, Federalist 48, 1999, p.281

[166] Hayek, 1976, .68–69

[167] See Muller, 2002, pp.370–377 for an excellent summary

[168] Skidelsky, 2006, p.100

[169] Gamble, 2006, p.129

[170] Schumpeter, 1950, p.251; Schumpeter had much more sympathy with socialism than his compatriots, Mises and Hayek.

[171] Hayek, 1978, p.33

[172] A. Ebenstein, 2001, p.145; D. Jones, 2012

[173] Hayek, 1960, p.411

[174] J. Mayer, 2016, p.3

[175] Mirowski & Plehwe, 2009, pp.1–42

[176] D. Jones, 2012

[177] Wapshott, 2011, p.213

[178] Hayek, "The Intellectuals and Socialism," 1949/1967, pp.178–194

[179] Ashton, in Hayek, 1954, p.33; Thompson, 1963; cf. Griffen, 2013, for a good update

[180] Long, 1960

[181] See the other essays in Hayek, 1967

[182] Rumsfeld, May 2002, quoted in Klein, 2007, p.144

[183] Machlup, 1976, pp.xxi–xxiv

[184] M. Friedman, 1951, pp.91–92

[185] M. Friedman, 1953, p.134

[186] Ibid., pp.135–156

[187] L. Ebenstein, 2007, pp.135–145

[188] Quoted in Burgin, 2012, p.155

[189] See, for example, Van Horn, 2009

[190] M. Friedman, 1962/2002, p.25

[191] Ibid., p.34

[192] M. Friedman, Ibid., p.2

[193] See Ingham, 2015, pp.282–308 for some historical background

[194] Dempsey, 2012, pp.1155–1156
[195] M. Friedman, 1962/2002, p.29
[196] Cushman, 1972
[197] Simons, 1948, p.43
[198] Van Horn, 2009, pp.215, 219
[199] M. Friedman & S. Kuznets, 1945
[200] M. Friedman & R. Friedman, 1980, pp.213–218
[201] M. Friedman, 1962/2002, pp.85–107
[202] M. Friedman, in Sole, 1955, pp.
[203] See Ingham, 2015 for the historic battle over parochial schools
[204] M. Friedman & R. Friedman, 1980, p.153; further on Mann in my next chapter
[205] Ibid., p.166; the next chapter will present the actual results of their experiment
[206] M. Friedman & R. Friedman, 1980, pp.128–149
[207] Ibid., p.132
[208] M. Friedman, 1962/2002, pp.119–136, p.133
[209] Sumner 1887/1992, pp.234–236
[210] Reason Magazine, October 2005
[211] Nozick, 1974, p.ix
[212] Ibid.
[213] Nozick, ibid., p.214
[214] Ibid., p.226
[215] Ibid, pp.169–172, 265–268
[216] Locke, 1689/1965, pp.133–146, section 27t chapter, p.134
[217] Nozick, 1974, p.163

## Chapter 2,Con:

[218] Saez & Zucman, 2015; also, Center for Budget & Policy Priorities; further below; note that all such income and other statistics are only best estimates
[219] Krueger, 2016
[220] See Freeland, 2012, pp.242–275
[221] Mayer, 2o16
[222] See, for example, Hacker & Pierson, 2010
[223] Stiglitz, 2002; Blyth, 2013; Piketty, 2014; Freeland, 2012
[224] Quoted in McGerr, 2003, p.98
[225] Piketty, 2014, pp.493–514, p.493
[226] Piketty, ibid.
[227] I hope to publish more about the real meaning science in my next book
[228] Bureau of Justice Statistics
[229] Gottschalk, 2015, pp.10–14; Waquant, 2009
[230] LIS Cross-National Data Center
[231] Ibid., cf., also, Piketty, 2014; Grusky & Kricheli-Katz eds, 2012; Gordon, 2016, pp.605–652; Sachs, 2012; Stiglitz, 2012
[232] Source, Stanford University Center on Poverty and Inequality
[233] See, for example, Deaton, 2013, pp.9–10, and throughout this noted economist's book
[234] Quoted in Ellis, 1993, p.47
[235] Alesina, Glaeser, & Sacerdote, 2001

[236] Sources, 2012 U.S. Census & 2014 Bureau of Labor Statistics

[237] See, for example, Brennan, 1961, pp.214–223

[238] See Gould, 1981 for an important critique and history of similar misuse; Murray, 1994; Kaus, 1986

[239] Aizer, Eli, Ferrie, & Lleras, 2014; Handler & Hasenfeld, 2007; Schram, 2000

[240] See, Basu, et al., 2016, for negative health effects; Edsall, 1984, pp.227–226; Krugman, 2007, pp.57–78, p.178; A. Hacker, 1997, pp.175–178; Hoyner, 1995; Banerjee, 2014

[241] Jowett & O'Donnell, 2012; Koob, 2015; Center for Effective Government;Federal Reserve Bank of St. Louis; Bureau of Labor Statistics

[242] Quoted in Freeland, 2012, p.241

[243] Haidt, 2012, pp.350–356

[244] Freeman & Pontusson, in Grusky & Kricheli-Katz, 2012, pp.63–112

[245] Szántó, 2007, p.xii

[246] See, for example, Danner in Szántó, 2007, pp.16–36

[247] Smith, 1776/1937, Book 5, Ch. 2, p.808

[248] Smith, ibid., Book 1, chapter 10, pp.140–143

[249] Ibid., Book 1, Chapter 8, p.81

[250] Ibid., Book 1, chapter 8, pp.79–82

[251] Ibid., Book 1, Chapter 8, pp.85–86

[252] Quoted in Muller, 1993, p.63; for Smith's influence on Madison and the other founders, cf., Fleischacker, 2002 and 2003

[253] Kindleberger, 2000

[254] See Mallaby, 2016; Tuccille, 2002

[255] Attributed to Thatcher by Newt Gingrich and others

[256] Bourdieu, 1998, p.30

[257] Ingham, 2015; Smith, 1776/1937, Book 1, Chapter 1, pp.11–12

[258] Hayek, 1976, Volume 2, p.74

[259] Stern, quoted in Pole, 1978, p.328

[260] See Hacker & Pierson, 2010 for further examples

[261] J. Adams, 1780/2008, vol.10, p.510

[262] Jefferson, 1789/1907, vol.7, p.300

[263] Washington, 1796/2012

[264] Bailyn, 1967, pp.281–284; Viroli, 2002

[265] Plato, 1963, p.785 (*Republic* VIII, 556e)

[266] Ingham, 2016

[267] Plato, 1961, *Republic*, Bk. VIII, 566, p.794

[268] Aristotle, 1985, *Politics,* Bk. VI, pp.2095–2096, 1320a–b

[269] Aristotle, 1941, pp.1220–1221 (*Politics*, Bk. IV, Ch. II, 1295)

[270] Plato, ibid., p.663 (Bk. IV, 421a–d

[271] Cappon, ed., 1959, vol.II, pp.350–438

[272] J. Adams, Taylor ed., vol.4, 1776/1980, pp.211–213

[273] Aristotle, ibid., Bk. II, 1253c1–12;Glassman, 2000

[274] Machiavelli, 1998, pp.79, 142, 244, 255; cf. also, Ingham, 1989 and 2015

[275] Ingham, 2015, references on p.328

[276] Harrington, ed. Pocock, 1992/1656, p.57

[277] Ibid., p.20

[278] Sidney, ed. West, 1698/1996, p.352

[279] Wood, 1972, and my works cited in the previous note

[280] Banning, 1994, pp.51–69

[281] Trenchard & Gordon, ed. Hamowy, 1995, vol. I, p.263

[282] Ibid., vol. II, p.614

[283] See the section on values, below, & Ingham, 2016

[284] He wrote some similar things in his *Life of* Lycurgus; cf. also, De St. Croix, 1981; G. Fabre, 1981; Finley, 1981

[285] Macneven, 1803

[286] Ingham, 2015, 130–168; Grab, 2003, pp.114–118; Fremont-Barnes, 2001, pp.84–89

[287] Quoted in Ingham, ibid., p.142

[288] Jefferson, 1823/1995, Smith ed., vol.III, pp.1862–1866

[289] Tocqueville, 1835/1980, vol., I, p. 201

[290] Polybius, *Histories*, VI, Bk,1, 6

[291] Tocqueville,1835/2003, II, Part B, Bk.3

[292] Tocqueville, ibid., vol. II, Ch.21; cf. also, Tocqueville, 1856/1955

[293] Ibid., vol.II, Ch. 10, p.531

[294] Tocqueville, 1837/1997, p.26

[295] See Ryan, 1994, pp.181–204 for examples and complexities

[296] Spinoza, 1958, p.359

[297] Spinoza, 1951, pp.226–236; 385–387

[298] Acemoglu & Robinson, 2012

[299] Ibid., pp.70–79

[300] Ibid., p.74

[301] Ibid., pp.152–158

[302] Ibid., p.153

[303] For a well-written short history, cf., Irany, 2013

[304] Acemoglu & Robinson, 2012, p.156

[305] Madison, 1999, pp.92–93

[306] Yates in Farrand, ed.,2016, vol.1, pp.421–422; compare, Madison, ibid., pp.110–111

[307] Jefferson, 1953, vol.8, ed. By Boyd, pp.681–682

[308] Jefferson, September 10, 1814/1999, pp.136–142

[309] Madison, 1999/1787, pp.160–167

[310] Ibid., p.162

[311] Webster, 1787/1998, eds., Sheehan & McDowell, p.400, emphasis in original

[312] Abigail Adams to Isaac Smith, Jr. April 20, 1771, in Butterfield, et al., eds., 1963, vol.1, pp.76–77

[313] R. Jones, 1992; Elkins & McKitrick, 1993, pp.272–276

[314] Kindleberger, 2000

[315] Madison, 1999, pp.480–490

[316] Quoted in, Elkins & McKitrick, 1993, p.243

[317] Banning, 1995, pp.352–365

[318] Madison in, ibid., p.356

[319] Wilentz, 2005, p.50

[320] Wilentz, 2016, pp.3–30

321 Hamilton, 2001, ed. Freeman, pp.176–182, p.176
322 See, for example, Acemoglu & Robinson, 2012; Brown, 2015
323 Ibid., p.178, emphasis in original
324 Ibid., pp.647–734
325 Ibid., pp.151–166; Farrand,1787/1911, vol. I, pp.424–432
326 Fatovic, 2015, pp.87, 92, 93, 112–116, 118–120
327 Holt, 1999, pp.1–20
328 Holzer & Garfinkle, 2015, p.75
329 Wilentz, 2016, p.41
330 Lincoln, 1858/1989, Fehrenbacher, ed., p.512
331 Pipes, 2000, p.35
332 Madison, 1792/1999, pp.515–517, p.515, emphasis in original
333 Locke, 1683/1965, p.146
334 Ibid., p.132
335 Lincoln, 1854/1989, pp.327–333
336 Ibid., p.449
337 See Morgan, 1975 for examples of pro-slavery arguments
338 Burt, 2013, p.84
339 Lincoln, ibid., p.585
340 Ingham, 2015, pp.1–22
341 Burt, ibid., p.177
342 Quoted in Hofstadter, 1955, p.47
343 Neely, Jr., 1995, pp.137–142
344 Lincoln, 1859/1967, ed. Current, pp.125–138
345 Quoted in, Hofstadter, 1960, p.81
346 Howe, 2009, p.126
347 Wilentz, 2016
348 Summers, 2014, p.154
349 Woodward, 1974, especially, pp.67–109
350 Frankfurt Institute, trans., Viertel, 1972, pp.169–181
351 Ibid., p.170
352 Summers, 2014,pp.179–193; Beatty, 2007, pp.232–268.
353 See, for example, Montgomery, 1983, pp.90–100; Dubofsky, 1975
354 Parrington, 1930, vol.3, p.23
355 Quoted in, Boas, 1993, p.35
356 Quoted in Hofstadter, 1960, p.182
357 Barnum, et al., 1888, p.56
358 Hofstadter, 1960, p.164
359 Beatty, 2007, p.195
360 P. Smith, 1984, pp.614–660; Trachtenberg, 1982, pp.76–96; Beatty, 2007
361 Vol. 148, p.391
362 Quoted in Hofstadter, ibid., p.168
363 Hofstadter, 1955, p.10
364 Ibid., p.41
365 See, for example, Sternhell, 1994, pp.9–14, 46, 105–118;Paxton, 2005
366 Fischer, 2009, in Mirowski & Plehwe, eds., pp.305–346
367 Sumner,1871–1909/1992, ed. by, Bannister.

[368] Quoted in, Hofstadter, 1955, p.41
[369] Sumner, 1883/1992, pp.206–212
[370] Ibid., p.51
[371] Quoted in Hofstadter, 1955, p.45
[372] Sumner, 1888/1992, pp.137–148, p.146
[373] Ibid., p.147
[374] Sumner, 1883/1992, pp.201–222
[375] William Gladden, quoted in McGerr, 2003, p.115
[376] Ibid., 1902/1992, pp.149–155
[377] King, 1915, pp. 219–231
[378] Ibid., p.233
[379] Ibid., p.249
[380] Quoted in Thomas, 1998; see also, Abramovitz, 2006
[381] Ibid., pp.250–251
[382] Hofstadter, 1955, pp.161–169
[383] McGeer, 2005, pp.97, 115–117
[384] Wilson, 1918, Section 1285, p.661
[385] Quoted in, Urofsky, 1981, p.70
[386] Quoted in, ibid., p.70
[387] Qhoted in ibid., p.73
[388] Quoted in ibid., p.72
[389] Quoted in, Brookhiser, 2006, p.190
[390] Hamilton, June 18, 1787/2001, p.156
[391] Frankfurter, 1962, pp.203–228
[392] Ibid., pp.305–313, p.306
[393] Croly, 1909/1965, p.205; he was not so progressive as to include women here
[394] Ibid., p.104
[395] Price, 1974, pp.1663–1678, p.1663
[396] Croly, 1909/1965, p.203
[397] Ibid., p.206
[398] Quoted in, Sandel, 1996, p.217
[399] Goodwin, 2013, pp.12, 157–156, 280–282, 339
[400] Quoted in Rockefeller, 1991, p.438
[401] Dewey, 1908, p.488
[402] Dewey, 1935/1987, vol.11, p.291
[403] Dewey, 1930, p.166
[404] Dewey, 1908, pp.435–509
[405] Klein, 2007
[406] Dewey, 1908, p.481
[407] Ibid., pp.35–50
[408] Ingham, 2015
[409] Dewey, 1927, p.24
[410] Twain, 1905
[411] Twain, 1927, p.67
[412] Dewey, 1916/2007, pp.203–212
[413] Dewey 1912–1914/1985, Vol.7, pp.79–104
[414] Dewey, 1916/2007, pp.249–260

[415] R. Rorty, 1998, p.6
[416] Ibid., p.30
[417] Ibid., p.43
[418] Croly, 1909/1965, p.23
[419] Merton, 1966
[420] R. Rorty, 1998, p.83
[421] For Britain, cf., A. Glyn & D. Milliband, 1994; B. Barry, 2005
[422] R. Rorty, 1998, p.87; for Rorty and Orwell on truth, cf., Conant, 2000
[423] For Hayek and Orwell, cf., Epstein, 2005, pp.58–62
[424] R. Rorty, pp.88–89
[425] Lipset & Raab, 1970, especially pp.428–483
[426] Madison, 1787/1999, p.165
[427] Signer, 2009, p.31; Hamilton, 1787/1979, p.173 (emphasis added).
[428] Herman, 2005, pp.112–123, p.113, p.120; cf., also, Szántó, 2007
[429] See Ingham, 2015 for much more on this modern form of control
[430] Stiglitz, 2012
[431] Ibid., p.xiii
[432] Quoted in Stiglitz, ibid., p.137
[433] Dürrenmatt, 1956/1990, p.13
[434] On the latter, cf., Postman, 1986
[435] Kontos, 1979, pp.153–165
[436] Ibid., p.157
[437] Paxton, 2004, p.207
[438] Cassels, 1975, pp.119–122
[439] Ibid., p.160
[440] Stiglitz, 2011
[441] Madison, 1788/1999, pp.281–285
[442] Niebuhr, 1947/1960, p.28
[443] Ibid., 1948/1960, p.214
[444] Niebuhr, 1944, pp.86–118, p.109
[445] Olson, 1970, pp.187–188, 218–226, 377
[446] Galbraith, 1952/2012; Galbraith, 1983
[447] Galbraith, 1983, pp. 5–6, 24–37
[448] Niebuhr, 1960, pp.223–225
[449] Quoted in Milgate & Stimson, 1991, p.54
[450] Stiglitz, 2012, p.157
[451] Ibid., pp.52–82
[452] See the award winning documentary, *Inside Job* for many details; also, Morgenson & Rosner, 2011; Hacker & Pierson, 2016
[453] Milgate & Stimson, 1991, pp.104–124
[454] Smith, 1776/1937, Book 1, Ch. 10, part 2, p.128
[455] Cooper,1838/2000. pp.430–434
[456] Ibid., p.430
[457] Ibid., pp.457–458
[458] Acemoglu & Robinson, 2012, p.80
[459] Stiglitz, 2012, p.180
[460] Friedman, 2002, p.xiv

461 Quoted in Klein, 2007, p.8
462 Acemoglu & Robinson, ibid., p.38
463 Mirowski & Plehwe, 2009, pp.139–180
464 Klein, ibid., p.104
465 Ravitch, 2013
466 Ibid., p.6
467 See, Dubose & Bernstein, 2006
468 Polybius, 1962, vol.1, bk. 9
469 Kant, 1795/1983, pp.107–143
470 Montesquieu, 1748/1975, p.316–317
471 Message to Congress on Curbing Monopolies, April 29, 1938
472 Schwartz, 2006, p.3
473 Chang, 2008, pp.170–171 and references
474 Suarez-Villa, 2015, p.79
475 J. Mayer, 2016, p.56
476 Ibid., p.150
477 Ibid., p.290
478 Suarez-Villa, 2015, pp.277–280
479 Ibid., pp.31–35, 296–297
480 Gore, 2007
481 Klein, 2007, p.399
482 Brown, 2015, pp.142–150
483 Acemoglu & Robinson, 2012, p.444
484 Quoted in Brown, 2015, p.143
485 See Yack, 1993, for an excellent study
486 Aristotle, 1985, *Nicomachean Ethics,* vol.2, bks.8–10, pp.1825–1867
487 Quoted in Cooper, 1980, p.305
488 Taylor, 1986, pp.187–210
489 Ibid., pp. 211–229
490 Ibid., p.215
491 I am following Bernard Yack, ibid., pp.33–43; contrast Cooper, 1980, pp.301–340
492 Yack, ibid., p.37n33
493 Price, 1991, p.104
494 Aristotle, *Rhetoric*, 1985, vol. II, 4, p.2200, 1381a–1381b
495 Aristotle, *Nicomachean Ethics*, 1984, vol. II, bk. VIII, p.1825, 1155a–1155b
496 Kraut, 1989, pp.78–154
497 Oliner, et al., eds., 1992
498 Sandel, 2009, p.75
499 Kant, 1785/2012,
500 Nozick, 1974, pp.30–31
501 See A. Wood, 1999 for an excellent analysis
502 Locke, 1689/1965, Section 34, p.137; sections 124–131, pp.184–186
503 Sandel, 2009, p.104
504 Ibid., p.131
505 For Britain, cf. Rose, 1990, pp.115–125; for the United States, cf., Tone, 1997.
506 Alexander, 2017

[507] Dewey, 1908/1983, p.481

[508] MacIntyre, 1984, especially pp.181–225

[509] Sandel, 2012, p.28

[510] Stout, 1988, pp.266–292; MacIntyre, 1998

[511] See Smith, 1948 for a good collection of his writings on this subject

[512] MacIntyre, 1984, p.23

[513] Kant, 1785/1998, 4:43 –435, p.42 (emphasis in original)

[514] See Brown, 2015, pp.9–111

[515] For Jefferson, cf., Wills, 1978, pp.167–255

[516] Madison, 1815/1999, p.717

[517] Mann, 1848/1965, pp.119–131

[518] Dewey, 1938, p.61

[519] See the essays in Euben, Wallach & Ober, eds., 1994

[520] See Bellah, Sullivan, & Tipton, eds, 1985; Nussbaum, 2013; Ingham, 2016

[521] Nussbaum, 2010; Brown, 2015, pp.175–200

[522] Fleischacker, 1999

[523] Rothchild, 1992; Fleischacker, ibid., pp.161–183

[524] Quoted in ibid., p.164

[525] Ibid., p.166

[526] Kant, 1784/1992, pp.54–60; cf., the important collection, ed. by Schmidt, 1996

[527] Hinchman, 1996, p.500

[528] See Herman, 1993

[529] Kant, 1790/1951, bk. 2, sec.40, pp.135–138

[530] Ibid., p.136 (emphasis in original; the influence of Smith here is clear)

[531] Ibid., sec. 43, p.146

[532] Kant, 1793/1992, pp.61–92; Fleischacker, ibid., pp.193–196

[533] Dewey, 1930, p.163

[534] Rawls, 2003, pp.176–180; Nussbaum & Sen, 1993

[535] Ibid., p.237 (emphasis in original)

[536] Sen, 1987, 2000, 2011; Nussbaum, 2001; Crocker & Robeyns, 2010

[537] Crocker & Robeyns, 2010, p.64

[538] Westbrook, 1991, p.166

[539] King, 2012, pp.171–173

# Bibliography

Abramovitz, Mimi. "Welfare Reform in the United States: gender, race and class," *Critical Social Policy*, 26, no.2 (May, 2006), 336–354.

Acemoglu, Baron and James A. Robinson. *Why Nations Fail: The Origins of Power, Prosperity, and Poverty,* New York: Crown Business, 2012.

Adams, Henry. *The Education of Henry Adams*, New York: Modern Library, 1931.

Adams, John. *The Political Writings of John Adams*, George W. Carey, ed., Washington, D.C.: Regnery Publishing, 2000.

Aizer, Anna, Shari Eli, Joseph Ferrie, Adriana Lleras-Mune. "The Long Term Impact of Cash Transfers to Poor Families," *National Bureau of Economic Research Papers*, May, 2014.

Aldrich, John H. *Why Parties? The Origin and Transformation of Party Politics in the United States*, Chicago: University of Chicago Press, 1995

Alexander, Brian. *Glass House: The 1% Economy and the Shattering of the All-American Town,* New York: MacMillan, 2017.

Appiah, Kwame Anthony. *Experiments in Ethics*, Cambridge, MA: Harvard University Press, 2008.

Aristotle. Richard McKeon, (ed.). New York: Random House, 1941.

Aristotle. Jonathan Barnes, (ed.). *The Complete Works of* Aristotle, 2, Princeton: Princeton University Press, 1985.

Atkinson, A.B., *The Economic Consequences of Rolling Back the Welfare State*, Cambridge: MIT Press, 1999.

Backhouse, Roger E. and Bradley W. Bateman, (eds.). *The Cambridge Companion to Keynes*, Cambridge, U.K., 2006.

Bader, Ralf and John Meadowcraft, (eds.). *The Cambridge Companion to Nozick's Anarchy, State, and Utopia*, Cambridge, U.K.: Cambridge University Press, 2011.

Bailyn, Bernard. *The Ideological Origins of the American revolution*, Cambridge, MA: Harvard University Press, 1967.

Balleisen, Edward J. and David A. Moss, (eds.). *Government and Markets: Toward a New Theory of Regulation*, Cambridge: Cambridge University Press, 2010.

Banaji, Mahzarin and Anthony Greenwald. *Blindspot: Hidden Biases of Good People*, New York: Delacorte, 2013.

Banning, Lance. *The Jeffersonian Persuasion: Evolution of a Party Ideology*, Ithaca: Cornell University Press, 1994.

———. *The Sacred Fire of Liberty: James Madison & the Founding of the Federal Republic*, Ithaca: Cornell University Press, 1995.

———. *Jefferson & Madison: Three Conversations from the Founding*, Madison, Wisconsin: Madison House, 1995.

Barry, Brian. "Review of *Anarchy, State, and Utopia* by Robert Nozick, *Political Theory*, 3 (3), (1975), 331–336.

———. *Why Social Justice Matter*, Cambridge, UK: Polity, 2005.

Barry, Norman. "The Tradition of Spontaneous Order," *Literature and Liberty*, 5 (2), (1982), Arlington, Va: Institute for humane Studies, 7–58.

———. "Hayek on Liberty," In Z. Pelczynski & John Gray (eds.). *Conceptions of Liberty in Political Philosophy*, 263–288, New York: St. Martin's Press, 1984.

Basu, S, D. Rothkopf, M. Glymour, I. Kawachi. "Health Behaviors, Mental Health, and Health Care Utilization Among Single Mothers after Welfare Reform in the 1990s," *American Journal of Epidemiology*, 183(6), (March 2016), 531–538.

Bavel, Bas Van. *The Invisible Hand? How Market Economies Have Emerged and Declined Since A.D. 500*, Oxford: Oxford University Press, 2016.

Beatty, Jack. *Age of Betrayal: the Triumph of Money in America, 1865–1900*, New York: Alfred Knopf, 2007.

Bellah, Robert N., et al. *Habits of the Heart: Individualism and Commitment in American Life*, Berkeley: University of California Press, 1985.

Bentham, Jeremy. *Jeremy Bentham's Writings on Economics*, 3 Vols. W. Stark (ed.), London: George Allen & Unwin, 1952–1954.

Berlin, Isaiah. "Two Concepts of Freedom," In Isaiah Berlin, *Liberty*, Henry Hardy, (ed.) Oxford: Oxford University Press, 2002.

Berofsky, Bernard. *Liberation From Self: A Theory of Personal Autonomy*, Cambridge, U.K.: Cambridge University Press, 1995.

Binswanger, Harry. *The Ayn Rand Lexicon*, New York: New American Library, 1986.

Bird, Colin. *The Myth of Liberal Individualism*, Cambridge: Cambridge University Press, 2007.

Blasé, Joseph R., Richard B. Freeman, Douglas L. Kruse. *The Citizen's Share: Putting Ownership Back into Democracy*, New Haven: Yale University Press, 2013.

Boas, David. *The Libertarian Mind: a Manifesto for Freedom*, New York: Simon & Schuster, 1997.

———. *Libertarianism: A Primer*, New York: Free Press, 1998.

———. *The Libertarian Reader: Classic & Contemporary Writings from Lao-Tzu to Milton Friedman*, New York: Simon & Schuster, 1999.

Boas, Tayor and Jordoan Gans-Morse. "Neoliberalism: from Liberal Philosophy to Anti-Liberal Slogan," *Studies in Comparative International Development*, 44(2) (2009), 137–161.

Boorstein, Daniel. *The Lost World of Thomas Jefferson*, Chicago: University of Chicago Press, 1993.

Bouillon, Hardy. *Libertarians and Liberalism: Essays in Honour of Gerard Radnitzky*, Aldershot, Hants, U.K.: Avebury, 1996.

Bourdieu, Pierre. *Acts of Resistance: Against the Tyranny of the Market*, New York: Free Press, 1998.

Brandeis, Louis B. Ervin Pollack, (ed.). *The Brandeis Reader*, New York: Oceana Press, 1956

———, *Other People's Money and How te Bankers Use It*, New York: Harper Books, 1967.

Brennan, Jason. *Libertarianism: What Everyone Needs to Know*, New York: Oxford University Press, 2012.

Brittan, Samuel. "The Economic Contradictions of Democracy Revisited," *Business and Economics Review*, 3 (Summer 1988), 37–44.

Brown, Henry Phelps. *Egalitarianism and the Generation of Inequality*, Oxford: Oxford University Press, 1997.

Brown, Wendy. *Undoing the Demos: Neoliberalism's Stealth Revolution*, New York: Zone Books, 2015.

Burgin, Angus. *The Great Persuasion: Reinventing Markets since the Depression*, Cambridge: Harvard University Press, 2012.

Burt, John. *Lincoln's Tragic Pragmatism: Lincoln, Douglas and the Moral Context*, Cambridge, MA: Harvard University Press, 2013.

Butterfield, L.H., W.D. Garrett, and M. Sprague (eds.). *Adams Family Correspondence*, Cambridge: Harvard University Press, 1963.

Caldwell, Bruce. *Hayek's Challenge: an Intellectual Biography of Friedrich A. Hayek*, Chicago: University of Chicago Press, 2005.

Cappon, Lester J. (ed.). *The Adams-Jefferson Letters*, 2 vols., Chappel Hill, NC: University of North Carolina Press, 1959.

Carey, George W. *Freedom and Virtue: the Conservative/Libertarian Debate*, Wilmington: Intercollegiate Studies Institute, 1998.

Cassells, Alan. *Fascism*, Arlington Heights, IL: Harlan Davidson, 1975.

Chang, Ha-Joon. *Bad Samaritans: the Myth of Free Trade and the Secret History of Capitalism*, New York: Bloomsbury, 2008.

Clayton, Matthew and Andrew Williams (eds.). *The Ideal of Equality*, London: MacMillan, 2002.

Coburn, David. "Income Inequality, Social Cohesion and Health Status of Populations: the Role of Neo-Liberalism," *Social Science and Medicine*, 51 (1) (2000), 35–46.

———. "Beyond the Income Inequality Hypothesis: Globalization, Neoliberalism, and Health Inequalities," *Social Science and Medicine*, 58 (1), (2004), 41–56.

Cohen, G.A. *Self-Ownership, Freedom, and Equality*, Cambridge, U.K.: Cambridge University Press, 1995.

Cohen, Nancy. *The Reconstruction of American Liberalism, 1865–1914*, Chapel Hill, NC: University of North Carolina Press, 2002.

Conant, James. "Rorty and Orwell on Truth," In A. Gleason, J. Goldsmith, and M.C. Nussbaum, eds., *On Nineteen Eighty-Four*, (2005) 86–111.

Cooper, James Fenimore. *The American Democrat,* Washington, D.C.: Regnery Press, 2000.

Cooper, John M. "Ariistotle on Friendship," In Amélie Rorty( ed.). *Essays on Aristotle's Ethics,* 301–340, Berkeley: University of California Press, 1980.

Crèvecoeur, J. Hector St. John de. *Letters from an American Farmer and Other Essays*, D.D. Moore (ed.), Cambridge: Harvard University Press, 2013.

Crocker, David and Ingrid Robyns. "Capability and Agency," In Christopher W. Morris, ed., *Amartya Sen*, 60–90, Cambridge: Cambridge University Press, 2010.

Croly, Herbert. *The Promise of American Life* (ed.). Arthur Schlesinger, Jr., Cambridge: Harvard University Press, 1965.

Cushman, Barry. *Rethinking the New Deal: the Structure of a Constitutional Revolution*, New York: Oxford University Press, 1998.

Cushman, Robert E. *The Independent Regulatory Commissions*, New York: Octagon, 1972.

Dazell, Robert F. *The Good Rich and What They Cost Us*, New Haven: Yale University Press, 2013.

Danner, Mark. "Words in Time of War: On Rhetoric, Truth, and Power," In András Szántó (ed.). *What Orwell Didn't Know: Propaganda and the New Face of American Politics*, 16–36, New York: Public Affairs, 2007.

Dawley, Alan. *Struggles for Justice: Social Responsibility and the Liberal State*, Cambridge: Harvard University Press, 1991.

Deaton, Angus. *The Great Escape: Health, Wealth, and the Origins of Inequality*, Princeton: Princeton University Press, 2013.

Dempsey, Paul S. "The Rise and Fall of the Interstate Commerce Commission: the Tortuous Path from Regulation to Deregulation of America's Infrastructure," *Marquette Law Review*, 95 (4) (2012), 1151–1189.

Desmond, Matthew. *Evicted: Poverty and Profit in the American City*, New York: Crown Publishers, 2016.

Dewey, John. *The Public and Its Problems*, Chicago: Swallow Press, 1954.

———. *Individualism Old and New*, New York: G.P. Putnam's Sons, 1962.

———. *Freedom and Culture*, New York: G.P. Putnam's Sons, 1963.

———. *Liberalism and Social Action*, G.P. Putnam's Sons, 1963.

———. *Ethics: the Middle Works of John Dewey,* 5, Carbondale: Southern Illinois University, 1983.

———. *Essays on Philosophy and Psychology: the Middle Works of John Dewey*, 7, Carbondale: Southern Illinois University, 1985

Diamond, Peter A., ed. *Issues in Privatizing Social Security: Report of* an *Expert Panel of the Academy of Social Insurance*, Cambridge: MIT Press, 1999.

Dionne, Jr., E.J. *Why the Right Went Wrong: Conservatism from Goldwater to the Teaparty and Beyond*, New York: Simon and Schuster, 2016.

Dobb, Maurice. *Theories of Value and Distribution Since Adam Smith: Ideology and Economic Theory*, Cambridge: Cambridge University Press, 1973.

Douglas, Mary. *Natural Symbols: Explorations in Cosmology*, London: Routledge, 1996.

Drennan, Matthew. *Income Inequality: Why it Matters and Why Most Economists Didn't Notice,* New Haven: Yale University Press, 2015.

Dubose, Lou and Jake Bernstein. *Vice: Dick Cheney and the Hijacking of the American Presidency*, London: Pimlico, 2006.

Duménil, Gérard and Dominique Lévy. *The Crisis of Neoliberalism*, Cambridge: Harvard University Press, 2011.

Duncan, Greg, Tibor Machan, and Martha Nussbaum. *Libertarianism: For and Against*, Lanham, Md: Rowan & Littlefield, 2005.

Dürrenmatt, Friedrich. *The Visit: A Tragi-Comedy*, Translated by Patrick Bowles, New York: Grove Weidenfeld, 1962.

Dworkin, Ronald. *Is Democracy Possible Here? Principles for a New Political Debate*, Princeton: Princeton University Press, 2006

———. *Justice for Hedgehogs*, Cambridge: Harvard University Press, 2011.

Ebenstein, Alan. *Friedrich Hayek: A Biography*, New York: MacMillan, 2001.

———. *Hayek's Journey: The Mind of Friedrich Hayek*, New York: MacMillan, 2003.

Edsall, Thomas B. *The New Politics of Inequality*, New York: W.W. Norton, 1984.

Elkins, Stanley and Eric McKitrick. *The Age of Federalism: The Early American Republic, 1788–1800*, New York: Oxford University Press, 1993.

Ellis, Joseph. *Founding Brothers: the Revolutionary Generation*, New York: Alfred Knopf, 2000.

———, *First Family: John and Abigail Adams*, New York: Alfred Knopf, 2010.

Ellis, Richard J. *American Political Cultures*, New York: Oxford University Press, 1993.

Elshtain, Jean Bethka. *Democracy on Trial*, New York: Basic Books, 1995.

Englehardt, H.T. *The Foundations of Bioethics*, New York: Oxford University Press, 1986.

Epstein, David F. *The Political Theory of the Federalist*, Chicago: University of Chicago Press, 1984.

Epstein, Richard. *Mortal Peril: Our Inalienable Right to Health Care?*, Reading, MA: Addison Wesley, 1997.

Euben, J.P., J.R. Wallach, Josiah Ober (eds.). *Athenian Political Thought and the Reconstruction of American Democracy*, Ithaca, N.Y.: Cornell University Press, 1994.

Falk, Richard. *Predatory Globalization: A Critique*, Cambridge, U.K.: Polity Press, 1999.

Farber, Daniel, *Lincoln's Constitution*, Chicago: University of Chicago Press, 2003.

Farmer, Paul. *Pathologies of Power: Health, Human Rights, and the New War on the Poor*, Berkeley: University of California Press, 2003.

Farrand, Max. *Records of the Federal Convention of 1787*, 3 Vols. New Haven: Yale University Press, 1987.

Fatovic, Clement. *America's Founding and the Struggle Over Inequality*, Lawrence, KAN: University of Kansas Press, 2015.

Feser, Edward, ed. *The Cambridge Companion to Hayek*, Cambridge: Cambridge University Press, 2006.

Ferejohn, John. "Rising Inequality and American Politics," In D.B. Grusky and T. Kricholi-Katz, eds. *The New Gilded Age*, Stanford: Stanford University Press, (2012), 115–130.

Filler, Louis, ed., *Horace Mann on the Crisis in American Education*, Yellow Springs, Ohio: Antioch Press, 1965.

Fink, Leon. *Progressive Intellectuals and the Dilemmas of Democratic Commitment*, Cambridge: Harvard University Press, 1997.

Finn, Daniel K. *The Moral Ecology of Markets: Assessing Claims about Markets and Justice*, Cambridge: Cambridge University Press, 2006.

Flanagan, Owen and Amélie O. Rorty, eds. *Identity, Character, and Morality: Essays in Moral Psychology,* Cambridge: MIT Press, 1993.

Fleischacker, Samuel. *A Third Concept of Liberty: Judgment and Freedom in Kant and Adam Smith*, Princeton: Princeton University Press, 1999.

Fogel, Robert W. *The Fourth Great Awakening and the Future of Egalitarianism*, Chicago: University of Chicago Press, 2000.

Foucault, Michel. *Biopolitics: Lectures at the Collège de France, 1978–1979*, New York Picador, 2008.

Frank, Robert H. *Falling Behind: How Rising Inequality Harms the Middle Class*, Berkeley: University of California Press, 2007.

Frankfurter, Felix. edited by E. F. Prichard, Jr. and Archibald MacLeish, *Law and Politics*, New York: Harcourt, Brace, 1962.

Freeland, Chrystia. *Plutocrats: the Rise of the New Global Super-Rich and the Fall of Everyone Else*, New York: Penguin Press, 2012.

Friedman, Milton and Simon Kuznets. *Income from Independent Professional Practice*, New York: National Bureau of Economic Research, 1945.

———. *Essays in Positive Economics*, Chicago: University of Chicago Press, 1953.

———. "The Role of Government in Education," In Robert A. Solo, ed., *Economics and the Public Interest*, New Brunswik, NJ: Rutgers University Press, (1955), 123–144.

———. *Capitalism and Freedom,* Fortieth Anniversary Edition, Chicago: University of Chicago Press, 2002.

——— and Anna J. Schwartz. *A Monetary History of the United States, 1867–1970*, Princeton, N.J.: Princeton University Press, 1963.

———. *Dollars and Deficits: Inflation, Monetary Policy, and the Balance of Payments*, Englewood Cliffs, N.J.: Prentice Hall, 1968.

———. *An Economist's Protest: Columns on Political Economy*, Glen Ridge, N.J.: Thomas Horton, 1972.

——— and Rose Friedman. *Free to Choose: A Personal Statement*, Orlando: Harcourt, 1990.

———. *On Economics: Selected Papers*, Chicago: Chicago University Press, 2007.

Gadamer, Hans-Georg. *Truth and Method*, New York: Crossroad, 1982.

Galbraith, John Kenneth. *The Anatomy of Power*, Boston: Houghton Mifflin, 1983.

———. *American Capitalism: the Concept of Countervailing Power*, New Brunswik, N.J.: Transactions, 1993.

———. *The Economics of Innocent Fraud: Truth for Our Time*, Boston: Houghton Mifflin, 2004.

Gamble, Andrew. "Hayek on Knowledge, Economics, and Society," In E. Feser (ed.), *Cambridge Companion to Hayek*, Cambridge: Cambridge University Press, (2006), 111–131.

Garson, Barbara. *Up the Down Escalator: How the 99% Live in the Great Recession*, New York: Random House, 2013.

Gaylin, Willard and Bruce Jennings. *The Perversion of Autonomy: Coercion and Constraints in a Liberal Society*, New York: Free Press, 1996.

Gillespie, Nick and Matt Welch. *The Declaration of Independents: How Lincoln's Politics Can Fix What's Wrong with America*, New York: BBS, 2011.

Glassman, Ronald M. *Caring Capitalism: A New Middle-Class Base for the Welfare State*, New York: MacMillan, 2000.

Gleason, Albert, Jack Goldsmith, and Martha Nussbaum, eds. *On Nineteen Eighty-Four: Orwell and Our Future*, Princeton: Princeton University Press, 2005.

Glyn, Andrew and David Milliband (eds.). *Paying for Inequality: the Economic Cost of Social Injustice*, London: Rivers Oram Press, 1994.

Gordon, Robert J. *The Rise and Fall of American Growth: the Unites States Standard of Living Since the Civil War*, Princeton: Princeton University Press, 2016.

Gore, Albert. *The Assault on Reason*, New York: Penguin Press, 2007.

Gottschalk, Marie. *Caught: The Prison State and the Lockdown of American Politics*, Princeton: Princeton University Press, 2015.

Gould, Stephen Jay. *The Mismeasure of Man*, New York: W.W. Norton, 1981.

Gray, John. *Hayek on Liberty*, third edition, London: Routledge, 1996.

Greenberg, Stanley B. *Middle Class Dreams: the Politics and Power of the New American Majority*, New York: Random House, 1995.

Greene, Joshua. *Moral Tribes: Emotion, Reason, and the Gap Between Them*, New York: Penguin, 2013.

Griffen, Emma. *Liberty's Dawn: a People's History of the Industrial Revolution*, New Haven: Yale University Press, 2013.

Gruber, Helmut. *Red Vienna: Experiment in Working-Class Culture, 1919–1934*, New York: Oxford University Press, 1991.

Grusky, David B. Tamar Kricholi-Katz (eds.). *The New Gilded Age: the Critical Inequality Debates of Our Time*, Stanford: Stanford University Press, 2012.

Gulick, Charles A. *Austria from Habsburg to Hitler*, Vol.1, Berkeley: University of California Press, 1948.

Hacker, Andrew. *Money: Who Has How Much and Why*, New York: Scribners, 1997.

Hacker, James and Paul Pierson. *American Amnesia: How the War on Government Led Us to Forget What Made America Prosper*, New York: Simon and Schuster, 2016.

———. *Winner-Take-All Politics: How Washington Made the Rich Richer—and Turned its Back on the Middle Class*, New York: Simon and Schuster, 2009.

Haidt, Jonathan. *The Righteous Mind: Why Good People are Divided by Politics and Religion*, New York: Vintage Books, 2013.

Halteman, James and Edd [sic.] Noell. *Reckoning with Markets: Moral Reflection in Economics*, New York: Oxford University Press, 2012.

Hamilton, Alexander. *Writings*, New York: Library of America, 2001.

Hamowy, Ronald, ed. *The Encyclopedia of Libertarianism*, Thousand Oaks, CA: Sage, 2008.

Handler, Joel F and Yeheskel Hasenfeld. *Blame Welfare, Ignore Poverty, and Inequality*, New York: Cambridge University Press, 2007.

Häring, Bernard. *Ethics of Manipulation: Issues in Medicine, Behavior Control, and Genetics*, New York: Seabury Press, 1975.

Harrington, James. *The Commonwealth of Oceana and A System of Politics*, Cambridge: Cambridge University Press, 1992.

Haslett, D.W. *Capitalism with Morality*, Oxford: Oxford University Press, 2002.

Haugren, David, Susan Musser, Vickey Kalambakal (eds.). *The Middle Class: Opposing Viewpoints*, Detroit, MI: Greenhaven Press, 2010.

Hayek, Friedrich. *Individualism and Economic Order*, Chicago: University of Chicago Press, 1948.

Hayek, Friedrich, A. (ed.). *Capitalism and the Historians*, Chicago: University of Chicago Press, 1954.

Hayek, Friedrich. *The Counter-Revolution of Science*, New York: Free Press, 1955.

———. *The Constitution of Liberty*, Chicago: University of Chicago Press, 1960.

―――. *Studies in Philosophy, Politics, and Economics*, Chicago: University of Chicago Press, 1967.

―――. *New Studies in Philosophy, Politics, Economics, and the History of Ideas*, London: Routledge, 1978.

―――. *Law, Legislation, Liberty: a New Statement of Liberal Principles of Justice and Political Economy*, 3 vols. Chicago: University of Chicago Press, 1973–1979.

―――. *The Road to Serfdom*, Chicago: University of Chicago Press, 1994

Heller, Anne C. *Ayn Rand and the World She Made*, New York: Random House, 2010.

Herman, Barbara. *The Practice of Moral Judgment*, Cambridge: Harvard University Press, 1993.

Herman, Edward S. "From Ingsoc and Newspeak to Amcap, Amerigood, and Marketspeak," In A. Gleason, J. Goldsmith, and M.C. Nussbaum, eds. *On Nineteen Eighty-Four*, 112–124, (2005).

Hetzel, Robert L. *The Great Recession: Market Failure or Political Failure?* Cambridge: Cambridge University Press, 2012.

Hild, Marc Lamont. *Nobody: Casualties of the American War on the Vulnerable, from Ferguson to Flint and Beyond*, New York: Atria Books, 2016.

Hindess, Barry. *Freedom, Equality, and the Market: Arguments on Social Policy*, London: Tavistock, 1987.

Hofrichter, Richard (ed.). *Health and Social Justice: Politics, Ideology, and Inequality in the Distribution of Disease: a Health Reader*, San Francisco: Jossey-Bass, 2003.

Hofstadter, Richard. *Social Darwinism and American Thought*, Boston: Beacon Press, 1955.

―――. *Anti-intellectualism in American Life*, New York: Alfred Knopf, 1963.

―――. *The Paranoid Style in American Politics and Other Essays*, New York: Random House, 1967.

Hollander, Samuel. *The Economics of Karl Marx: a Contemporary Analysis and Application*, Cambridge: Cambridge University Press, 2008.

Holmes, Stephen and Cass Sunstein. *The Cost of Rights: Why Liberty Depends on Taxes*, New York: W.W. Norton, 1999.

Holt, Michael F. *The Rise and Fall of the American Whig Party: Jacksonian Politics and the Onset of the Civil War*, New York: Oxford University Press, 1999.

Holzer, Harold and Norton Garfinkle. *A Just and Generous Nation: Abraham Lincoln and the Fight for American Opportunity*, New York: Basic Books, 2015.

Horn, Robert Van, P. Mirowski, and T.A. Stapleton (eds.). *Building Chicago Economics: New Perspectives on the History of America's Most Powerful Economics Program*,

Horton, John and Susan Mendes, eds. *After Virtue: Critical Perspectives on the Work of Alasdair MacIntyre*, Notre Dame, Ind.: Notre Dame University Press, 1994.

Howe, Daniel Walker. *Making of the American Self: Jonathan Edwards to Abraham Lincoln*, New York: Oxford University Press, 2009.

Humboldt, Wilhelm Von. *The Sphere and Duties of Government*, trans. Joseph Coulthard, Bristol, U.K.: Thoemmes Press, 1996.

Hunt, Louis and Peter McNamara, eds. *Liberalism, Conservatism, and Hayek's Idea of Spontaneous Order*, New York: MacMillan, 2007.

Huyssen, David. *Progressive Inequality: Rich and Poor in New York, 1890–1920*, Cambridge: Harvard University Press, 2014.

Ignatieff, Michael. *The Needs of Strangers*, New York: Picador, 1984.

———, *Human Rights: As Politics and Idolatry*, Princeton: Princeton University Press, 2001.

Ingham, George R. *Irish Rebel, American Patriot: William James Macneven, 1763–1841*, Amazon Books, 2015.

———, *Love of Having: Compulsive Buying, Spending, and Hoarding*, Amazon Books, 2016.

Isbister, John. *Capitalism and Justice: Envisioning Society and Fairness*, Bloomfield, CT: Kumarian Press, 2001.Ronald Hamowy (eds.), *The English Libertarian Heritage*, San Francisco: Fox & Wilkes, 1965.

Jefferson, Thomas. *Political Writings*, Joyce Appleby (ed.), Cambridge: Cambridge University Press, 1999.

Jones, Daniel Stedman. *Masters of the Universe: Hayek, Friedman, and the Birth of Neoliberal Politics*, Princeton: Princeton University Press, 2012.

Jones, Robert F. *The King of the Alley: William Duer, Politician, Entrepreneur and Speculator, 1766–1799*, Philadelphia: American Philosophical Society, 1992.

Jowett, Garth and Victoria O'Donnell. *Propaganda and Persuasion*, 5th ed., Los Angelas: Sage, 2012.

Kant, Immanuel. *Critique of Judgment*, New York: Hafner Publishing, 1968.

————. *Perpetual Peace and Other Essays*, Indianapolis: Hackett Publishing, 1983.

————. *Political Writings*, Hans Reiss, ed., Cambridge: Cambridge University Press, 1992.

————. *Groundwork of the Metaphysics of Morals*, ed. Mary Gregor, Cambridge: Cambridge University Press, 1998.

Kaus, Mickey. *The End of Equality*, New York: Basic Books, 1992.

Keats, John, *The Letters of John Keats*, edited by H.E. Rollins, vol.1, 193–194, Cambridge: Cambridge University Press, 1968.

Kelly, Mathew. *The Politics of Income Inequality in the United States*, Oxford: Oxford University Press, 2009.

Kett, Joseph F. *The Pursuit of Knowledge Under Difficulties: From Self-Improvement to Adult Education in America, 1750–1990*, Stanford: Stanford University Press, 1994.

Keynes, John Maynard. *Essays in Biography*, New York: W.W. Norton,1951.

————. *Essays in Persuasion*, New York: W.W. Norton, 1963.

————. *The General Theory of Employment, Interest, and Money*, New York: Harcourt, Brace, Jovanovich, 1964.

Kibbe, Matt. *Don't Hurt People and Don't Take Their Stuff: A Libertarian Manifesto*, New York: Harper Collins, 2014.

Kindleberger, Charles P. *Manias, Panics, and Crashes: A History of Financial Crashes*, 4th ed., New York: Wiley & Sons, 2000.

King, Martin Luther, Jr. *"Thou Dear God:" Prayers that Open Hearts and Spirits*, Boston: Beacon Press, 2012.

King, Wilford I. *The Wealth and Income of the People of the United States*, New York: MacMillan, 1915.

Kirk, Russell. *The Conservative Mind*, Revised Edition, Chicago: Gateway, 1960.

Klein, Naomi. *Shock Doctrine: the Rise of Disaster Capitalism*, New York: Henry Holt, 2007.

Knight, Frank H. *The Ethics of Competition and Other Essays*, M. Friedman, H. Jones, G. Stigler, W.A. Wallis, eds., New York: Harper, 1835.

Kohl, Lawrence. *The Politics of Individualism: Parties and the American Character in the Jacksonian Era*, New York: Oxford University Press, 1989.

Kontos, Alkis. "The Dialectics of Domination: An Interpretation of Friedrich Dűrrenmatt's *The Visit*, In C.B. Macpherson & Alkis Kontos, *Powers,*

*Possessions, and Freedom: Essays in Honour of C.B. Macpherson*, Toronto: University of Toronto Press, (1979), 153–166.

Koob, Jeff. *Ad Nauseum: How Advertising and Public Relations Have Changed Everything*, Bloomington, Ind.: Indiana University Press, 2015.

Kraut, Richard. *Aristotle and the Human Good*, Princeton: Princeton University Press, 1989.

Kukathos, Chandran. "Hayek and Liberalism," in E. Feser, ed., *The Cambridge Companion to Hayek*, Cambridge: Cambridge University Press, (2006), 182–205.

Kymlicka, Will. *Contemporary Political Philosophy: An Introduction*, Oxford: Oxford University Press, 1990.

Lal, Deepak. *Reviving the Invisible Hand: the Case for Classical Liberalism in the Twenty-First Century*, Princeton: Princeton University Press, 2006.

Lasch, Christopher. *The Revolt of the Elite and the Betrayal of Democracy*, New York: W.W. Norton, 1995.

Lasswell, Harold D. *Politics: Who Gets What, When, How*, New York: World Publishers, 1971.

Lehmann, Chris. *Money Cult: Capitalism, Christianity, and the Unmaking of the American Dream*, Brooklyn: Melville House, 2016.

Leonard, Peter *Personality and Ideology: Towards a Materialist Understanding of the Individual*, London: MacMillan, 1984.

Levins, Richard. "Is Capitalism a Disease? The Crisis in U.S. Public Health," *Monthly Review*, 52 (4), (September 2000), 8–33.

Levy, David W. *Herbert Croly of the New Republic: the Life and Thought of an American Progressive*, Princeton: Princeton University Press, 1985.

Leys, Colin and Leo Panitch (eds.). *Morbid Symptoms: Health Under Capitalism*, London: Merlin Press, 2009.

Lichtenstein, Nelson. *State of the Union: a Century of American Labor*, Princeton: Princeton University Press, 2002.

Lincoln, Abraham. R.N. Current (ed.), *The Political Thought of Abraham Lincoln*, Indianapolis: BobbsMerrill, 1967.

Locke, John. *Two Treatises of Government and Robert Filmer Patriarcha*, Thomas Cook (ed.), New York: Hafner Publishing, 1965.

Lomasky, Loren E. *Persons, Rights, and Moral community*, New York: Oxford University Press, 1987.

Long, Clarence D. *Wages and Earnings in the United States, 1860–1890*, Princeton: Princeton University Press, 1960.

Lowenthal, Leo and Norbert Guterman. *Prophets of Deceit: a Study of the Techniques of the American Agitator*, New York: Harper & Brothers, 1949.

Lukes, Stephen. *Power: A Radical View*, second edition, London: MacMillan, 2005.

Lux, Kenneth. *Adam Smith's Mistake: How a Moral Philosophy Invented Economics and Ended Morality*, New York: Random House, 1990.

MacEwan, Arthur. *Neo-Liberalism or Democracy? Economic Strategy, Markets, and Alternatives for the 21st Century*, London: Zed Books, 1999.

MacIntyre, Alasdair. "Utilitarianism and Cost/Benefit Analysis: an Essay on the Relevance of Moral Philosophy to Bureaucratic Theory," In Tom Beauchamp & Norman Bowie, *Ethical Theory and Business*, Englewood Cliffs, NJ: Prentice-Hall, (1979), 266–276.

———. *After Virtue*, 2nd. ed., Notre Dame: Note Dame University Press, 1984.

———. *The MacIntyre Reader*, ed. Kevin Knight, Notre Dame: University of Notre Dame Press, 1998.

Macpherson, C.B. and Alkis Kontos. *Powers, Possessions, and Freedom: Essays in Honour of C.B. Macpherson*, Toronto: University of Toronto Press, 1979.

McCoy, Drew R. *Elusive Republic: Political Economy in Jeffersonian America*, Chapel Hill: University of North Carolina Press, 1980.

McGeer, Michael. *A Fierce Discontent: The Rise and Fall of the Progressive Movement in America*, New York: Oxford University Press, 2003.

McGraw, Thomas K. *Prophets of Regulation*, Cambridge: Harvard University Press, 1984.

Machlup, Fritz. *Essays on Hayek*, Hillsdale, MI: Hillsdale College Press, 1976.

Mack, Eric. "Hayek on Justice and the Order of Actions," In E. Feser, ed., *Cambridge Companion to Hayek*, Cambridge: Cambridge University Press, (2006), 259–286.

Madison, James. *Notes of Debates in the Federal Convention of 1787*, New York: W.W. Norton, 1966.

———. *Writings*, New York: Library of America, 1999.

Mallaby, Sebastian. *The Man Who Knew: the Life and Times of Alan Greenspan*, New York: Penguin Press, 2016.

Manza, Jeff. "Unequal Democracy in America: the Long View," In D.B. Grusky & T. Kricholi-Katz, eds. *The New Gilded Age*, Stanford: Stanford University Press, (2012), 131–158.

Mayer, David N. *The Constitutional Thought of Thomas Jefferson*, Charlottesville: University Press Virginia, 1997.

Mayer, Jane. *Dark Money: the Hidden History of the Billionaires Behind the Radical Right*, New York: Random House, 2016.

Mencken, H.L. *Minority Report: H.L. Mencken's Notebooks*, New York: Alfred Knopf, 1956.

Michelman, Irving S. *The Moral Limitations of Capitalism*, Aldershott, Hants: Avebury Publishers, 1994.

Milgate, Murray and Shannon Stimson. *Ricardian Politics*, Princeton: Princeton University Press, 1991.

————, *After Adam Smith: a Century of Transformation in Politics and Political Economy*, Princeton: Princeton University Press, 2009.

Miller, Rose. *Paving Wall Street: Experimental Economics and the Quest for Perfect Markets*, New York: John Wiley & Sons, 2002.

Miron, Jeffrey. *Libertarianism: from A to Z*, New York: Basic Books, 2010.

Mirowski, Philip and Dieter Plehwe. *The Road from Mont Pèlerin: the Making of the Neoliberal Collective*, Cambridge: Harvard University Press, 2009.

Mises, Ludwig von. *Socialism: an Economic and Sociological Analysis*, New York: MacMillan, 1937.

————. *Human Action: a Treatise on Economics*, New Haven: Yale University Press, 1949.

Mises, Ludwig von, and Richard Ebeling. *Human Action: a 50-Year Tribute*, Hillsdale, MI: Hillsdale College Press, 2000.

Mises, Ludwig and Bettina Grieves. *Theory and History: an Interpretation of Social and Economic Evolution*, Indianapolis, IN: Liberty, 2005.

————. *Omnipotent Government: the Rise of the Total State and Total War,* Indianapolis: Liberty, 2011.

Mitchell, Mark T. *Michael Polanyi*, Wilmington, DE: ISI Books, 2006.

Mochlup, Fritz, ed. *Essays on Hayek*, New York: New York University Press, 1976.

Monbiot, George. *How Did We Get Into This Mess?: Politics, Equality, Nature*, London: Verso, 2016.

Montesquieu, Baron De. *The Spirit of the Laws*, Translated by Thomas Nugent, New York: Hafner Publishing, 1975.

Morgan, H. Wayne (ed.). *The Gilded Age*, Syracuse: Syracuse University Press, 1970.

Morgenson, Gretchen and Joshua Rosner. *Reckless Endangerment: How Outsized Ambition, Greed, and Corruption led to Economic Armageddon*, New York: Henry Holt, 2011.

Mueller, John. *Capitalism, Democracy, and Ralph's Pretty Good Grocery*, Princeton: Princeton University Press, 1999.

Mulhall, Stephen and Adam Swift. *Liberals and Communitarians*, Oxford: Blackwell, 1992.

Muller, Jerry Z., *The Mind and the Market: Capitalism in Modern European Thought*, New York: Alfred Knopf, 2002.

Murray, Charles. *What it Means to be a Libertarian: a Personal Interpretation*, New York: Broadway Books, 1997.

Nash, George H. *The Conservative Intellectual Movement in America since 1945*, 3oth edition, Wilmington: ISI Books, 2008.

Nehamas, Alexander. *On Friendship*, New York: Basic Books, 2016.

Niebuhr, Reinhold. *The Children of Light and the Children of Darkness: a Vindication of Democracy and a Critique of its Traditional Defense,* New York: Scribner, 1944.

———. *Reinhold Niebuhr on Politics: His Political Philosophy and its Application to our age as expressed in Writings*, H. R. Davis & R. C. Good, eds., New York: Scribner, 1960.

Nielson, Kai. *Equality and Liberty: a Defense of Radical Egalitarianism*, Totawa, NJ: Rowan & Allenhead, 1985.

Nozick, Robert. *Anarchy, State, and Utopia*, New York: Basic Books, 1974.

Nussbaum, Martha. *The Fragility of Goodness: Luck and Ethics in Greek Tragedy and Philosophy*, Cambridge: Cambridge University Press, 1986

Nussbaum, Martha and Amartya Sen (eds.). *Quality of Life*, Oxford: Oxford University Press, 1993..

———. *Women and Human Development: the Capabilities Approach*, Cambridge: Cambridge University Press, 2001.

———. *Not for Profit: Why Democracy Needs the Humanities*, Princeton: Princeton University Press, 2010.

———. *Creating Capabilities: the Human Development Approach*, Cambridge: Harvard University Press, 2011.

———. *Political Emotions: Why Love Matters for Justice*, Cambridge: Harvard University Press, 2013.

O'Hear, Anthony. "Hayek and Popper: the road to Serfdom and Open Society," In E. Feser (ed.), *Cambridge Companion to Hayek*, Cambridge: Cambridge University Press, (2006), 132–147.

Oliner, Pearl M. et al., eds. *Embracing the Other: Philosophical, Psychological, and Historical Perspectives on Altruism*, New York: New York University Press, 1992.

Olson, Marvin. *Power in Societies*, London: MacMillan, 1970.

O'Neill, John. *The Market: Ethics, Knowledge, and Politics*, London: Routledge, 1998.

Otsuka, Michael. *Libertarianism without Inequality*, Oxford: Oxford University Press, 2003.

Parfit, Derek. *Equality and Priority*, Lawrence, Kan: University of Kansas Press, 1995.

————. *Reasons and Persons*, Oxford: Oxford University Press, 2002.

Parrington, Vernon L. *Main Currents in American Thought*, Vol.3, New York: Harcourt, Brace, 1930.

Paul, Jeffrey, ed. *Reading Nozick: Essays on Anarchy, State, and Utopia*, Totawa, NJ: Rowan & Allenheld, 1983.

Paxton, Robert O. *The Anatomy of Fascism*, New York: Vintage Books, 2005.

Peck, Don. *Pinched: How the Great Recession Has Narrowed Our Futures and What We Can Do About It*, New York: Brown Publishing, 2011.

Pellegrino, Edmund, and David Thomasma. *For the Patient's Good: the Restoration of Beneficence in Health Care*, New York: Oxford University Press, 1988.

Perlstein, Rick. *Before the Storm: Barry Goldwater and the Unmaking of the American Consensus*, New York: W.W. Norton, 2009.

Petsoulas, Christina. *Hayek's Liberalism and its Origins: His Idea of Spontaneous Order and the Scottish Enlightenment*, London: Routledge, 2001.

Piketty, Thomas. *Capital in the Twenty-First Century*, Cambridge: Harvard University Press, 2014.

Piketty, Thomas, and Emmanuel Saez. "Income inequality in the United States,1913–1998," *Quarterly Journal of Economics*, 118 (1) (February, 2003), 1–41.

Pipes, Richard. *Property and Freedom*, New York: Vintage Books, 2000.

Polanyi, Karl. *The Great Transformation: the Political and Economic Origins of Our Time*, Boston: Beacon Press, 1944.

Polanyi, Michael. *The Tacit Dimension*, New York: Anchor Books, 1967.

Polybius, *The Histories of Polybius in Two Volumes*, trans. By F. Hultsch & E.S. Shuckburgh, Bloomington: Indiana University Press, 1962.

Porta, Donatella Della. *Social Movements in Times of Austerity*, Cambridge, U.K.: Polity, 2015.

Posner, Richard. *A Failure of Capitalism: the Crisis of '08 and the Descent into Depression*, Cambridge: Harvard University Press, 2009.

Postman, Neil, *Amusing Ourselves to Death: Public Discourse in the Age of Show Business*, New York: Penguin Books, 1986.

Price, A. W. *Love and Friendship in Plato and Aristotle*, Oxford: Oxford University Press, 1991.

Price, David E. "Community and Control: Critical Democratic Theory in the Progressive Period," *The American Political Science Review*, 68 (4), (December, 1974) 1663–1678.

Rabinbach, Anson. *The Crisis of Austrian Socialism: From Red Vienna to Civil War, 1927–1934*, Chicago: University of Chicago Press, 1983.

Rahe, Paul A. *Republics: Ancient and Modern Classical Republicanism and the American Revolution*, Chapel Hill: University of North Carolina Press, 1992.

Ranelagh, John. *Thatcher's People: an Insider's Account of the Politics, the Power and the Personalities*, London: Fontana, 1992.

Rank, Mark, Thomas Hirschl, and Kirk Foster. *Chasing the American Dream: Understanding What Shapes Our Future,* New York: Oxford University Press, 2016.

Ravitch, Diane. *Reign of Error: the Hoax of the Privatization Movement and the Danger to America's Public Schools*, New York: Alfred Knopf, 2013.

Rawls, John. *A Theory of Justice*, Revised Edition, Cambridge: Harvard University Press, 2003.

Reeves, Richard. *John Stuart Mill: Victorian Firebrand*, London: Atlantic Books, 2007.

Reid-Henry, Simon. *The Political Origins of Inequality: Why a More Equal World is Better for Us All*, Chicago: University of Chicago Press, 2015.

Rich, Frederic O. *Getting to Green, Saving Nature: a Bipartison Solution*, New York: W.W. Norton, 2016.

Risen, James. *Pay Any Price: Greed, Power, and Endless War*, Boston: Houghton Mifflin, 2014

Roark, Eric. *Removing the Commons: a Lockean Left-Libertarian Approach to Natural Resources*, Lanham, Md: Lexington Books, 2003.

Root, Wayne Allen. *The Conscience of a Libertarian: Empowering the Citizen Revolution with God, Guns, Gambling, and tax Cuts*, Hoboken, NJ: John Wiley & Sons, 2009.

Rorty, Amélie Oksenberg, ed. *Essays on Aristotle's Ethics*, Berkeley: University of California Press, 1980.

Rorty, Richard. *Achieving Our Country: Leftist Thought in Twentieth Century America*, Cambridge: Harvard University Press, 1998.

Rose, Mary B. *Paternalism, Industrial Welfare, and Business Strategy: Britain to 1939*, Leuven: Leuven University Press, 1880.

Rosenblum, Nancy L.. *Good Neighbors: the Democracy of Everyday Life in America*, Princeton: Princeton University Press, 2016.

Rothkopf, David. *Superclass: the Global Power Elite and the World They Are Making*, New Yor: Farrar, Straus & Giroux, 2008.

Rothschild, Emma. *Economic Sentiments: Adam Smith, Condorcet, and the Enlightenment*, Cambridge: Harvard University Press, 2001.

Rousseau, Jean-Jacques. *Rousseau's Political Writings*, Alan Ritter and J.C. Bondanella (eds.), New York: W.W. Norton, 1988.

Ryan, Alan. *John Dewey and the High Tide of American Liberalism*, New York: W.W. Norton, 1995.

Saez, Emmanuel and Gabriel Zucman. "Wealth Inequality in the United States Since 1913: Evidence from Capitalized Income Tax Data," National Bureau of Economic Research Paper no.20624, (2015).

Sally, Razeem. *Classical Liberalism and International Economic Order: Studies in Theory and Intellectual History*, London: Routledge, 1998.

Sandel, Michael J. *Liberalism and the Limits of Justice*, Cambridge: Cambridge University Press, 1982.

———. *Democracy and its Discontents: America in Search of a Public Philosophy*, Cambridge: Harvard University Press, 1996.

———. *Justice: What's the Right Thing to Do?* New York: Farrar, Straus, & Giroux, 2009.

———. *What Money Can't Buy: the Moral Limits of Markets*, New York: Farrar, Straus & Giroux, 2012.

Sartorius, Rolf. Ed. *Paternalism*, Minneapolis: University of Minnesota, 1983.

Schaar, John H. "Liberty/Authority/Community in the Political Thought of John Winthrop," *Political Theory*, 19 (4), (November 1991) 493–518.

Schmidt, James, ed. *What is Enlightenment? Eighteenth-Century Answers and Twentieth- Century Replies*, Berkeley: University of California Press, 1996.

Schollmeier, Paul. *Other Selves: Aristotle on Personal and Political Friendship*, Albany: State University of New York, 1994.

Schram, Sanford F. *After Welfare: the Culture of Postindustrial Social Policy*, New York: New York University Press, 2000.

Schwartz, Andrew H. *The Politics of Greed: How Privatization Structured Politics in Central and Eastern Europe*, Lanham, MD: Rowan & Littlefield, 2006.

Scott, James C. *Seeing Like a State: How Certain Schemes to Improve the Human Condition Have Failed*, New Haven: Yale University Pres, 1998.

Scruton, Roger. "Hayek and Conservatism," In E. Feser (ed.) *Cambridge Companion to Hayek*, Cambridge University Press, (2006), 208–231.

Schumpeter, Joseph A. *Capitalism, Socialism, and Democracy*, third edition, New York: Harper & Row, 1962.

Sen, Amartya. *On Ethics and Economics*, Oxford: Basil Blackwell, 1987.

———. *Development as Freedom*, New York: Random House, 2000.

———. *Theory of Justice*, Cambridge: Harvard University Press, 2011.

Shearmur, Jeremy. "Hayek's Politics," In E. Feser, (ed.), *Cambridge Companion to Hayek*, Cambridge: Cambridge University Press, (2006), 148–170.

Sheehan, Colleen and Gary McDowell, eds. *Friends of the Constitution: Writings of the "Other" Federalists, 1787–1788*, Indianapolis, IN: Liberty Fund, 1998.

Signer, Michael. *Demagogue: The Fight to Save Democracy From Its Worst Enemies*, New York: MacMillan, 2009.

Silk, Leonard. *The Economists*, New York: Basic Books, 1974.

Simons, Henry. *Economic Policy for a Free Society*, Chicago: University of Chicago Press, 1948.

Singer, Joseph William. *No Freedom Without Regulation: the Hidden Lesson of the Subprime Crisis*, New Haven: Yale University Press, 2016.

Skidelsky, Robert. "Hayek versus Keynes: the Road to Reconciliation," In E. Feser (ed.), *Cambridge Companion to Hayek*, Cambridge: Cambridge University Press, (2006), 82–110.

———. *Keynes: the Future of the Master*, New York: Public Affairs, 2010.

Skocpol, Theda and Vanessa Williamson. *The Tea Party and the Making of Republican Conservatism*, Oxford: Oxford University Press, 2012.

Smith, Adam. *An Enquiry into The Nature and Causes of the Wealth of Nations*, Edward Cannon, ed., New York: Modern Library, 1937.

———. *Adam Smith's Moral and Political Philosophy*, Herbert Schneider, (ed.) New York: Harper & Row, 1948.

———. *The Theory of Moral Sentiments*, D.D. Raphael & A.L. Macfie (eds.) Oxford: Oxford University Press, 1979.

Smith, James Norton. *The Republic of Letters: the Correspondence between Thomas Jefferson and James Madison, 1776–1826*, New York: W.W. Norton, 1995.

Smith, Page. *The Rise of Industrial America: a People's History of the Post-Reconstruction Era*, New York: McGraw Hill, 1964.

Sowell, Thomas. *Wealth, Poverty and Politics: an International Perspective*, New York: Basic Books, 2015.

Spinoza, Benedict De. *A Theological-Political Treatise*, New York: Dover Publications, 1951.

———. *The Political Writings of Spinoza*, Oxford: Oxford University Press, 1958.

Spragens, Thomas Jr. *Civic Liberalism: Reflections on Our Democratic Ideals*, Lanham, Md: Rowan & Littlefield, 1999.

Starr, Paul. *The Social Transformation of American Medicine: the Rise of a Sovereign Profession and the Making of a Vast Industry*, New York: Basic Books, 1982.

Steger, Manfred and Ravi Roy. *Neoliberalism: A Very Short Introduction*, Oxford: Oxford University Press, 2010.

Stenner, Karen. *The Authoritarian Dynamic*, New York: Cambridge University Press, 2005.

Stern, Fritz. *Gold and Iron: Bismarck, Bleichröder, and the German Empire*, New York: Alfred Knopf, 1977.

Sternhell, Zeev. *The Birth of Fascist Ideology: From Cultural Rebellion to Political Revolution*, Princeton: Princeton University Press, 1994.

Stettner, Edward A. *Shaping Modern Liberalism: Herbert Croly and Progressive Thought*, Lawrence, Kansas: University Press Kansas, 1993.

Stiglitz, Joseph. *Globalization and Its Discontents*, New York: W.W. Norton, 2002.

———. *The Price of Inequality: How Today's Divided Society Endangers Our Future*, New York: W.W. Norton, 2012.

———. *The Great Divide: Unequal Societies and What We Can do about Them*, New York: W.W. Norton, 2015.

Stone, Geoffrey R. *Perilous Times: Free Speech in Wartime, From the Sedition Act of 1798 to the War on Terror*, New York: W.W. Norton, 2004.

Storing, Herbert J. *What Anti-Federalists Were Fir: the Political Thought of the Opponents of the Constitution*, Chicago: University of Chicago Press, 1981.

Story, Ronald and Bruce Laurie. *The Rise of Conservatism in America, 1945–2000: a Brief History with Documents*, Boston: St. Martin's Press, 2008.

Stout, Jeffrey. *Ethics After Babel: the Languages of Morals and their Discontents*, Boston: Beacon Press, 1988.

Summers, Mark W. *Party Games: Getting, Keeping, and Using Power in Gilded Age Politics*, Chapel Hill: University of North Carolina Press, 2004.

Suarez-Vila, Louis. *Corporate Power, Oligopolies, and the Crisis of the State*, Albany: Suny Press, 2015.

Sumner, William Graham. *On Liberty, Society, and Politics: the Essential Essays of William Graham Sumner*, R.C. Bannister (ed.) Indianapolis: Liberty Fund, 1999.

————. *Folkways*, Salem, NH: Ayer, 1992.

————. *The Science of Society*, New Haven: Yale University Press, 1947.

Sunstein, Cass and Richard H. Thaler. "Libertarian Paternalism is Not an Oxymoron," *Public Law and Legal Theory Working Papers*, No.43, (second series), Chicago: University of Chicago Press (May, 2003).

Szántó, András, ed. *What Orwell Didn't Know: Propaganda and the New Face of America*, New York: Public Affairs, 2007.

Taylor, Charles. *Philosophy and the Human Sciences: Philosophical Papers*, Vol.2, Cambridge: Cambridge University Press, 1986.

Thaler, Mark H. *Misbehaving: the Making of Behavioral Economics*, New York: W.W. Norton, 2015.

Thomas, Susan L. "Race, Gender and Welfare Reform: the Antinatalist Response," *Journal of Black Studies*, 28 (4), (March 1998), 319–446.

Thompson, E.P. *The Making of the English Working Class*, London: Penguin, 1963.

Tocqueville, Alexis de. *The Old Régime and the French Revolution*, translated by Gilbert Stuart, New York: Random House, 1955.

————. *Democracy in America*, ed. by Phillips Bradley, 2 Vols., New York: Alfred Knopf, 1980.

————. *Memoir on Pauperism*, Chicago: Ivan Dee, 1997.

Tone, Andrea. *The Business of Benevolence: Industrial Paternalism in Progressive America*, Ithaca: Cornell University Press, 1997.

Trachtenberg, Alan. *The Incorporation of American Culture and Society in the Gilded Age,* New York: Hill & Wang, 2007.

Trenchard, John and Thomas Gordon, ed. by Ronald Hamowy, *Cato's Letters: or Essays on Liberty, Civil, Religious and Other Serious Matters*, 2 Vols. Indianapolis: Liberty Fund, 1995.

Tuccille, Jerome. *Alan Shrugged: Alan Greenspan, the World's Most Powerful Banker*, New York: John Wiley & Sons, 2002.

Twain, Mark and Charles Dudley Warner. *The Gilded Age*, ed. by S.F. Fishkin, New York: Oxford University Press, 1996.

Urofsky, Melvin I. *Louis D. Brandeis and the Progressive Tradition*, , Boston: Little Brown, 1981.

Vallantyne, Peter and Hillel Steiner, eds. *Left-Libertarianism and its Critics: the Contemporary Debate*, Houndsville, Bassingstoke: Palgrave, 2000.

Vickers, Douglas. *The Tyranny of the Market: a Critique of Theoretical Foundations*, Ann Arbor: Michegan University Press, 1995.

Viroli, Maurizio. *Republicanism*, New York: Hill & Wang, 2002.

Wacquant, Loic. *Punishing the Poor: the Neoliberal Government of Social Insecurity*, Durham, NC: Duke University Press, 2009.

Wapshott, Nicholas. *Keynes and Hayek: the Clash that Defined Modern Economics*, New York: W.W. Norton, 2011.

Westbrook, Robert B. *John Dewey and American Democracy*, Ithaca: Cornell University Press, 1991.

White, Lawrence H. *The Clash of Economic Ideas: the Great Policy Debates and Experiments of the Last Hundred Years*, Cambridge: Cambridge University Press, 2012.

White, Morton. *Philosophy, The Federalist and the Constitution*, Oxford: Oxford University Press, 1987.

Wilentz, Sean. *The Rise of American Democracy: Jefferson to Lincoln*, New York: W.W. Norton, 2005.

―――. *The Politicians and the Egalitarians: The Hidden History of American Politics*, New York: W.W. Norton, 2016.

Wills, Gary. *Inventing America: Jefferson's Declaration of Independence*, New York: Doubleday, 1978.

―――. *A Necessary Evil: a History of American Trust of Government*, New York: Simon & Schuster, 1999.

Winters, Jeffrey and Benjamin Page. "Oligarchy in the United States," *Perspectives in Politics*, 7 (4) (2009), 731–751.

Wolff, Jonathan. *Robert Nozick: Property, Justice, and the Minimal State*, Stanford: Stanford University Press, 1991.

Wood, Allan W. *Kant's Ethical Thought*, Cambridge: Cambridge University Press, 1999.

Woodward, C. Van. *The Strange Career of Jim Crow*, New York: Oxford University Press, 1974.

Veatch, R.A. *A Theory of Medical Ethics*, New York: Oxford University Press, 1981.

Yack, Bernard. *The Problems of a Political Animal: Community, Justice, and Conflict in Aristotelian Political Thought*, Berkeley: University of California Press, 1993.

Zakaras, Alex. *Individualism and Mass Democracy: Mill, Emerson, and the Burdens of Civilization*, Oxford: Oxford University Press, 2009.

Zakaria, Fareed. *From Wealth to Power: the Unusual Origins of America's World Role*, Princeton: Princeton University Press, 1998.